The Complete Yachtsman
A Cruising Manual

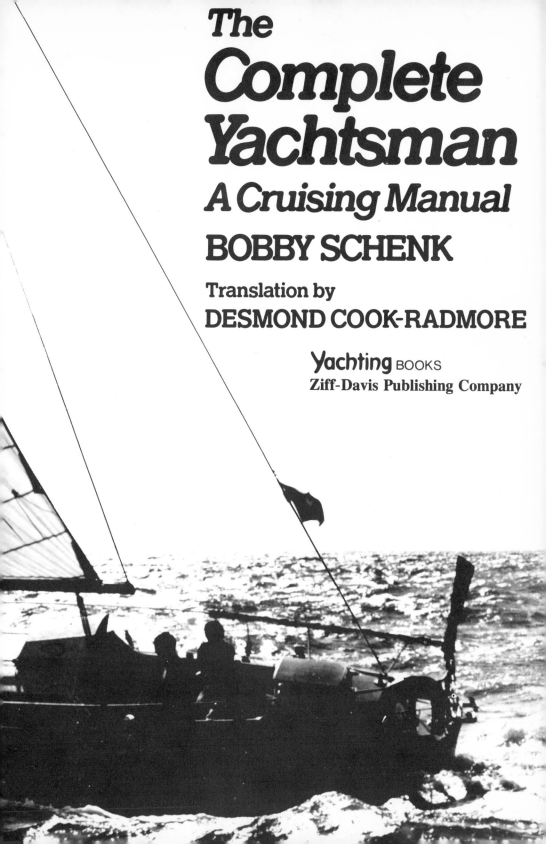

The
Complete Yachtsman
A Cruising Manual
BOBBY SCHENK

Translation by
DESMOND COOK-RADMORE

Yachting BOOKS
Ziff-Davis Publishing Company

Copyright © BLV Verlagsgesellschaft mbH, Munich 1977
Translation © Desmond Cook-Radmore 1978
First published in the United States by
Ziff-Davis Publishing Company
One Park Avenue
New York, N.Y. 10016

Library of Congress Catalog Number 78-58509
ISBN 0-87165-018-5

The publishers would like to thank John Driscoll
of *Yachting World* and Bill Anderson of The Royal
Yachting Association for their advice and help in
the details of the translation. Basil D'Oliveira
made a substantial contribution to the chapter on
Navigation, in particular to the section on
Pocket Calculators.

First published in West Germany in 1976
by BLV Verlagsgesellschaft mbH, Munich
Printed in Great Britain

Foreword

Nowhere are you so independent as on the open sea and it is not surprising that in this technological age more and more people are taking to the water. There, in a small sailboat, they seek the freedom so sadly lacking in modern life. But in cruising under sail they also experience the romance and thrill of a successful passage and a safe landfall – shared by man over centuries – using only the wind, a chart and a tiny magnetic needle. It is just as rewarding whether you make a short coastal passage or cross a great ocean.

Though the lore of seamanship has remained unaltered for centuries, technology with its modern materials and recent developments in electronics has made sailing for enjoyment so much easier that today anyone, irrespective of sex or age, can cruise anywhere they like so long as the boat is suitable and they have the necessary knowledge.

That knowledge is what this book sets out to provide. I have tried to present the problems as simply as possible so that every reader can, even without prior technical know-how, readily grasp the point being made. Where 'reader-participation' is called for in the chapter on navigation, all the material needed (chart, tables, etc.) is provided in the book.

My thanks are due to Dr Walter Dirr and Dr Gert Meyer-Uhl, two experienced and much-travelled yachtsmen, who wrote the sections on Medicine and Avoidance of collisions. A great many friends in the sailing fraternity have helped write the book; during innummerable chats in picturesque anchorages all over the world they have given me tips from the wealth of their experience, and these I am glad to pass on here. Conversely, any comments or suggestions from readers will be very welcome.

Bobby Schenk

Contents

**Important facts
about
this and that**

Index

The cruising boat

Over recent years the demands made on a seagoing boat have changed a great deal. While in the past people would talk about a yacht being suitable for coastal cruising or ocean-going, there is nowadays quite rightly no longer any difference made; any sail boat can quite easily meet such bad weather conditions that it needs to have just the same seakeeping qualities as an ocean-going yacht. Besides, I and a good many other sailors believe it is a great deal easier to cross the Atlantic by the trade-wind route than, for instance, to cruise uneventfully in our own North Sea waters for a few weeks on end. And there are even 6m boats that have proved their offshore worth, though these may be individual cases that ought not necessarily to be imitated. How big a boat you choose is first and foremost a matter of the size of your purse. If the idea is only to spend holidays sailing along the Yugoslav coast, stopping every night in harbour, I can imagine that a couple would be quite happy with a boat of 7m or so; it is mainly a matter of personal taste and, of course, of sporting inclinations. One friend of mine sailed from Canada to Australia with his wife and two-year-old child in a 7m yacht; certainly not everyone's choice, but it does show that – if

A small glassfibre coastal cruiser may be suitable for the open sea with proper equipment and an experienced skipper.

The owner of this French Meltem can go anywhere in the world – travelling first class, for its 16m length gives space for everything from a deep-freeze to the shopping trolley!

needs be – it is possible to live in a very small space. In the tropics, where in any case you spend more time in the open air, it is of course much easier.

Those who can afford only a small boat should not be too down-hearted about this, because it offers several not unimportant advantages. First, a smaller boat is much simpler to cope with – both afloat and on land, where it can be trailed comfortably behind a car to change cruising grounds. And besides, it makes for less maintenance work; from a certain size – say, 13m – upwards, this can very easily become a full time job, depending on the age and equipment of the boat and the condition it is in. Finally, and this is something one should already have in mind when buying, the financial risk is much lower with a small boat. When selling, the number of prospective buyers is relatively large even in bad times, and the loss is proportionally much less.

When buying bear two factors in mind:

■ safety

■ comfort

Speed is less important, and should

Only 7.75m long, yet this Neptune 26 is a full-blooded motor sailer.

never be allowed to detract from either safety or comfort. Getting into harbour an hour sooner or later at the end of a day's cruising is not going to mean the end of the world. Of course it's fun to be faster than other boats – there's a bit of the racing helmsman in every skipper – but racing successes should not be the only thing affecting the decision to buy a certain boat.

The hull

The development of hull shapes over the past few years is the clearest possible example of the fact that it is not always right to be guided by what goes on in the racing world. The short keel, standard on the majority of boats today, has few advantages to offer in cruising. I will readily concede that good manoeuvrability and a quick, responsive helm – qualities we owe to the modern hull shape – are essential for many sailing areas. Many cruising helmsmen frequently take part in races, too, and would not enjoy themselves much with an old-fashioned hull design – meaning a long keel.

But the biggest drawback of a short keel is its inability to hold a course. The boat, being quick on the rudder, will tend to swing off her heading, especially when down wind. The short keel also affects stowage space – the ballast has to be put in the keel, so the

A long keel – kindly at sea, and no trouble when hauling-out.

A free-hanging rudder gives excellent manoeuvrability, but needs plenty of feel on the tiller.

If the rudder is additionally supported by a skeg, it is not quite as vulnerable as a free-hanging (balanced) rudder.

natural place for accommodating fuel and water stores is no longer available. There may also be problems hauling the boat out, since many boatyards are not equipped for slipping short-keel yachts.

For me, a further major disadvantage is that the rudder mounting cannot help being substantially weaker than when the rudder is supported, not just by a skeg or shaft, but by a long keel. Damage to this highly vulnerable part of the boat is very serious indeed; far more so than, for instance, losing the mast. In the latter case one can usually manage somehow, by jury-rigging a boom or one of the other spars or – if the nearest harbour is not too far away – by simply using the auxiliary.

But if you lose your steering, rigging an emergency rudder will often (especially with a big boat of more than 10m) prove impossible. Many books put forward the idea that a yacht can be steered using the sails. Now this may be feasible for a short while in calm water in a sheltered area; but it is usually impossible in the open sea with a swell running. Just unship the tiller one day, and try it!

Round bilge: expensive to build, it looks nice but for the cruising boat offers no real advantage.

In the argument between round-bilge and hard-chine, the cruising man really has no choice. Admittedly a hard chine may not look as attractive as the pleasant shape of a curved bilge, but apart from that there is nothing at all to be said against a single or double chine. Quite the opposite, in fact, because this design is bound to be a great deal cheaper to build, particularly in the case of steel hulls where flat surfaces are easier to cope with.

Hard-chine: gives a harder ride in a seaway, but is cheaper to build, particularly in steel.

A single-hull boat must be capsize-proof; this means there must be enough ballast to bring her back upright (on the same principle as the tumbler doll with its weighted foot) even in the extreme case of being knocked flat on the water. Ideally, a cruising boat would be unsinkable as well, and would not go down even when completely waterlogged; but this is possible, using built-in buoyancy, only with

very small boats, and unfortunately out of the question with anything bigger than 7m overall or thereabouts.

How high the proportion of ballast should be is for the designer
alone to decide. It should never be as high as in a racing hull (50
per cent, or more, of the total weight), since the boat's movements
will then be so harsh and violent that comfortable cruising will be
impossible. The ability of a racing yacht to carry the greatest possible amount of canvas, even hard on the wind where the heeling
moment is greatest, is only a secondary consideration in a cruising
boat. At sea, in a heavy swell, you never try to sail close-hauled at
the quite fantastic angles to apparent wind that many racing
designs can manage. One can be quite satisfied with a cruiser if it
points as high as 50°. It is incidentally quite easy to check how high
a yacht is pointing by reading off the compass course first on one
tack and then on the other. The difference divided by two will give
the angle to the true wind that you can just manage to hold.

Building materials

There has been a real revolution in boat-building over the last 10
years, and wood has almost entirely disappeared as a material for
building seagoing yachts. The reason lies in the enormous progress made in chemistry. Plastics such as polyester and epoxy
resin offer such impressive properties that using them for building
boats has become almost inevitable; wood, on the other hand, has
some quite decisive disadvantages. First, it is an organic sub-
stance which can go mouldy and rot. Then, one piece can never be
joined integrally to another – it either has to be stuck together
(which brings problems because it 'works') or else the gaps between planks have to be caulked, as in our forefathers' days, to
keep the boat watertight. A wooden boat would nowadays
(because it is much more labour-intensive) cost more than a
glassfibre boat with all its advantages. And, finally, wood is highly
vulnerable in southern waters where the teredo worm flourishes.

Against this, a glassfibre yacht has a number of major advantages. First of all, 'plastic' is watertight, something that can be said
about very few wooden boats. When we talk here about plastics,
this does not mean straight polyester, or even epoxy resin (which is
a good deal dearer, and less flexible), but usually glassfibre mat
impregnated with polyester. The polyester serves merely to hold
the glass mat together, which is why the material is usually known

Plastics

This rung from a new
swimmers' ladder was
hung in the water for only
five weeks: it gives an idea
of what the teredo worm
can do to a wooden hull.

13

as glassfibre reinforced plastic, or GRP. The more glassfibre there is in the plastic, the stronger the result. Before long, glass is likely to be ousted by carbon fibre, which will provide even more strength.

GRP is not, however, entirely unaffected by water, Polyester can be dissolved by water (albeit very, very slowly) unless it is protected by what is termed a gel coating. If this coating is damaged, the water will find its way into the plastic, along the fine glass fibres, by capillary action, and will slowly dissolve the polyester (the process takes years). A good gel coating should last six years, however, and a glassfibre hull will not need repainting until small cracks have appeared. Nowadays the quality of paints is so good that there will then be nothing to worry about for another few years.

It is a shame that, because many boatbuilders make such a poor job of screwing on fittings and bolting together the deck and hull shell, the advantage of watertightness that plastic offers tends to be thrown away. Care must be taken to see that every bolt-hole is properly sealed with silicone rubber to prevent water seepage. One source of trouble is the join between deck and hull. Generally, the two are glued together and then bolted at close intervals.

This has not proved satisfactory, mainly because many yards – for reasons of cost – rely solely on the adhesive in the gaps of 30cm or more between the bolts. When the boat works in a heavy sea, the relatively brittle adhesive breaks up, and water gets in through the resulting hairline cracks. A different method is now being used, employing a non-hardening adhesive to glue the parts together. A good deal of attention needs to be given to this question of keeping the hull watertight, because the wellbeing of the crew on a long voyage depends to a great extent on whether they, and their belongings, stay dry or not. I will confess that I have still not come across an entirely watertight glassfibre boat. One friend of mine had what sounds a good idea, though I doubt that it would actually work: he planned, the next time he was buying a boat, to have a clause written into the contract requiring the boat, before acceptance, to withstand 30 minutes under a firehose, played especially round the hatches and ports. In many cases, unfortunately, leaks do not show up until the boat is in a seaway, or is heeling hard, and even the firehose test would not guard against this.

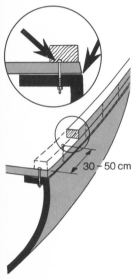

This is where water gets in, a drop at a time, and spreads out over the bunks and lockers; it is seldom possible to find the exact location of the leak.

30 – 50 cm

Steel

There is no doubt that in the event of a collision or going aground steel is the toughest material to have a yacht built of, and it is an

14

advantage for which many sailors will gladly put up with a whole range of minor drawbacks. Today corrosion is no longer the main bugbear of building in steel, though it used to be said that a steel yacht is always red – either with rust or with lead oxide paint! Today there is almost total agreement on how steel should be dealt with: it must, without fail, be sandblasted in the works, inside and out, until every trace of rust has been removed, and the first coat of protective paint then applied within a matter of minutes. It takes only ten minutes for a film of corrosion to re-form on the surface of the steel. This applies even to the rather more resistant Corten steel, which has become extremely popular in shipbuilding; its virtue is that though it rusts just like ordinary steel, the layer of rust that forms then acts as a protective coating. We can mainly thank outstandingly good tar-epoxide paints for the fact that steel is now comparatively problem-free; they give steel protection as reliable as that given to GRP by the gel coating. And here, indeed, is where the two materials are alike: as soon as the protective layer has been damaged something must be done about it, for both steel and glassfibre.

Steel is also at risk from galvanic corrosion. When there is an electrical connection between two dissimilar metals, or they come very close together in salt water, the baser of the two metals will be corroded; ions will migrate from the less to the more electropositive metal (this is incidentally, the principle of the electric battery, since

Typical steel-hull cruising yacht from Holland.

a current is a shift of ions). If we were to immerse a couple of brass bolts in the bilge water of a steel yacht, the steel, being the more electronegative of the two metals, would be eaten away. Unhappily this electrochemical process occurs even if you use a single, uniform metal, because parts made from the same metal can take on a different voltage potential during welding. Special measures, therefore, always need to be taken to prevent corrosion.

Passive protection: here, we try by using special tar-epoxide paints to keep the electrolyte (salt water) away from the steel, for without this contact corrosion cannot take place. This is a cheap method, and there is no problem in getting the paint to adhere; but as soon as mechanical damage lays the steel surface bare, there is no further protection.

Active protection: electronegative zinc metal is coated on to the sand-blasted steel by flame spraying (very expensive), spray galvanising (possible adhesion problems) or zinc-epoxide painting to give a conductive bond, and the seawater is then kept away with a tar paint (as with passive protection methods). If the top paint gets scratched, the electronegative zinc coating then protects the steel.

In the Jongert method, tar-epoxide is put on immediately after sand-blasting.

It is not yet clear which system is to be preferred. Most steel yachts belonging to long-distance cruising owners (eg. the old and new *Kairos* sailed by the Kochs) and from the Dutch Noord Nederland yard who built my new boat have active protection, while the Jongert shipyard believes that passive protection is enough. With both methods you need to provide further protection by attaching small lumps of an even baser metal at the danger points, to as it were 'divert attention'. Usually, small streamlined lumps of zinc are used as these sacrificial anodes. It is not all that easy to identify the points on a hull that are most at risk; generally they are aft, near the propellers. It is an excellent idea to put a boat in the water as a test, diving during the next few days and weeks to watch the hull for the first signs of galvanic action, which will show where to attach the zinc anodes. There are people who believe that if a boat were made in pure stainless steel, all corrosion problems would be over. But they are wrong, because stainless steel suffers just as much from galvanic action; you can see this quite clearly if you look

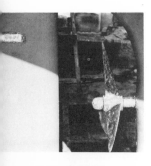

The right place for a sacrificial anode is nearly always close to the prop and rudder.

carefully at a stainless propeller shaft after it has been in salt water for a year of two. Even on a glassfibre boat one can find appreciable corrosion of the metal parts, so it is common practice in tropical waters (which are especially bad in this respect) to fit zinc anodes to glassfibre and wooden hulls as well.

Apart from cost (steel ought, in fact, to be the cheapest of all boatbuilding materials) the absolute watertightness of a welded seam is an advantage. One need not even bolt fittings through the deck of a steel yacht; they can be welded on from the outset, though the builder will naturally need to have a very clear picture of the deck plan beforehand. There are certain points on the deck that are particularly prone to rusting, where blocks strike and chip away the paintwork, or where the anchor chain is dragged across a sharp edge. It should be possible to persuade a yard that has pride in its work to weld on small stainless steel plates at these points, and these will solve the problem. It must, at all events, be possible in a steel yacht to get into even the most remote corners with a wire brush, to get rid of every bit of rust and repaint should this be needed. The protection provided by tar-epoxide paints has probably made this unnecessary, though a hole as small as a pinhead in the protective coating can, if it is in the wrong place, lead to trouble. This is why, with steel construction, one needs to be consistent in other respects, and never to make the toe-rails from wood. Teak planking laid on top of a steel deck is absurd, even though it may look like a proper boat. A steel deck painted in a light colour is, besides, much cooler in warm regions than a teak deck. When listing the snags of building in steel, many people insist that condensation would build up particularly easily in a steel hull. This can only happen when there is a very big difference between the air and water temperatures. In our latitudes, for example, this occurs in spring when we occasionally get a warm day while the water is still at 12 or 13°C. In general, however, the risk of condensation is exaggerated. It helps to have the boat well ventilated, or to have good internal insulation (the modern foam plastics are very good for this). For the same reason as I would not want a teak deck on a steel hull, I am not very keen on this last idea, however, and it would be better to try first without the insulation.

A 42-foot steel ketch – very sensibly built.

Aluminium

Despite its advantages, aluminium has never become all that popular. Though expensive, the material is lighter than steel while providing almost the same strength, and does not rust (aluminium corrodes, of course, but this immediately forms a coating that gives reliable protection against further damage). It is, however, far and away the most vulnerable to electrolytic action. Aluminium comes well towards the end of what is known as the electromotive series, so the problem must be paid very close attention with regard to everything one wants to build into an aluminium hull. It is recommended that one insulates winches and other fittings electrically before bolting them down, though I doubt whether, with suitably solid fixing, this needs doing 100 per cent. In spite of everything, there are many well known aluminium yachts that have been sailing the seven seas for years and are still in excellent condition. As in most things to do with sailing, the choice of the right building material for a boat is very much a personal matter. An owner of an aluminium craft whom I asked about his experience said 'I'm very satisfied, and couldn't want for a better material. You do have to be a bit careful, and in harbour I will on no account lie alongside a steel boat; it would be bound to cause damage to mine.' For me as a cruising man another drawback of aluminium is that, unlike steel and GRP, you cannot get it repaired everywhere (it needs welding with a gas-shielded 'argon-arc').

Ferro-cement

This boatbuilding material has become very popular lately, because far more than any other it is suited to home-building. No expensive mould is needed, and the concrete is supported by a steel frame and an armature of chicken-wire. The main advantages of this cheap material, which so far has not caught on everywhere, are strength and an almost total absence of galvanic corrosion problems. Against steel there is the disadvantage that ferro-cement is comparatively brittle, and thus much more likely to spring a leak after a collision or going aground. Because of its weight, 'ferro' is suitable only for boats of 9m length or more.

Catamaran

Multihulled boats

When the first catamarans, and then trimarans, were built shortly after the war, they initially attracted enormous enthusiasm in the sailing world, mainly because they allowed unimaginable speeds impossible with slow, good-tempered monohull designs. After there had been a few accidents, when catamarans capsized and could not be righted again and there were even fatalities; as a result the initial enthusiasm died away. Looking at the international boat market today one is struck by how few multihulls are being marketed and sold; yet you get quite a different picture when you are in moorings frequented mainly by blue-water skippers. All

Trimaran

those who have opted for a multihull boat are absolutely sold on the idea. People who have spent half their life sailing monohulls and then made the change not infrequently say that it was only with their catamaran that they learned the real joys of sailing. The main problem with multihulls – as conservative helmsmen see it – is that they can capsize and then are unable (unlike a monohull) to right themselves again. But it is wrong to conclude from this that catamarans or trimarans are worse; they are simply different. Cat enthusiasts rightly point out that their boats have the advantage that they cannot sink. So just as a big hole in a single-hull boat will mean the end of everything, the one thing the catamaran skipper must try to avoid is a capsize. There is really only one way of doing this, and that is:

shorten sail in plenty of time.

Recognising just when the time has come to reef is not easy with a multihull. The danger signal of excessive heeling is absent; when one hull starts lifting out of the water it may, depending on the type of boat, already be too late. For this reason, I think a wind-speed indicator is essential on a multihull boat. The sheets must never be cleated in such a way that they cannot be let fly in a matter of seconds. There have even been automatic sheet cleats designed for just this purpose, which at a preset angle of heel (say, 20°) will open by themselves and free the sheet. In this case the mainsheet must, of course, be coiled-down and laid so that it can run out through the block freely, and will not undo all the good work of the automatic sheet-cleat by kinking and jamming. One of the world's most experienced cat skippers, Wolfgang Hausner, has thought up a marvellously simple (and above all cheap) device that works along the same lines. Finding that his automatic cleat was opening when there was no wind pressure, but merely because the boat was sliding steeply down the side of a high wave, he now simply keeps the boom held by several turns of an ordinary fishing-line. The mainsheet is eased, before attaching this, just enough to ensure that if the fishing-line snaps the boom will not slam out hard against the shrouds, but will be checked by the 'give' in the main-sheet. How many turns of the fishing line are needed to give the right breaking strain is a matter of individual trial-and-error.

I am a little distrustful of the method Ernie Crampton thinks is right for protecting his trimaran from capsizing: the rig of his *Soraya VIII* is designed so that she will lose her mast before capsizing. I

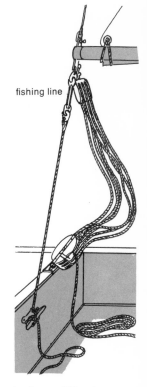

fishing line

Another good idea: the wedge at the end of the boom helps the sail set better when reefed.

cannot believe that the practical breaking strain of a rig can be calculated that accurately. The same basic idea lies behind an invention by Professor F. X. Wortmann, who has designed the rig of his Sigma so that with heavy wind pressure the mast will tilt off to the lee and spill wind, thus reducing the effective pressure. So far, this design has been successful. For an oceangoing catamaran (Hausner says 'Ocean-going cats under 10m are criminal') there is still no way of righting the boat without outside help. You see many big-name catamarans fitted with a disc-like buoyancy body at the top of the mast, intended to prevent the boat from going right

The rigging of the Sigma clearly gives when struck by a gust.

over and upside-down. Hausner rightly thinks this method is unsuitable. To be effective, the disc has to be quite large, and will thus be a surface offering a strong wind a purchase. As the boat heels this streamlined disc very considerably increases the surface offered to the wind, actually *promoting* the capsize.

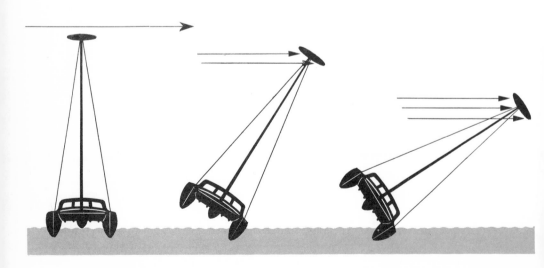

Much the better answer with a catamaran or trimaran is to do everything, and I mean everything, possible to avoid a capsize. Once it has happened, you must realise you have a distress on your hands. All is not lost, so long as preparations have been made to cope with it. There should always be a survival kit, in a watertight packing, attached to the underside of the catamaran (including an axe for getting inside the hull without having to dive underneath).

The quite exceptional *speed* provided by a catamarn will be jeopardised if one tries to build-in extreme stability, which means weight. A multihull must always be built as a 'light displacement' boat, so that it can utilise its higher speed potential. The catamaran *Wanderbird of Devon* (LOA 12.20m) was rather too heavy, and was overloaded as well, and was thus able to put up daily averages of only 120 sea miles or so; not a bad figure for a monohull, but disappointing for a catamaran. If a cat is under 13m in length, there can be no question of building in GRP, steel or solid wood; it will have to be in plywood, and sheathed with GRP for protection.

The poor *manoeuvrability* of a catamaran does not seem to me to be a real disadvantage. Most of the time will in any case be spent out at sea, not in cramped harbours, so this need not affect our choice. Nor need we be worried because a cat is a good deal less handy going about; in the open sea it is always possible to spend more time tacking at leisure, or instead of going about you can always wear ship (ie. go round stern to wind), a manoeuvre that presents no special problems even with a catamaran. It must, however, be said here that with the constantly growing popularity of sailing as a sport the catamaran, with its width, is creating more and more trouble in harbours, where moorings are already in short supply. On the other hand, a flat-on-the-water catamaran is able to creep into tucked-away corners of a harbour where no keel boat, with its draught, will be able to anchor.

The problem of *weight* in a multihull becomes specially acute when building an engine into a catamaran or trimaran. A cat in particular, with its limited manoeuvrability, needs a good auxiliary when in harbour. Cat skippers usually fall back on an outboard, which is only a makeshift solution. Wolfgang Hausner lost his catamaran *Taboo* on a reef on New Guinea, and it is interesting that he feels that if he had had a good inboard engine he would have been able to save the boat. Yet an inboard on a cat presents a whole host of problems.

Buoyancy discs commonly used at tops of masts are dangerous as they promote capsizing.

21

Because of the weight, it ought to be sited amidships, which means fitting a costly propeller layout in between the hulls. Experiments have already been made with a central engine and hydraulic drive to a screw in each of the two hulls. Only with the bigger catamarans could one afford the luxury of a separate inboard engine in each hull; these can have either a normal propeller layout as in a monohull, or (the usual solution) a Z-drive. Seen from the cost and engineering viewpoints (the Z-drive needs to tilt), this is still not the ideal answer.

I have many friends in the sailing world for whom the main argument in favour of the catamaran is that its *movement* is a great deal kinder on the stomach. Many of those who are not troubled by seasickness may scoff at letting the choice of the right boat depend on something like this; but if you have seen the unfortunate sufferers, almost literally at death's door as they lie prostrate on the deck of a rolling, pitching monohull, you can well understand that for them a multihull offers the last hope.

Naturally, sailing in a catamaran is somewhat different, especially its *behaviour in a storm*. While with a monohull the sea-anchor is a quite useless – even dangerous – thing to have, it seems so far to be very successful with a catamaran. This is

Catamarans – not popular in crowded harbours.

undoubtedly due to the fact that multihulls almost invariably lie very shallow in the water, and will lie downwind of a fixed point (ie. a drogue) very much better than a deep-keeled yacht with the greater wind resistance offered by its bows.

The pros and cons I have been listing for multihulls apply almost equally to catamarans and trimarans. By and large, catamarans achieve more speed, but on the other hand they are also more prone to capsizing. Arranging the accommodation should be rather simpler with a trimaran, especially if the coachroof stretches over all three hulls. The development of the trimaran, and its spread in popularity, owes much to a designer by the name of Piver. He designed trimarans mainly for the d-i-y builder (in plywood), and they were so cheap that, especially in America, it was hippies in particular who took up building these low-cost floating homes. This did nothing to make Piver trimarans popular in harbours, and unhappily led one of the world's most interesting yacht clubs, the otherwise quite sane and sensible Seven Seas Cruising Association, to put a blanket ban on accepting any more multihull owners as members.

The pros and cons of multihulls

- Multihulls can capsize (the smaller they are, the sooner they do it).
- Multihulls are virtually unsinkable.
- Multihulls need to be built light; in 'our size' of boat, this rules out steel and GRP.
- Multihulls provide, for the money, much more space than monohulls.
- Multihulls are sensitive to weight, so the space often can't be used.
- Multihulls are more difficult to manoeuvre.
- Multihulls present problems in cramped harbours.
- Multihulls are a great deal faster.
- Multihulls cannot point as high.
- Multihulls can lie to a sea-anchor in a storm.
- Multihulls sail upright, and have a more comfortable movement.
- Building-in an engine presents major problems.
- Self-steering gear presents a problem, because when surfing multihulls temporarily travel so fast that the apparent wind direction shifts.

The rig

The ketch

Above: Euros 41, a popular ketch-rigged cruiser from France with a centre cockpit and seven berths.

This is a two-masted boat with the smaller mast aft but stepped forward of the rudder. With biggish yachts this rig used to be a necessity; in the days of block-and-tackle and cotton sails the sail area had to be divided up, because a sail of more than 30m^2 was more than one man could cope with on his own. Nowadays the only thing I think can be said for a ketch rig is that it allows the sail area

Left: sloop. Right: ketch, with the smaller (mizzen) mast aft. With a schooner, the smaller mast is stepped forward.

to be spread over the ship better in heavy weather. While the skipper of a single-master is going to have his hands full reefing the mainsail when it begins to blow hard, on a ketch he could quite simply take the main in and leave the jib and mizzen standing. The problems start when sailing free. Off the wind, a well-trimmed sailboat will always carry a good deal of weather helm; and this is just when sail area aft does the most harm. Many offshore helmsmen who have chosen a ketch rig have later realised that the mizzen can seldom be used, for this reason. For most of the time the ketch is sailed as nothing more than a sloop, which is then of course somewhat undercanvassed. Even before the wind the ketch rig is not ideal when running 'goosewinged', ie. with the main and mizzen boomed out on opposite sides with a fore-guy. The aft sail then throws so much dirty wind into the mainsail that the latter loses much of its drive.

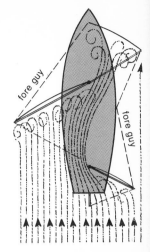

Ketch 'goosewinged'; only the wind on the mizzen is not disturbed by eddies.

The sloop

Of all the different rigs – schooner, yawl, junk or lateen – the only one that has lasted apart from the ketch is the sloop. It is the simplest, cheapest and most versatile rig. With the high quality of modern stainless steel there is nowadays no difficulty in staying even an exceptionally high mast effectively, and for this reason more than 95 per cent of all cruising yachts under 12m prefer the

These two girls sailed the GRP sloop *Kirk* (10.75m) from France to America.

sloop rig. I would keep this single-mast rig as simple as possible, that is to say with just the stays and shrouds needed to ensure the safety of the mast. There is no need for a second forestay, even though it may seem that having a double forestay will make ship-handling easier. On a cruiser, the few minutes this might save under favourable conditions really do not matter. The snag of having two forestays is that the two wires are never tensioned exactly the same, so there is continually a varying amount of slack. Experience shows that this leads to severe vibration in the wires, and this soon makes stainless steel brittle. I have been all round the world with my single forestay without it breaking, while on a sister ship three of the double forestays snapped during the voyage to the West Indies alone. A double forestay does not, in any case, do anything for safety. When beating we have a 'second forestay' anyway, in the luff-wire of the jib. On the other hand, I do rig a double backstay for safety reasons; if you have only one of these and it breaks, there is nothing left to hold the mast, which will undoubtedly carry away.

Roller jib

This will become a standard feature on cruising boats, because its advantages are impressively obvious. A simple tug on a line rolls up the jib, and the wind surface is immediately dowsed. During anchoring there is room to work on the fore-deck, yet the jib can be used to restore manoeuvrability within a matter of seconds. Roller jibs have been about for 20 years or more, but up to now they have not been a popular fitting because the roller mechanism has been

Below: The sheeting point for the genoa needs to be shifted.

trouble-prone and has let skippers down badly just when things on board were getting difficult. In these days of stainless steel and

nylon bearings the problems have, however, been overcome. The only precaution that needs to be taken is for it still to be possible to set an orthodox jib if the roller does go wrong. A common cause of trouble in the mechanism is the bottom joint tilting over because there is insufficient tension, so when a roller jib is fitted the pull on the mast should be through this, and not through the forestay. Our modern artificial fibre sails are very vulnerable to UV light, so with a roller jib (which is of course permanently bent on) the sail must be well protected by a cover stretching from the foot to the top of the mast.

Nowadays there are special roller jibs that can be used to carry varying areas of sail – with a good deal of wind, the jib is simply not unfurled all the way. With the sail area reduced like this one cannot, of course, expect to hold an ideal course on all points of sailing, but for a cruising skipper it should be quite adequate (particularly when not hard on the wind, where a well-cut sail becomes specially important). Systems which involve simply wrapping a special jib round the wire forestay have not proved satisfactory, mainly because the hanks tear the sail to pieces. Instead of this a rod with a groove for the buff-rope needs to be fitted.

Gauge and strength of standing rigging

Nowadays stainless steel is used almost without exception for the shrouds and stays. Standing rigging uses wire rope made up from 19 individual strands. The following gauges are recommended:

Boat's weight	Diameter
1t	4mm
2t	5mm
4t	6mm
6t	7mm
10t	8mm

This 19-strand rope is not suitable for halyards, for which we use a rope made up of a total of 133 strands.

Boat's weight	Diameter
up to 2t	4mm
up to 6t	5mm
up to 10t	6mm

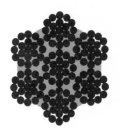

7 × 19 wire rope

Whether it is better to have the terminals for the shrouds swaged on, crimped on or screwed on has long been a subject of argument.

Left: Norseman screwed terminal

Centre: swaged terminal

Right: thimble as terminal

I personally have most confidence in Norseman terminals; these may not be quite as strong as rolled-on terminals, but they are easier to fix and far easier to keep an eye on.

Bottlescrews are usually made from stainless steel, though there is nothing wrong with satin bronze; the only thing to watch is that they are matched to the breaking strain of the wire rope. The theoretical breaking load of stainless wire rope is about:

4mm	1.5t	7mm	4.7t
5mm	2.4t	8mm	6.1t
6mm	3.4t	10mm	9.5t

Rigging screws should be fitted with a toggle to prevent twisting, which would lead to breakages. I do not like to see locknuts used on bottlescrews: strictly speaking they weaken the rigging screw, since they put an extra stress on it if they are done up tight enough to do their job properly. The same security can be obtained with stainless wire wound through the sleeve of the bottlescrew in a figure-eight. The end of the wire should be bent inwards and protected with sticky tape, so that no-one can scratch themselves.

Toggle

Left: locknut to secure rigging screw

Right: stainless steel wire to secure rigging screw.

The strength of the whole rigging depends on its weakest part, so the bottom point of attachment of the wire rope, the *chainplates*, must be solid enough; this is one of the points to watch when buying a new boat. Avoid like the plague chainplates that are sim-

Chainplate laminated-in.

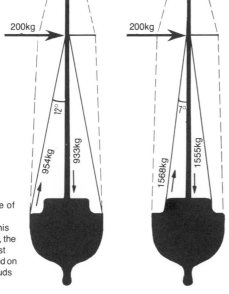

200kg

12°

954kg   933kg

With a pressure of 200kg at the crosstrees of this 3m beam yacht, the load at the mast foot is 933kg and on the lower shrouds 954kg.

200kg

7°

1568kg   1555kg

The same yacht, but with inboard lower shrouds; mast loading now 1555kg, shroud loading 1568kg, putting heavy stress on the superstructure.

ply bolted on to the deck. On GRP boats, they should be laminated into the side of the hull. On cruisers there is no point having inboard shrouds attached to the superstructure rather than to the hull: the down-pull on the mast is at a shallower, less effective angle and the coachroof is in any case never enormously strong.

Shroud tension

Setting up the shrouds correctly seems to give many people a good deal of trouble. We should not let ourselves be influenced by racing skippers, who like a flexible rig; it is very dangerous for stainless steel rigging to be subjected to changing tensile stress, since this makes a wire rope far more likely to break than if it carries a constant heavy load. Eric Hiscock, the doyen of the cruising world, has set out three rules for shroud tension which if followed to the letter will make 'tuning' simplicity itself.

On older wooden hulls it will be hard to produce these settings, but any GRP boat – and especially every steel yacht – should be able to stand up to the loads. The mast must stand straight and upright, and this can only be checked from ashore. A slight forward lean is permissible, though not of course any curvature (this is easy to detect by looking up the mast from the foot). The final tuning will have to be done at sea, when the boat is heeling at around 10° (use an inclinometer).

Care and maintenance of the rigging

Luckily, stainless steel does not need much looking after, though any film of rust should be wiped away since it can damage the steel. I have found a cheap polish for use on plastic excellent for this purpose, and far more effective than the special and vastly expensive steel preservative preparations. The threads of the bottlescrews should be greased before fitting; spraycan oils and silicone preparations are not suitable for this job, because they evaporate very quickly. It is important to check wire rope and terminals (including those at the top end of the shrouds) regularly, and at least every 1000 nautical miles. A snagged strand in a halyard may not mean any weakening of the rope, but it does indicate pretty surely either that the diameter of the sheave is too small, or that it is not running freely.

Lightning protection

The probability of being struck by lightning is extremely slight. Nonetheless, it has been a great help to my peace of mind having 3m lengths of 5mm copper wire attached with seizing and a jubilee-clip to all shrouds and stays, and to the foot of the mast. In a thunderstorm I simply trail these wires in the water; a very firm warning against streaming them permanently, however, because this could damage the rigging through galvanic corrosion. A steel yacht needs no special lightning conductor since it is completely protected on the principle of the Faraday cage.

The sails

For me the standard suit of sails for a sloop would comprise mainsail, genoa, working jib, small jib and storm ('spitfire') jib. You may be able to persuade the sailmaker to cut a main that does not need sail battens. It may not look as nice – but it will give you far less trouble, and the main can be handed or set on all points of sailing quite easily. A trysail (storm mainsail) is not, I feel, necessary; if the wind is so strong that a trysail is needed for beating, then the conditions are surely such that holding a course into the wind is not going to be possible. On all other points one can manage quite well under just a foresail. I would advise very strongly indeed against fitting a boom to the jib. Its sole advantage is that the jib does not need tending when going about, and against this there is a whole list of sizeable disadvantages: the bulky boom takes up much valuable space on the foredeck; in a swell with little wind the boom slatting to and fro can make foredeck work very dangerous indeed; and on a run it is in any case almost unusable if we do not want to run the risk of gybing all-standing. A fore-guy, like that used for securing the main, is difficult to rig.

Sailing on a close-reach under genoa and main.

If, as long-passage sailors, we want to carry running sails, the laborious business of setting and lowering can be made very much simpler if we can furl both sails on a roller stay. The foot of this double roller-jib should be fixed about 20 per cent of the boat's length forward of the mast.

Though it is almost self-evident, I will stress once again that everything to do with the rigging should be too large rather than too small, and that we must never let ourselves be influenced on this point by racing helmsmen. They, for reasons of weight and wind-resistance, are always on the danger-limit where calculating their rigging is concerned. These considerations are totally irrelevant to the cruising skipper. A somewhat heavier rigging is, naturally, a bit more expensive; but if we give thought to this when first buying the boat the extra cost can be kept within limits – and making the changes later on can be costly.

The engine

Inboard or outboard

This problem arises only up to a length of 7m overall. The draw-backs of an outboard can readily be listed:
1. Petrol is carried on board (giving a fire risk).
2. In heavy seas it may be impossible to use the engine, as the propeller comes out of the water.
3. Fuel consumption is high.

In spite of these drawbacks, one cannot really avoid using an outboard on very small yachts because there simply is not enough space to install an inboard with its costly propeller installation. The major shortcoming is that even if you fit the long-shaft type of outboard the screw is not deep enough in the water to guarantee that it will stay submerged in a heavy swell. It will not matter, of course, if it occasionally comes out of the water for a few seconds and the engine screams, but the efficiency will be very definitely reduced. If the lifting-free becomes at all frequent, however, it can do serious harm to the bearings. It is advisable to fit the outboard in a well, if at all possible. With it hung on the stern, there is the danger of a following sea completely swamping a valuable engine. Hard though it is to understand why, many famous firms making outboards use parts that have only a limited resistance to salt water, and are worn out within three to four years; so the engine must be protected scrupulously against seawater.

When ordering an outboard for a yacht, it must be made clear that it is not wanted for a runabout, but for a slow, displacement craft. Many makers will then fit it with a special prop, allowing better use to be made of the available power while moving relatively slowly. I would look on an engine of 5hp or so as the smallest size suitable for use in coastal waters.

The following are recommended engine sizes:

Weight of boat	Engine power
up to 700kg	approx. 5hp
up to 800kg	approx. 8hp
up to 1000kg	approx. 10hp

It must be understood that these engine ratings are certainly not enough for making way against, for instance, a very strong wind or in a storm. In such conditions an outboard is anyway unsuitable, and even a substantial increase in engine size would not bring much improvement.

The inboard petrol engine

The major disadvantage of the petrol engine is the explosion and fire hazard. Even if the engine is fitted with a number of protective devices to reduce the risk, it cannot be entirely excluded. The least that must be done is to fit a fan which, when the ignition key is turned, will drive fumes out of the engine compartment for a time before the engine can be started. A 'gas sniffer' is also worthwhile, though switching this on and off must not cause any sparks that might ignite a petrol-and-air mixture (only this will explode – petrol on its own only burns) before the sniffer has time to indicate anything. A disaster can still occur if, for example, there is a leak in a fuel pipe that goes unnoticed. This means that all the time petrol is carried on board painstaking care is called for, and one must never adopt the car-driver's nonchalant attitude to the fuel. In a car leaking fuel lines are comparatively harmless, because the petrol fumes disperse into the atmosphere and a dangerous petrol-and-air mixture cannot occur.

The reason why despite this so many sailors opt for a petrol engine has less to do with price than with its low weight. This is its main advantage over the diesel engine. The higher cost of petrol hardly comes into the argument, I feel, bearing in mind the modest quantities used on small boats. A further advantage of the petrol engine is, of course, its very much quieter running compared to a diesel.

A big drawback, on the other hand, is the far more trouble-prone ignition system, inescapable in a petrol unit. Especially in a boat, where the air is always laden with moisture and salt water does everything it can to help along corrosion of the points and other contacts, an ignition circuit like this is a real headache. It is some measure of safeguard to start up the engine every morning, if possible, throughout the voyage; the heat produced will dry out the engine thoroughly, especially the plugs, distributor and so on.

The diesel engine

The diesel, on the other hand, has nothing but advantages apart from being heavier and causing much more vibration. Fuel consumption is low, diesel oil is cheaper, and diesel fuel does not evaporate at normal temperatures so there is no gas to mix with air and form an explosive mixture. There are almost no components given to breaking down.

Installing a diesel engine is a job for an expert. Nowadays flexible mountings are normally used, since the vibration transmitted to the hull needs to be kept to an absolute minimum. If an engine were put on solid mountings this could (especially in the case of GRP boats) considerably shorten the life of the whole vessel. A single cylinder diesel presents particular installation problems; considerable skill, and a measure of luck as well, is needed to fit the engine so that it can be described as anything like 'quiet-running'; usually the results, even with a twin-cylinder, will not be satisfactory throughout the rev-range. At tickover, in particular, the shuddering goes through the entire boat and gets on one's nerves. Consequently the cruising engine speed cannot, if one has any feeling for the boat at all, be governed solely by considerations of economical fuel consumption; we also have to think about the vibration that is being produced. The more cylinders the engine has, the less of a problem there is.

How big an engine should be fitted? You often hear it said that for a sailboat's auxiliary an engine power of 3hp/t of the ship's weight is ample. I do not agree, and look on this as the lower limit. The engine is not going to be used only in a flat calm – it will also be needed to get out through a harbour mouth, for instance, against a

34

2-cylinder diesel

valves

flexible mounting

fuel filter

thermostat

exhaust

bleed valve

fuel supply pump

dipstick

oil filter

generator

injectors

valves

air filter

control box

strong wind and tide. I can speak from experience: my yacht was powered with 3hp/t, which in calm water with no wind would give a speed of nearly 6 knots (her hull speed!). But with a Force 4 blowing, and a head sea to match, I could manage only something between 2 and 3 knots. It is interesting to find just how misinformed the so-called experts can be. Before I started on my round-the-world trip, I went to see the makers of the boat's engine. One of the heads of the firm, no less, just could not believe that his very large engine would give my 6-tonner a speed of only 6 knots, and was firmly convinced that with 20hp at least 9 knots should be possible. He had never even heard of 'hull speed' (which for cruisers is 2.2 $\sqrt{\text{waterline length}}$). If I, personally, ever had to choose an engine for a sailing boat again, I would work on the basis of 4hp/t; and correspondingly more for a motor-sailer.

Mechanical trouble Obviously you will, even if you may not regard yourself as very gifted mechanically speaking, have to work on the engine; it is impossible to go to a workshop every time something goes wrong, and small engine repairs will sometimes have to be carried out under way, with whatever is available on board in the way of tools. A main cause of problems is leaks in the fuel lines; they can be recognised from the engine running 'lumpily', or running for only a few seconds after starting and then dying and refusing to restart. It should be possible to cope with this with the means to hand, though it is not as simple as it looks. One will, of course, have made sure of a set of gaskets and seals from the manufacturer; it is, anyway, advisable to throw old seals away. Copper washers should never be re-used. It is essential to keep things spotlessly clean, because even a tiny particle of dirt or trace of paint can lead to another leak at the same spot. Before assembly, all parts should also be washed clean of diesel fuel, using petrol; diesel oil is in fact a penetrating oil, like that we use in the home (or indeed on a boat) to get a rusted nut moving again. After any work on the fuel lines the engine will have to be bled of air, and many engines are fitted with a bleed valve for this purpose. In this case all that need be done is to operate the fuel pump by hand until no more air bubbles come out of the bleed valve, only pure fuel oil. If there is no bleed valve provided, the operating instructions will explain how to bleed the engine.

Every effort must be made to obtain the fullest possible literature on the engine. Even though a workshop manual describing, say, work on the cylinder head, may not mean much to you personally, you may still manage to find a skilled mechanic in some remote harbour: and the workshop manual will make his work very much easier. The manufacturer should also be asked for the torque settings for the various bolts. When working on an engine it is possible to do a lot of damage by pulling the threads of some bolt or other; and if the spanner is long enough this is not difficult, even for a woman's wrist muscles. The ideal answer is always to use a torque wrench, so that you do not have to rely on 'feel' – which those who are not mechanics do not have anyway.

A sound basic principle is that there is no harm in carrying too many tools and spares. For long passages in particular the tool kit supplied by manufacturers is certainly not enough. For a petrol engine I would take a spare set of gaskets, plugs, coil, distributor contacts and perhaps even a spare carburettor. For a diesel, one would need to carry spare seals and gaskets, oil filters and injector nozzles. There is nothing one can do in the way of working on injectors, so in the (rare) event of trouble there is only one thing to do – if you suspect the injectors, change the lot (ie. both, in the case of a twin-cylinder engine).

If there is a choice of colours in which the engine can be painted, it is best to ask for the lightest possible; this makes it easy to spot where fuel or oil is leaking, and to investigate the reason at once. Most of all, it is imperative to keep the engine readily accessible; this will of course need to be thought about when first installing the engine, and it will have a major bearing on its longevity and reliability. Ideally, it should be possible to remove all the engine casings so that routine jobs can be done on it easily from all sides. A smaller diesel (up to 2 cylinders) has the advantage that it can, given the right circumstances, still be started up by hand; this enormously useful feature should be borne in mind when fitting the engine, and enough room left for turning the starting handle.

A diesel engine, too, can only benefit from being started up and run as often as possible. This will stop rust from forming in the cylinders and on the piston rings; rust here dramatically shortens the life of an engine, and this is something that should be kept in mind during winter storage (when it is easy to avoid by shifting the position of the pistons, by hand, at intervals throughout the winter). Looked after properly, a diesel engine like that used in our yachts should have a life of about 5000 hours, which is equal to about once round the world under engine! Without wishing to advertise one make or the other, I will list briefly the firms which in the experience of my friends make reliable auxiliary diesels for yachts. These are Sabb, Faryman, Mercedes, Peugeot, Renault and Perkins, with the superb but horribly expensive Gardner engine for yachts over 15t.

Cooling There is a good deal of disagreement on this. On paper, the *air-cooled* engine seems totally devoid of problems: but it is practical only from a very definite minimum size of boat. Special air-ducts have to be carefully designed to ensure effective cooling, and if you reckon up how much every cubic metre of space in a yacht costs you will see that the space lost with this ducting makes it a very expensive answer to the problem. There will have to be provision for keeping out water when waves break over the deck, and the exhaust system (which can reach more than 400°C) will almost certainly have to be water-cooled.

For this reason I personally prefer *water-cooling*, though here again opinions differ about using a single or dual-circuit system. In the former 'direct' system seawater is drawn in by a pump and passed through the cooling circuit of the engine and exhaust. This is a simple arrangement, which needs only one pump. The snag is that at temperatures over 65°C the salt and lime in seawater start to separate out, and sooner or later this is bound to block up the cooling system. The engine can therefore only be run cold – meaning, here, 60°C – and this increases wear and shortens its working life. This disadvantage is avoided with a dual-circuit, 'indirect' system in which the engine (like that of a car) has its own closed cooling system filled with fresh water. The engine can be run at temperatures close to boiling point, which is much better for it. The cooling work which in a car is done by the wind passing through the radiator is here left to a second cooling circuit which uses seawater. The drawback of this arrangement is that a second pump is needed; but when it comes down to it a dual-circuit system is more reliable because even if a pump does fail the temperature climbs only slowly, and the engine is not immediately in dire trouble. If the pump in a single-circuit system packs up, or the intake valve gets blocked, you have only a few seconds in which to switch the engine off before it seizes. In steel-hulled boats a single-circuit freshwater system has been used successfully; the piping is welded to the inside of the hull (or the steel rudder blade), and the heated water is then able to give off its heat through the steel plate to the seawater as it flows past.

Instruments are essential for keeping a close watch on what the engine is doing. The most important is a temperature gauge, even if there is a thermostat fitted to keep the temperature within the prescribed range. Thermostats can fail, and generally only a temperature gauge can tell you this has happened. Secondly, there must be an oil pressure gauge to show whether there is enough oil in the engine and whether the oil pump is working properly. On starting, the pressure will usually be very high, dropping off during running. Find out from the manufacturer how low the pressure can go without endangering the engine. Finally, of course, one needs an engine-speed indicator so that the throttle setting can always be adjusted to what has been found to be the best 'cruising-revs'.

Practical experience shows that the greatest danger for a yacht engine is overheating, so it undoubtedly is a good idea to have the temperature gauge coupled to an audible warning signal; this is not a difficult job for a handyman, though so far as I know there is still nothing available commercially.

Tanks For safety reasons these should always be fitted so that the fuel is pumped to the engine. With a diesel it is best for this to be a mechanical pump, since in an emergency one is then quite independent of electricity supplies.

Care must be taken especially with a diesel to keep the fuel tank as clean as possible; this rules out the use of a copper tank for diesel fuel, because this produces a rubbery deposit that will soon block the filter. A fuel tank must, of course, be fitted with a 'breather' opening upwards to the deck. There will always be a certain amount of water from condensation in the tank, depending on how much air there is in it, and for this reason the tank should (especially in the case of a diesel engine) be kept constantly topped up as far as possible. In regions where there is a big difference between air and water temperatures the condensed water will have to be drained off from time to time; water is heavier than diesel oil, so it will collect at the bottom of the tank. The ideal set-up is then to have a drain-tap at the bottom of the tank so that the water can be quite simply allowed to run out; the colour of the liquid will show when the diesel fuel itself is beginning to drain. The pipe drawing fuel from the tank should obviously not reach right down to the bottom, as it would then often be sucking up water, or even sediment. To avoid having constantly to bleed the system, a diesel fuel tank should never be allowed to run completely dry. Even though the intake pipe may not reach right down to the bottom, the boat's movement may well stir up 'dirt' (consisting mainly of algae, which thrive in condensed water) or water in the tank, and this will be drawn up. This will show up immediately through faltering of the engine; as a rule it will not stop the engine running, but power will be drastically reduced.

Many boats have what is known as a 'day-tank'; this may not look very pretty, but it is straightforward to the point of primitiveness, and utterly reliable since the engine no longer has to rely on a fuel pump. The day-tank principle is simple: a small tank holding just a few litres is fixed above the engine, and is filled either by hand or by pumping up fuel from the main tank. It should be fitted with a gauge, or be transparent, to avoid running it dry and getting air into the engine.

At cruising revs, a diesel will – calculated very roughly – use fuel at a rate of 0.1 litre per horsepower per hour. It should consume practically no lubricating oil, though oil changes as often as possible will certainly do the engine no harm. Usually the manufacturer will specify exactly which type of oil to use, and these recommen-

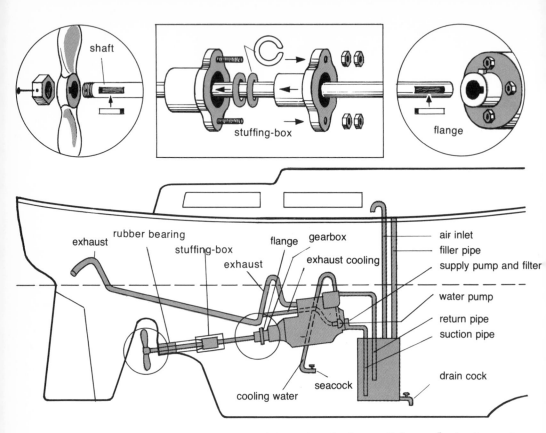

shaft

stuffing-box

flange

dations should be followed to the letter. If, for example, the maker stipulates 20 SAE oil whatever the time of year, every effort must be made to obtain this thin grade of oil, even in hot countries. It is a good idea, therefore, to keep some in stock.

Propeller and gearbox As a rule, the power of the engine is transmitted to the propeller via a mechanical gearbox; this *must* have a reverse gear, which provides the only means of 'putting on the brakes'. It must not be forgotten that the gearbox, too, needs its oil changed, though not so often. After the gearbox comes the propeller shaft, joined on by a flange and usually running from close behind the gearbox, through the boat and out into the water. This is normally now mounted in rubber ('silentbloc') bearings. In southern waters, by the way, one must not only run the engine frequently, but also ensure that the prop shaft is turned over from time to time. Tiny, hard shellfish containing a lot of lime get in between the rubber bearings and the shaft, to which they attach themselves, and if these are not soon removed by turning the shaft they can severely damage or even destroy the rubber bearings.

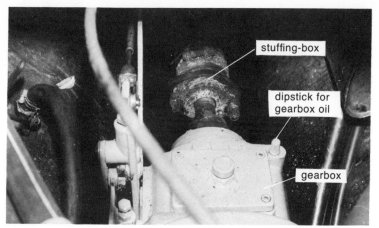

stuffing-box

dipstick for gearbox oil

gearbox

The bearings are water-lubricated. Water has to be prevented from getting along the shaft and into the hull, and this is done by a *stuffing-box*. This device merits special attention; inside it is a packing which is pressed against the rotating shaft more, or less, tightly depending on the pressure exerted by the two glands. This packing is quite simply a wedge of cotton yarn saturated in grease. Generally there is also a greasecup on the outside of the stuffing-box, and this is screwed down slightly every time after stopping the engine to force more grease into the cotton waste. The pressure can be adjusted by altering the setting of the nuts, and the art of adjusting a stuffing-box correctly lies in not letting it run dry while at the same time allowing as little water as possible to get into the hull. The correct setting will let one drop of water through the stuffing-box, with the shaft running, roughly every 5 to 10 seconds. This adjustment can really only be made with the shaft turning, and care must be taken never to tighten up the gland on one side only; this would almost certainly snap one or other of the bolts. It is better to be patient, tightening first the lefthand nut half-a-turn, then the righthand nut half-a-turn, and so on. Once the right setting has been found, secure it with the locknuts. Check at regular intervals (of 20 hours running) to see if readjustment is needed. When no more adjustment is left, the packing will have to be renewed. This can, in fact, be done with the boat afloat; if the fresh packing is prepared beforehand, it takes only seconds to push the ring of material into place and staunch the flow of water.

Calculating the propeller diameter and pitch is something to leave to the specialist. On a sailboat the prop will, as a general rule, preferably be two-bladed, because of its lower water resistance. It is not generally realised that a free-wheeling propeller will, when spinning at low speed, cause a very considerable amount of water resistance, so that it is much better to hold the prop fixed, vertical, behind the deadwood by engaging a gear. A piece of adhesive tape stuck to the prop shaft in the engine compartment can be used to show the 'right' position of the blades. Holding the shaft still will also cause less wear on the bearings and stuffing-box.

I am not keen on folding propellers, which offer very little resistance even when they are not behind the deadwood. Small shellfish, or dirt, can all too often interfere with their opening up automatically, and in any case reverse running with them is poor. There is really no justification for them on a cruising yacht, where differences of tenths of a knot do not matter. Far more useful for our purposes would be a variable-pitch screw in which the pitch of the blades can be adjusted by a rod mechanism. It would even be possible then to dispense with a mechanical reverse gear, since the blades can be adjusted right round to the reverse setting. Even when sailing with the engine running, it is an advantage to be able to set the pitch slightly coarser so that the engine can work more effectively. Unfortunately the smaller the installation the less efficient it is, so that it is not an ideal arrangement for boats under 13m. Moreover, a second stuffing-box is needed, as the rod for adjusting the blade pitch has to be led out to the propeller.

Checklist		
	weekly	battery: electrolyte level and density
	before running	engine oil level
	at start of running	stuffing box, with shaft turning (one drop every 10 seconds)
		exhaust leaks (detected by blackened patches; hold white paper over suspect places to see if it discolours)
	while running	engine temperature and oil pressure (every 10 minutes)
	after running	screw down greasecup of water pump and stuffing-box
		throttle lever at full speed setting with propeller engaged
	every 20hr	water level in dual-circuit system
	every 50hr	oil level in gearbox; engine oilchange (as stated by maker); valve clearances
	every 250hr	change oil filter

The accommodation

This will naturally be governed by the overall size of the boat. It would not be sensible in a small yacht to split up what is already a small enough space with bulkheads and the like; yet on larger craft (over 10m) I am in fact in favour of dividing up the space – it satisfies Man's instinct to retire into his cave, and makes for cosier living.

The usual arrangement on a small cruising boat is a saloon and a fo'c'sle. If the latter is to be used as living quarters, as little as possible should be stowed there, and certainly not any sails; these belong in the forepeak or – by no means the worst place – simply on deck. The fo'c'sle is the most uncomfortable part of the whole ship when under way; berths there can be almost uninhabitable in a rough sea, when in any case life tends to centre around the bunks near the companionway. Comfortable though wide bunks may be in harbour, they are not good things to have at sea. A double bunk may look attractive in an advertising brochure, but it is an absolute nonsense on a cruising yacht; on a reach or a beat it will make restful sleep quite impossible. Bunks must, of course, be fitted so that the occupant is prevented from falling out, and this can be done either with tensioned sailcloth or with leeboards. On our world trip we used leeboards hinged to fold down under the mattress, so that they merely needed raising when a sea got up. We found them very satisfactory. A 'pram-cover' above the companionway greatly extends the living space in a small yacht, because the hatch need be closed only seldom (when it is raining, or with a following wind) and at least subjectively one has the feel of the cabin being bigger.

An **aft cabin** becomes a possibility on larger boats, and is obviously ideal when cruising with several friends, who then have their own separate quarters. However, it needs to be a fair size if it is not to be a 'rat-hole', as I have heard one famous designer refer to a tiny after-cabin.

In hulls over 12m there can even be a *centre cockpit*, something that I prefer even though it does have a whole range of disadvantages. The biggest of these is that this is far and away the wettest part of the whole boat. Furthermore, one is 'wasting' on the engine beneath the cockpit floor what is, from the point of view of motion under way, the most comfortable part of the vessel. Ideally, the

43

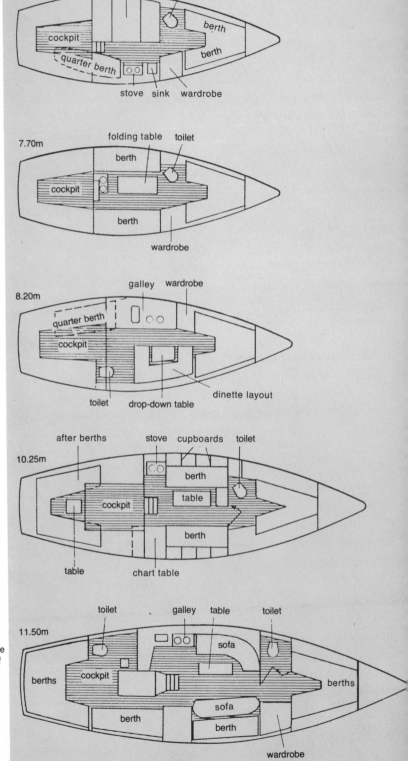

7.30m
drop-down table toilet
berth
cockpit
berth
quarter berth
stove sink wardrobe

7.70m
folding table toilet
berth
cockpit
berth
wardrobe

8.20m
galley wardrobe
quarter berth
cockpit
toilet
toilet drop-down table
dinette layout

10.25m
after berths stove cupboards toilet
berth
cockpit
table
berth
table chart table

11.50m
toilet galley table toilet
sofa
berths cockpit
berths
berth sofa
berth
wardrobe

The bigger the boat, the
more ways there are of
arranging the
accommodation.

boat would be big enough for us to pass from the saloon and under the centre cockpit into the aft cabin, so that in foul weather we would not even need to open the hatches over the companionways. If the engine is installed under the cockpit floor it is nicely accessible for maintenance and repairs; the only thing to keep a careful watch on is that water coming into the cockpit does in fact all run out through the drain tubes and does not get into the engine compartment. This is difficult to ensure, though certainly possible.

An important 'must' in a seagoing yacht is naturally a self-draining cockpit, together with a bridgedeck as an essential. Designs which have, in practice, nothing but an ordinary wooden bulkhead to keep the water in the cockpit from getting down into the cabin are highly dangerous. When a sea crashes into the cockpit, this generally fills right up for a short while; though admittedly the boat's motion immediately tips a large part of the water out again, there are still hundreds of litres left which may sometimes stay in the cockpit for minutes on end. A plain wooden bulkhead will let it run almost unhindered into the cabin; quite apart from the discomfort this will cause, this must be avoided at all costs from the safety viewpoint.

It is a matter of taste whether you have a 'wet zone' next to the companionway, accommodating the toilet, shower, galley, oilskin hanging stowage and so on. One learns that in bad weather, even without seas breaking over the boat, an incredible amount of wetness is brought below on one's oilskins, and can make life very

A folding hood looks ungainly, but enormously increases the amount of living space.

45

Navigator's corner on an Optima. Being close to the companionway can be wet, but kinder on the stomach.

miserable indeed. This will, to a certain extent, be prevented if the crew change out of their wet oilskins by the companionway, and then leave them in this wet zone. Such an arrangement is, of course, possible only with a biggish yacht where losing living space at the widest part of the boat does not matter.

The navigator's position, with its expensive instruments well shielded from spray, needs to be close to the companionway. It is of course easy to say that the chart table should be big enough for a normal chart to be laid out flat; but there is seldom that much space on a yacht. A surface measuring 70 × 50cm is quite sufficient, and on a boat used for a round-the-world cruise I would go so far as to say that a chart table is unnecessary. One has to remember that yachts nowadays are so expensive that there is no excuse for wasting space. On passage, out of sight of land, there is no need for a chart at all (at most it is wanted once a day, for plotting the midday position). This will surely not be while the table is laid for a meal, so the table can be used as a working surface. Close inshore, ie. when making a landfall, I cannot imagine a skipper navigating by the chart and eating at the same time – you usually only sit down and eat at peace, once all the excitement is over.

I have had nothing but good experience of the gimballed type of saloon table, though I know many well-travelled yachtsmen who have only bad reports to give of the system. Its main virtue, for me, is not so much that I can eat at it without worrying about the saltcellar suddenly flying across the cabin, but that, when the boat is rolling, the ship's cook has somewhere to dump various bits and pieces safely at any moment. The swinging saloon table hung from the deckhead seldom works trouble-free straight away, and needs a good deal of trial-and-error experiments before the pendulum motion can be damped with shock-cord to get it roughly into step with the boat's roll frequency. There is no harm in fitting a gimballed (or, to be exact, semi-gimballed) table with small edge-rails, or 'fiddles', though these will have to be removable if eating when in harbour is not to be a misery. If you decide to do without a swinging table, then a whole series of makeshifts are going to be needed. A fiddle at least 5cm high round the table edge will obviously help, and a damp cloth spread over the tabletop will stop plates from sliding about to a certain extent. A useful tip is that in very bad weather conditions eating and sleeping is most comfortable on the cabin sole.

Whether to have the table in the centre of the saloon or as a dinette arrangement is largely a matter of personal taste. I much prefer the dinette layout (especially in yachts over 9m) because I think it gives a cosier feel to the cabin. If you are a gregarious kind of person and like having lots of visitors when in harbour, the more traditional layout with the table in the middle would be better, as it allows a bigger get-together; apart from this, however, the central table is in everybody's way when moving about the boat.

Left: dinette layout

Right: on small boats, a central table is the only answer.

The galley

I have a thing against plastic plates, which I find not all that practical, anyway. Their only advantage is unbreakability; otherwise, they are vulnerable to knife cuts and they attract dirt. On our round-the-world cruise we used ordinary china crockery, and not a thing was broken. It is essential, of course, for galley lockers to be fitted with suitable compartments and fiddles to stop the plates, etc. from sliding to and fro. Where knives and forks are concerned, it should be remembered that if you wash the 'good silver' in salt water very often, electrolytic corrosion will affect it so badly that knife blades will (even if stainless) be eaten away by galvanic action and soon have an unintended sawtooth edge.

The galley should always be close to the companionway.

If you buy big mugs with the idea of being able to thrust a cup of hot coffee into the hand of the half-frozen man at the wheel, try them out first to see that they do not conduct heat so much that the helmsman won't be able to hold the thing! We found soup dishes in enamelware were not a good idea because we were continually burning our fingers on them.

Enamelled metal saucepans are dangerous, because the enamel splinters. Many experienced ship's cooks find a pressure-

Colour plate: Life is hard for the cook on a beat. While the skipper and crew collect in the cockpit with the boat heeling at 20 or 30°, the cook is down below coping with kerosene fumes, crashing crockery and nausea.

cooker a must; this avoids the annoyance of steam in the cabin making everything damp, it reduces cooking times considerably, and in parts of the world where you cannot buy top-quality fillet steak even quite tough meat can be made into a tasty stew by cooking it right through under pressure. Fears of a minor explosion are quite groundless with the modern, foolproof pressure-cooker, so long as the instructions are followed.

The stove

Bottled gas It is undoubtedly only a matter of time before there will have been so many accidents with bottled gas used on yachts that the use of this fuel will be prohibited by law. Few people are fully aware of the hideous dangers. Propane gas is somewhat heavier than air, so when there is a leak in a pipe or from a poorly-tightened screw-coupling it sinks down and collects in the bilges where, one day, it gets ignited. True, you can smell the escaping gas – so long as you don't have a cold. True, too there are such things as 'gas-sniffers' to give a reliable warning of gas in the bilges – so long as they are in working order, and are switched on. I could understand people preferring this type of fuel if it had really convincing advantages, and it does admittedly have a high calorific value and makes the stove simple to use. But that is all. The installation work has to be done very thoroughly, and to some extent has to be allowed for in the design of the boat. The bottles need filling from time to time, and this – particularly abroad – can cause enormous bother; in some Spanish ports, in fact, the taxi-drivers refuse to carry sailors who are toting gas bottles under their arm. And, finally, the screw-coupling on the bottle has to match that in the filling station (and abroad it hardly ever does). Many people have found that it is cheaper to throw away your own bottles and buy a new one each time.

Alcohol or kerosene If we have any care for the lives of our companions, and our own, the only answer left is alcohol (methylated spirits and the like) or kerosene, since electricity supplies on a sailboat are never adequate for cooking. Alcohol provides the safest form of fuel, and though its calorific value is fairly low it will fry a piece of meat in a pan even if not fast enough to seal it. Alcohol does not explode, but will burn. If any is spilt and catches fire, there is no need to panic; even quite large fires can be put out easily with a pan of water. In my opinion, kerosene (paraffin) is best for shipboard use. It heats almost as well as propane gas, and once you have got used to it operating the stove is no problem. The burner of a kerosene stove has to be heated up before use so that when the kerosene flows through it, it is immediately vaporised.

Primus stove with saucepan guard. Below it is an electric refrigerator with a door that lets all the cold out – hardly practical on a sailboat.

The preheating is done with methylated spirit, poured over the burner (naturally before the tap is opened to allow the kerosene, kept under slight pressure, to reach the burner). If the burner is not hot enough, what happens next is what makes kerosene so unpopular with the uninitiated: quite a long flame leaps up. But so long as there are no curtains in the way, this is completely harmless if you keep calm; shut off the tap, and in a moment or two the flame will die away. In any case, there is no need for this to happen at all if you are patient in heating the burner. It is, in fact, possible to buy little measures that let you pour out exactly the right amount of methylated spirit needed. If you have had to douse the flame, let the burner cool down before starting the procedure again from scratch. If there are draughts inside the galley, the measured amount of spirit may not give enough heat, so that the burner is still too cold when the tap is opened; and in some countries you can buy only low-concentration alcohol (70 per cent or less), so that rather more has to be used to preheat the burner.

Kerosene stoves are available (mainly from Primus, whose parts can be bought anywhere in the world) with two or three burners, gimballed or fixed, and with or without an oven. The latter will not be needed on a cruiser that hops from port to port and is seldom at sea for more than three days at a stretch; for the long-passage sailor, however, an oven will greatly enhance the choice of menu. Imagine, for example, being able to bake your own bread! In a luxury yacht which carries a freezer (see below) an oven is almost essential.

Galley stoves can also be used quite effectively as a means of heating, and are extremely efficient in small cabins. Care must be taken, however, to have enough fresh air coming into the cabin, because stoves burn up incredibly large amounts of oxygen. Getting headaches is a serious warning symptom.

Refrigerator

This could well be the most important piece of equipment for comfortable living on board. A careful look at the advertising leaflets, and thinking about the matter will, however, make you realise that an electric fridge on a sailing boat is ridiculous; simple mathematics will bring this fact home. The leaflet claims 'Economical consumption of 5 amps; once the food is chilled, only 3 amps'. Even the latest electric refrigerators working on the vibrating diaphragm principle need 2-3 amps. Reckoning on a chilling-time of three hours, this already means taking 15 ampere-hours (Ah) out of a boat's 72Ah battery, and after a further 10 hours overnight the figure will have reached 45Ah. With a battery giving, in practical terms, about 55Ah, this obviously means that the refrigerator alone will have flattened it by the next morning, and the engine will need to churn away for 10 hours on end to recharge it (see Electricity, page 69).

It is, however, also possible to run an absorption-type refrigerator on gas, kerosene or methylated spirit (you would naturally not even consider using petrol). What I have said about the lethal risks of having gas on board for cooking applies even more strongly to a gas refrigerator. A draught blowing out the flame behind the fridge would, unless there were a protective device, allow gas to escape unhindered even without there being any leak in the piping. Much better is a kerosene refrigerator, which works extremely well in harbour, though it should be borne in mind in the case of a small yacht that the flame will generate a good deal of

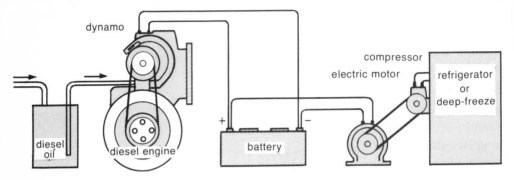

dynamo

compressor

electric motor

refrigerator or deep-freeze

+ –

diesel oil

diesel engine

battery

Five energy-consuming steps to generating cold.

heat close to the fridge. At sea, with the boat heeling, neither a gas nor a kerosene refrigerator will work.

American yachtsmen have, I believe, found a satisfactory answer to the problem in recent years. Let us look, for a moment, at the energy sequence in a normal compressor refrigerator: the energy contained in the fuel is changed by combustion into mechanical energy in the engine and then, via a dynamo, converted into electrical energy. The dynamo stores the energy it produces in a battery, which in turn gives up part of it to drive the electricity-guzzling electric motor in the refrigerator. The latter, finally, operates the compressor. Power is lost at each stage of the process.

The Americans have now adopted the shorter, and logical sequence shown here:

The much higher efficiency will be obvious at once. But the principal advantage lies in not putting any load on what is in any case the weakest link in our power supply system, the battery. Mechanical energy from the boat's engine is used, and is capable of meeting the needs of a small refrigerator compressor many times over. There is of course one difficulty: though the refrigerator thermostat is able to switch an electric motor on and off at frequent intervals to prevent a rise in temperature, we clearly cannot be starting up the main engine every 5 minutes to keep things cool. This problem is overcome with

Fuel – mechanical energy → cold

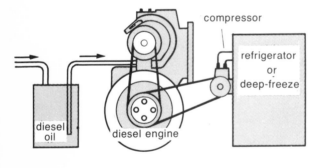

compressor

refrigerator or deep-freeze

diesel oil

diesel engine

In this system there are only two steps (in practice, the compressor is mounted on the ship's engine).

'cold banks', which are slim stainless steel tanks filled with an alcohol/water mixture and built into the refrigerator around the contents. Using the compressor, driven from the engine through a magnetic clutch, we need only refrigerate these cold banks which thereafter retain the cold; the engine will not then need to be started up again until the next day. With good insulation, this system can approach the performance of a chest freezer. Actual operating figures with a high-quality installation show that the engine needs five to six hours to freeze the entire contents down to $-35°C$; once this temperature has been reached, the engine need be run only 60 minutes or so each day. The installation does however need to be designed for a refrigerator or deep-freeze from the outset. If the fluid in the cold banks is selected with a freezing point of $-18°C$, for instance, the set-up will only work efficiently if the fluid is properly frozen ie. has reached at least $-18°C$. This needs a much bigger compressor than a refrigerator run at just under 0°C.

The various components, including a seawater-cooled condenser, need to be carefully matched to each other. It is not possible to convert an existing refrigerator on a do-it-yourself basis; it is much better to get a specialist firm to provide a simple-to-operate installation, which will cost from about £600 up. Adler Barbour Yacht Services Inc of 43 Lawton Street, New Rochelle, NY 10801, USA, have been making yacht freezer equipment for 10 years or more.

Toilet

The ship's toilet consists, in fact, of nothing more than a container (bowl) and two pumps. One pump removes the contents, while the other sprays in seawater to flush out the bowl. Nowadays toilets are a good deal more robust than they used to be, because membrane pumps are used almost exclusively. But even these are not entirely trouble-free, so it is wise to use only soft toilet paper and also to make sure that the pump is never asked to cope with any solid, non-natural material. If the pump at the bottom of the bowl is situated below the waterline, both the intake and outlet hoses must have an S-bend in them. To prevent a hose connector of this kind, with a permanent head of water, acting as a siphon there must be a

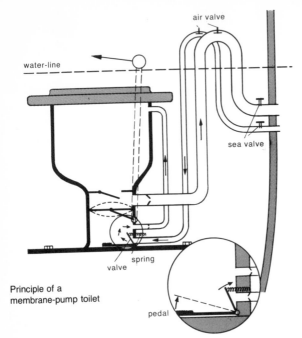

air valve

water-line

sea valve

spring
valve

pedal

Principle of a
membrane-pump toilet

valve at the top of the curve to let a little air into the flow of water, so that the resulting bubble of air can break up the hydrostatic head. The pump is usually operated by rocking a long lever to and fro, and the contents are pumped out or water flushed through depending on the valve setting. It is interesting to note that a single membrane normally does both jobs; the underside forces rinse-water into the bowl, and the upper surface evacuates the bowl contents.

Watch out for trouble!

- If the pump lever becomes hard to operate, this usually means that the sea-valves are not open, or a pipe is blocked.
- If small particles of the pumped-out contents come back into the bowl during flushing, this indicates a split in the membrane.

As with any membrane pump, the neoprene membrane has only a limited working life, in seawater not much more than a year, so it is as well when buying the toilet to ask for at least one kit of spare parts. Changing the membrane is an unpleasant, though not all that difficult, job which can be done by anyone on his own with the tools carried on board – after first closing the sea-valves!

Pipes routed in the open may not look very pretty, but make for easy maintenance.

Pumps on board

Besides the *bilge pumps*, on which the safety of the boat relies, there is a whole range of pumps needed on board, and as a basic rule enough spares should be carried for it to be easy to cope with breakdowns. A foot-pump has been found best for the *washbasin* in the heads, for washing the hands; if the pump can only be operated manually, this simple operation becomes a real feat. If you insist on washing-up the dishes in the *sink*, a pump with non-return valve will have to be fitted in the outlet, even if the sink is above the waterline – it is quite wrong to assume that the waste water will run away of its own accord.

In boats over 10m in length, a *shower* is well worth having. It is always pleasant to be able to wash salt water off the body, and besides this will keep the bunks dry for longer: the reason why bedclothes are usually very clammy is that, without realising it, you take a lot of salt to bed with you. Other than on very long passages there is no need to worry about the water consumption; a quick shower uses not much more than 5 litres of water, equivalent to half-a-bucket (try it, if you don't believe me!). For once I would, in the case of the shower, recommend an electric pump; though it uses a lot of power, it is seldom used for longer than a minute, so this matters less. Speaking for myself, I would lose all the enjoyment of a shower if I had to do acrobatics working a footpump at the same time. The water from a shower can quite happily be allowed to run into the bilges, since a few strokes of a large-capacity bilge pump will quickly get rid of it.

In cold latitudes a hot shower could be a godsend at times, but this involves big problems if you have not gone in for gas heating (which, as we have seen, is dangerous). So far as I know there are no kerosene 'instantaneous' water-heaters available yet, working on the same lines as the through-flow gas water-heaters we are used to over the kitchen sink at home. The smaller models of these would be just right for a modest shower on a cruising yacht; but they would, I must stress again, be extremely dangerous. There is, however, another answer: we can let the engine heat up the water. In fact, this is not all that simple to arrange. A heat-exchanger will need to be built into the engine's cooling system, drawing fresh water from a tank of its own, with an extra pump to take it from the engine to the shower. Nevertheless, there are already firms manufacturing such systems; the real problem lies in grafting them into the engine circuit. It is simpler, and cheaper, to fit an alternator to the ship's engine that will produce the household mains voltage (220V) needed for an electric instantaneous heater.

Cooking on board

Cooking is of immense importance for the wellbeing of the crew and, consequently, for the safety of the boat. One is, unfortunately, forced to make use of naked flames for cooking, so the risk of burn injuries is far from slight. Getting burnt at sea is an extremely serious business, and precautions must be taken to prevent it ever happening. The cook must never, even in a tropical climate, work at the stove wearing nothing but shorts. Gloves, made from oven-cloth material suitable for holding hot pans and dishes, must be kept ready to hand. Stoves are usually already equipped with a fence arrangement that can be adjusted to various sizes of saucepan, yet there is no harm in additionally securing deep pans, in particular, with a length of shock-cord.

Drinking water supplies are a very special problem to those planning long cruises, though in fact they present little difficulty if a few basic rules are followed. If you avoid frequent washing all over, and take a little care to keep consumption down, one person needs about 1½ litres a day. By drinking canned fruit-juice and soft drinks, and using seawater wherever possible, this can easily be brought down to 1 litre without discomfort. Washing-up must be done in seawater, which should be self-evident anyway. Eggs can be boiled in salt water, and pasta and potatoes can be cooked in salt and fresh water mixed half-and-half. There are special salt-water soaps for personal washing; if you cannot get these, Badedas and similar products will work as well.

Many *fresh water tanks* are not suitable for drinking from, and this is something one unfortunately often discovers only a long while after buying the boat. Some metal tanks are particularly troublesome, giving the water a bitter aftertaste. As a general rule, plastic tanks are less of a problem, and ordinary plastic jerricans can also be used. Poor drinking water is not made any better by keeping it in a suitable tank, so care must be taken in harbours to fill up, as far as possible, with the best quality water you can get. On the world trip I never boiled the water, nor put any additives in my tanks. Hygienically-minded Americans would never touch water like this; I did in fact find formations of algae when I came to clean the tanks, but these had not affected either the colour or the taste of the water. Whenever possible, I would always collect rain water and use that in preference to doubtful water taken aboard from supplies ashore. In the tropics, especially, a single shower is enough to fill the tanks, given effective collecting arrangements. Deck awnings, or a cabin roof specially fitted with guttering for the purpose, make excellent water traps, though the salt deposit should be given a chance to rinse off before starting to collect the rainwater. If the quality of the water is doubtful and there really is nothing better around, you can always play safe by boiling it for at least 10 minutes before use.

If extended holidays are to be spent on board and you are keen on keeping up housekeeping standards, it can be well worthwhile raiding grandma's attic for old-fashioned cooking utensils: a mechanical eggbeater, for instance, waffle-irons, a Dutch oven for baking bread and cakes, as well as a kerosene-heated iron or even a small hand-operated sewing machine.

Stores

I have myself often seen quite experienced seagoing housewives (or 'boatwives'?) driving themselves into a bundle of nerves dashing from shop to shop, anxiously scanning lists to make sure nothing has been missed out. Yet there are very few items that are really necessary: fuel for the stove, matches, pepper and salt, sugar, oil and vinegar. If you are out of pasta, there are always potatoes and rice. In any case, there is no need to get worked up about buying stores – if you go attentively through a big super-market, it will be almost a feat to overlook something.

Unhappily there is very little really appetising canned meat on the market, certainly not in countries outside Europe. So for our big trip our parents' old recipes were revived, and we salted down and bottled, and even dried and smoked, meat and fish. An excellent substitute for fresh meat (even in the tropics) is a whole ham, well smoked; it keeps for weeks, and will make a very reasonable roast if a couple of thick slices are soaked in water overnight. Freeze-dried food is expensive, but still better than corned beef. An American girl-friend of ours, Dawn, claimed to know 148 recipes for making meat-loaf into a palatable meal; but then palatable is a concept that can be stretched to cover a lot!

A major problem for European digestions is always the question of bread. There is no way of keeping ordinary brown bread, of the kind we prefer, for more than a couple of weeks at most, so like it or not bread will have to be replaced by things like crispbread, pumpernickel, cracker biscuits and the like. If you can find a friendly baker, get him to double-bake the bread; it may taste on the dry side, but it will keep for months. White bread can be sliced and dried out completely in the sunshine on deck; even several weeks later it can then be toasted over a stove burner if sprinkled with a few drops of water beforehand. If there is an oven on board, fresh-baked bread is a real delicacy on a long voyage.

Eggs are an important food for long-distance cruises. If really fresh when bought, they will keep for several weeks; their keeping qualities can be substantially improved if they are smeared with Vaseline, or plunged in boiling water for a couple of seconds, within a day of being laid. If you want to avoid opening up a rotten egg and stinking out the cabin, test it by plunging it in a pan of water: if it sinks, it is still good.

In large towns nowadays it is unfortunately not all that easy to buy really fresh fruit and vegetables. Food from the deep-freeze is not much use for our purposes, because it goes off fairly quickly (and the same is true of milk and other foods). The aim, on a long voyage, is still to be eating fresh fruit and vegetables at the end, so as far as possible these should be bought while still unripe. Tomatoes, for instance, will not keep longer than 10 days, but oranges, grapefruit and cabbage are still edible after four weeks (normally I dislike cabbage, but raw in a salad it becomes really tempting by the end of an Atlantic crossing!). Apples – ideal for a night watch – lemons, potatoes, onions, and garlic can be kept for several months, though this will naturally depend on proper storage and supervision. Anything that goes bad must be removed at once, and rotting parts (such as the outer leaves of cabbages) cut away. Wire baskets, like those in self-service shops, are specially good as storage containers. Bananas bought while still green, on the other hand, should be hung up in the forepeak until ripe (they ripen all at the same time, unfortunately).

If there is enough space, this is the best way of storing fruit.

On long, and often boring, voyages the changes need to be rung on the menus, if nothing else, and it helps to carry plenty of herbs, ketchup and other sauces, mustard, capers, olives, gherkins and so on.

It is often suggested that cans should be specially marked, or even lacquered against rust; but on today's relatively dry boats this should not be necessary. Even if a can is half-submerged in sea-water, it will still take at least six months for it to rust through. If you are afraid of the paper labels coming off, all that needs doing is to mark the can 'F', 'V' and 'M' (fruit, vegetables and meat) with a wax crayon. On long passages, there should be chocolate, dried fruit and biscuits within reach for those on the night watch. And when someone is suffering from seasickness, the relatively bland taste of biscuits is the best way of getting back an appetite.

Self-steering gear

Reduced to basics, the principle of self-steering gear for small yachts is that a wind-vane is pivoted to swing freely and to stay exactly in line with the wind. This is then coupled up to the tiller while the latter is exactly in the straight ahead position. Now, if the yacht deviates from her course, the vane will no longer be exactly in line with the wind and will offer enough surface to the wind for the pivoting vane to be pushed back into line. As the wind-vane is linked to the tiller through an arm or lines, this movement will also move the tiller; the yacht's course (relative to the wind) will alter

A large vane acting directly on the tiller.

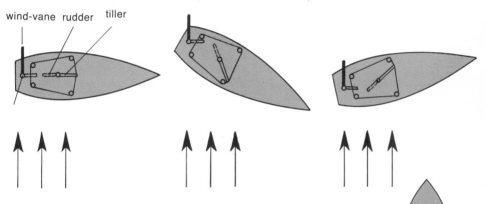

wind-vane rudder tiller

until the wind-vane is lined up with the wind again and at the same time the tiller is back in the straight-ahead position.

This system needs fairly large wind-vanes, so it cannot be used on the bigger cruising yachts. Instead of transmitting the force from wind-vane to tiller, a second rudder can be fitted, small enough to be moved by the vane. But in light winds it is not sensitive enough to 'tend' the rudder, although you do have a second rudder available.

These snags do not arise with self-steering gear working on the revolutionary design thought up

Here the wind-vane actuates a separate rudder, but will not work in light winds.

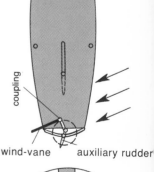

coupling

wind-vane   auxiliary rudder

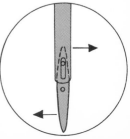

by 'Blondie' Hasler. In this, instead of applying the force from the vane direct to the rudder, Hasler has a thin, narrow blade at the stern going down about 1m into the water. This is not, however, meant to steer the boat. It is made to swivel, but at the same time is mounted so that it can swing to port or starboard like a pendulum. Let us assume that the yacht is moving along at 4 knots. The wind-vane now twists the slim servo-rudder slightly; this is then no longer able to stay midships in the boat's wake, but is pushed away to one side by the flow of water. This is done with quite considerable force, especially if the servo-blade is fairly long. If we now either simply attach a single line to the bottom of the blade, or extend it upwards past its pivot point and fix two lines to the top, we can quite easily transmit this force to the tiller via a series of pulleys. In other words, whenever the wind-vane is not lined up with the wind, the servo-blade will sheer off to one side or the other and move the tiller. The force of the wind is no longer being used to steer the boat, but merely to rotate the long, slim servo-blade; the force needed for steering comes from the passage of the boat through the water. The prime advantage of the system is that wind-vanes need be only very small, since they have only to turn the servo-blade. The effectiveness of steering thus depends not so much on the wind strength, as on the boat's movement. I used a Hasler steering gear on my round-the-world voyage, and it gave perfectly satisfactory steering at speeds as low as 1 knot. Of the 32,000 miles we covered sailing right round the globe, only 100 or so were done steering by hand: the rest of the time, Hasler's masterpiece of ingenuity took over the hard work. If a boat tends to luff up into wind very easily (ie. carries strong weather

A Hasler gear: it looks complicated, but the principle is most ingenious.

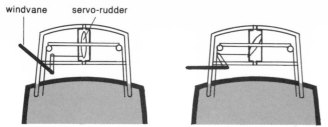

windvane   servo-rudder

The Hasler system: the vane moves a pendulum rudder, which tilts to one side.

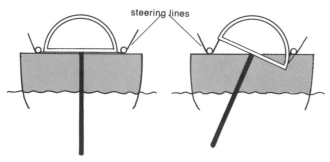

steering lines

The force developed by the pendulum rudder can be transmitted to a wheel.

helm), we can give the system a helping hand by means of shock-cord attached to the tiller. Obviously, the pull from the lines can be transmitted just as well to a drum fixed to the wheel, in the case of wheel steering. Thought must naturally be given to being able to uncouple the system quickly. This is important, because the force produced by the servo-rudder is so great that it cannot be over-ridden by steering by hand. I keep a pair of stainless-steel cutters ready so that the lines could be severed in an emergency.

The most important thing in set-ups like this is the self-centring action. All this means is that the servo-rudder will come back to the middle position of its own accord as soon as there is no more wind pressure on the vane; this is easily achieved by ensuring that the rod rotating the servo-rudder is not attached at the pendulum pivot point. If it is connected exactly at the centre point the pendulum has no inducement to return to its initial position, and will in fact need to be pushed to the other side by the vane. The result will be the boat steering an extremely zig-zag course.

It would be wrong to think that this ingenious arrangement is perfect. Skippers who are something of a handyman have been able to make improvements to the Hasler design. The basic idea stays the same, but the wind-vane is altered; in modern designs (the Aries) it is mounted on a horizontal axis. For the vane to remain upright when unaffected by wind, it has to be fitted with a

joint exactly on axis of rotation, so no self-centring action

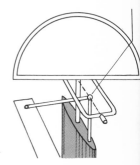

It will not work if the pendulum rudder does not go back of its own accord.

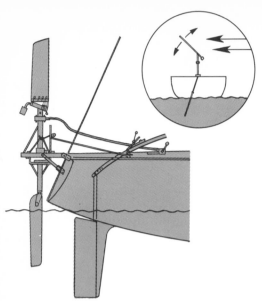

counterweight at the bottom. When the wind is blowing directly on to the edge of the vane it cannot tilt, because the force is exactly parallel to the axis of rotation: the counterweight holds the vane vertical. But if the boat strays off course, the wind is able to get a purchase on the surface of the vane and pushes it down to a greater or lesser degree, depending on the wind strength. Here again, the force is transmitted to the servo-blade.

Unlike an electrical system, wind-vane self-steering will not of course keep the boat to a compass heading, but alters course if, for example, the wind shifts direction. This happens, too, if the wind strengthens or falls off, because this also changes the direction of the apparent wind (the only wind that really matters to the skipper at sea). The advantage is that once set, the sails are used to optimum effect; the disadvantage lies in the changes in course. Electric self-steering gears keep a compass course; but this, too, can be a disadvantage, because if the wind shifts the setting of the sails will not be right. Their main drawback, however, is the high power consumption. However much manufacturers may bombard the boat-owner with meaningless phrases like modest consumption and small drain on the battery, one must remember that not even the well-intentioned maker of this kind of gear is able to turn the laws of physics upside down. An electric motor is switched on and off by commands received from a steering compass equipped with pickups. The more a yacht is 'leaning against her rudder', the more force the electric motor has to exert to turn it. And that means drawing current from the battery. Recently, there have been gears which steer by means of a small wind-vane instead of a compass. Because the vane has to provide virtually no force, but merely transmit information which is passed on electronically, it need have an area of not much more than a few square centimetres (like the vanes of wind-direction indicators). And in any case, I cannot see why I should use costly battery power to achieve an effect that I can get just as satisfactorily by mechanical means, thanks to Hasler.

Modern 'Pacific' pendulum layout by John Adam; as with the Aries, the vane pivots on a horizontal axis.

The tender

The tender (more familiarly, the dinghy) is part of the basic equipment of a cruising yacht. Allowance must always be made for only being able to anchor, or of having to moor Italian-style (see page 134), where the circumstances are sometimes so bad that the stern cannot be brought close enough in to the quayside to permit direct climbing aboard.

Inflatable or rigid?

The question hardly arises with a yacht of 7 or 8m, because there simply will not be enough room to carry a rigid dinghy on deck, and the choice will have to be an inflatable. When I talk about an inflatable, I do not of course mean the cheap kind you can buy from a department store, from as little as £20 or so; these are fit only for

Inflatables by Avon and Zodiac are popular with many cruising skippers; suitable for use with outboards of up to 3hp.

holiday use along the beach, and consist of a single buoyancy chamber. Manufacturers have for years been providing extremely efficient inflatable tenders for yachts, sturdy enough to be able to withstand even rough landings on rocky shores quite well. If these do occasionally get holed, the tear can be repaired with adhesive fairly easily. After about six years, however, the rubber becomes brittle and liable to split, and it is then better to invest in a new dinghy. A rubber dinghy is more stable in rough water, but is more difficult to row. Unfortunately, the makers have not so far managed to make the task of blowing the dinghy up, and deflating and folding it, simple enough to be only a matter of minutes, and this is the real disadvantage of an inflatable. If it is still wet when you are ready to get under way, it must on no account be stowed away in this condition. I think it is bad seamanship to tow the dinghy astern, and this will in any case be possible only in sheltered, coastal waters. It will

65

A French plastic dinghy – light and easy to manage, but suitable for an outboard only in the next size up.

hamper the sailing quite a lot, and there is always the danger of waves – particularly with a following wind – swamping the dinghy, whereupon the enormously heavy load will tear away the painter. If the weather gets up, the dinghy will have to be brought on board; yet there are usually so many other important things needing doing then that there is scant time left for recovering the dinghy.

If there is enough space on deck, up in the bows or right aft, my choice would always be a rigid dinghy. Plastic dinghies are unsinkable and – from a certain size – practically uncapsizable. They are virtually impervious to mechanical wear and tear and their working life is usually limited only by plastic's sensitivity to light. Tenders built in aluminium, with a welded-in air chamber to give buoyancy, have almost no disadvantages. If I had children, I would plump for the Optimist dinghy; when this is being used as a boat's tender, the daggerboard is used as a thwart, while the sail that goes with it makes it an ideal pastime for the junior skipper while in harbour.

Should you be lucky enough to be able to cruise in the tropics, it will not cost much to have a transparent perspex panel put in the bottom of the tender; it will then be possible, in crystal-clear tropical waters, to take a prudent look at the holding-ground before anchoring, without using a mask and snorkel. If the dinghy is carried on the cabin roof underway, as is usual with small yachts, the transparent panel will let light through to the skylight underneath; and in regions where there is coral, the 'glass-bottomed boat' will make it possible to study the fascinating underwater world without having to worry about the sharks that are plentiful in those waters.

The size of the tender will depend very largely on the size of the mother craft, and of the crew. A good rule of thumb would be that it should not be too heavy for the whole of the crew to be able to lift it aboard by hand, if needs be, without having to use the falls.

Outboard engines In the Baltic, North Sea or Mediterranean an outboard for the yacht's tender will be unnecessary, and indeed will not be popular because of the noise, and of the (minor) pollution it causes. On the other side of the Atlantic, however, moorings alongside are seldom available, and the best spots to anchor are so far away from the quayside that a small outboard is a worthwhile investment. If you have an outboard, being close to land is not the only point that matters when choosing your anchorage – you can look for the safest spot, even if it is rather further away. And heading into the wind and in a seaway, a small outboard will be many times more effective than even the most energetic oarsman!

This dinghy outboard may be rather exposed to salt water but stowed here it takes up no useful space and the petrol fumes stay outside.

The ideal cruising boat

The great charm of cruising under sail undoubtedly stems partly from the fact that there are only a few things for which there are rigid rules, and plenty of room is left for personal viewpoints and individual opinions. So it would be wrong, and totally against the spirit of the sport, to try to lay down to any sailing friend what his boat should be like. While I, for instance, look on a steel yacht as the ideal, some of my cruising friends may see a plywood hull as the best choice, for equally good and equally compelling reasons. It is, nevertheless, often interesting to hear the views of highly experienced skippers, and to draw one or two lessons from them. *Yachting World* has organised an extremely valuable survey of members of the Ocean Cruising Club, sending its questionnaire to people who are solely cruising men; one of them, T. H. Carr, has during his lifetime logged the almost unbelievable total of 100 000 miles! Famous, and scarcely less experienced names include people like Robin Knox-Johnson, Sir Alec Rose and Roderick Stephens. Behind the bald percentage figures listed lie the skill and knowledge gained in cruises totalling more than seven million miles. This was how these cruising skippers expressed their preferences:

Hull type	%	Length overall	%	Draft	%	Ballast	%
monohull	95	under 7m	0	under 1.50m	12	iron	11
catamaran	4	7–9m	1	1.50–2.00m	80	lead	80
trimaran	1	9–12m	58	over 2m	8	other	4
		over 12m	41			no ballast	5

Overhang	%
long	1
medium	71
short	28

Hull material	%
wood	24
mixed (wood and iron)	11
cold-moulded wood	8
GRP	15
GRP sandwich	13
steel	15
aluminium	10
ferro-cement	4

Deck	%
flush	34
short c'roof	28
long c'roof	18
c'roof with house	20

Deck surface	%
teak	65
ply	3
GRP	17
painted	3
non-slip	12

Keel	%
long	81
short, with separate rudder	10
bilge keels	1
fin	6
other	2

Rig	%
sloop	14
cutter	17
ketch	47
yawl	16
schooner	3

Running sails	%
spinnaker	15
twin jibs	20
squaresail	4
boomed jibs	61

Reefing	%
roller	66
slab	30

Steering	%
tiller	37
wheel	63

Self-steering control	%
sheets to tiller	6
vane horiz. axis	32
vane vert. axis	44
electric	10
none	8

Self-steering operation	%
direct to tiller	32
separate servo-rudder	44
trim tab on main rudder	24

Cockpit	%
central	28
aft	72

Sea anchor	%
essential	12
useful	26
not useful	62

Auxiliary engine	%
none	0
outboard	0
inboard, on centre line	94
inboard, off centre line	1
2 inboards	5

Horsepower	%
under 10	2
10–30	44
30–60	43
over 60	11

Fuel	%
petrol	1
diesel	96
kerosene	3

Range	%
0–200 miles	16
200–800 miles	70
over 800 miles	14

Generator/ alternator	%
on main engine	39
separate	22
wind	1
solar cells	0
combination of several methods	38

Electrical system	%
6V	2
12V	69
24V	27
32V	2

Battery capacity	%
0–100Ah	6
100–200Ah	45
200–400Ah	40
over 400Ah	9

Navigation lights	%
electric	87
kerosene	13

Riding light	%
electric	45
kerosene	55

Main anchor	%
CQR	60
Danforth	27
fisherman	12
other	1

Anchor with	%
chain only	66
chain & warp	44
warp only	0

How much chain?	%
40-80m	46
80-100m	41
over 100m	13

Warp length	%
60-100m	23
100-150m	56
over 150m	21

Tender	%
rigid	33
inflatable	67

Size	%
under 2.5m	14
2.5–3.5m	84
over 3.5m	2

Tender driven by	%
oars	52
outboard	42
sail	6

Tender construction	%
wood	16
metal	2
GRP	34
other plastics	48

Cooking Fuel	%
kerosene	31
gas	52
spirit	11
electricity	2
diesel oil	2

Would you carry:	%
life raft	95
radar	16
Decca	4
Loran	5
OMEGA	6
Radio DF	91
SW transmitter	12
MW transmitter	25
VHF transmitter	31
intermediate-wave transmitter	49
echo-sounder	96
anemometer	51
apparent wind indicator	43
radar reflector	80
patent log	72
deep freeze	18

Electrics and Electronics

Electricity aboard

Being scared of the technical problems connected with electricity on board a boat is really quite wrong, and indeed it is highly desirable for every cruising sailor to know a fair bit about the electrical gear he carries.

Power sources on a boat are the generator and the battery. The batteries one meets afloat are almost invariably what are known as lead accumulators; one lead battery cell provides, near enough, 2V (if you liken an electrical current to water passing along a hose, the voltage is equivalent to the water-pressure). In motorcars the usual voltage of the battery is 6 or (more commonly nowadays) 12V. Batteries are made up by linking together the appropriate number of cells, so a 12V battery will have six cells, and so on. As a basic rule the voltage chosen should be as high as possible, for reasons connected with the physics of electricity. If current is passed down a long wire with a voltage (or 'pressure') of exactly 12V, it will be found that what comes out at the other end is no longer exactly 12V, but slightly less: this is known as voltage drop. The lower the voltage, and the smaller the diameter of the wire (usually a copper wire, nowadays), the greater the voltage drop will be. It would, therefore, be better to choose a ship's voltage of 24V; but then many items of equipment that are intended mainly for use on cars (and are consequently quite cheap to buy) could not be used aboard. There would, indeed, be hardly any suitable starter motors for the engine, since these are almost exclusively designed for 12V. So a compromise is struck, and 12V is used for the yacht's power supply. To minimise voltage drop, the leads to the items using electricity should be as thick as possible; this will cost more initially, but it will be a once-for-all outlay. I would look on wire of 2.5mm diameter as the ideal.

The battery

This needs careful treatment and servicing.

Important! Batteries should never be left aboard for long periods discharged, as this will damage them.

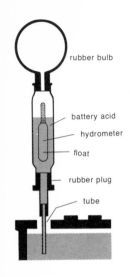

rubber bulb

battery acid

hydrometer

float

rubber plug

tube

The state-of-charge of the battery therefore needs checking from time to time. For this one uses a hydrometer, a device that measures the specific gravity of the battery acid. A freshly-charged battery will show a reading of 1.28; when the density has fallen to 1.15, the battery needs recharging at once. If a yacht cruises solely in a warm area like the Mediterranean, or in the tropics, the battery acid must be adjusted so that when fully charged the density is only 1.235 to 1.245, otherwise the battery's life will be shortened. If you sail into a warm climate, the adjustment procedure recommended by battery manufacturers is to empty the electrolyte from a fully-charged battery into a container and dilute it with distilled water to get a reading of 1.220. When poured back into the battery, the density should then be 1.235–1.245; if not, bring it to this density by adding fresh acid (at 1.28) or more distilled water.

A worn-out battery can be recognised from the fact that despite recharging it can no longer reach this full reading. In general, a battery is ready to be thrown away after four years or so. All the cells must give the same hydrometer reading; if one cell differs substantially from the others, this is a sure sign that it – and hence the whole battery – has had it.

The acid level in the battery must be checked at frequent intervals, and the plates should be kept covered at all times. If they are found to be dry, the battery must never be topped up with neat sulphuric acid, because the low level indicates that the water in the electrolyte has evaporated. Whenever possible, use distilled water to top up; clean rainwater will also do however, and is much cheaper.

A voltmeter connected to the battery is essential (as is an ammeter to measure the current being passed), but is not really the best way of checking the state of charge. A lead accumulator has the following discharge pattern:

Left: discharge curve of a lead accumulator

Right: discharge curve of a NC accumulator

lead accumulator

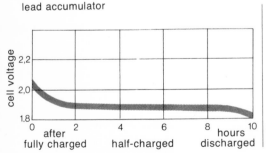

nickel-cadmium accumulator

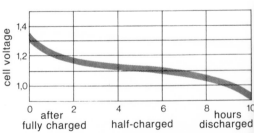

It will be seen at once that after a short time the voltage of the fully-charged battery drops to about 12V (6 cells at 2V each), and then remains at this level for quite a long time while the battery discharges. Only at the end of this period does the voltage fall off sharply. The voltmeter cannot show how far one has gone along this almost straight line towards the fully-discharged point.

Lead batteries can discharge of their own accord. This disadvantage is not present in the nickel-cadmium battery; the 'nicad' battery is virtually maintenance-free, and its working life is about ten times that of the lead battery – but so, unfortunately, is its price. There is, besides, another drawback that people who sing its praises tend to overlook, and which will be obvious from the discharge curve.

Since the electrical appliances on the boat need at least 12V, the nicad battery would give the necessary voltage for only a short

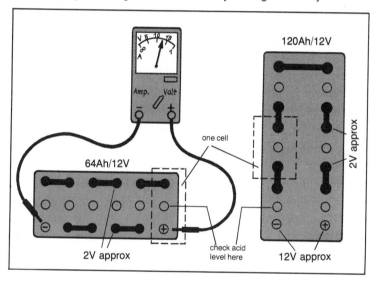

A simple voltmeter will let you measure the voltage of the whole battery or a single cell; each cell gives about 2V, whether the lead battery is large or small.

while. Further cells would then have to be connected in during operation so that the equipment always had a 12V supply to work with, and arranging this would be technically difficult and costly.

Not all 12V batteries are the same size. Depending on its *capacity* a battery will be able to supply a greater or lesser amount of current. This can be seen immediately in electrically-driven boats; in these the 12V batteries have six cells, just like other batteries, but are very much bigger than a car battery, because the highly-uneconomical propulsion motors of the electric boat consume vast amounts of current. The capacity of a battery is indicated in ampere-hours (Ah). If the cabin lamp, for instance, draws one ampere (1A) from the battery and is left to burn for one hour, the consumption will be 1Ah. Theoretically, therefore, a 100Ah battery should be able to keep the lamp burning for 100 hours; in reality the battery will be flat well before that, since under practical conditions on a boat one gets only 70 per cent at most of the nominal capacity out of a battery.

Using car starter batteries on yachts, though general, is far from ideal. These are built to yield high currents over short periods, for starting an engine. Apart from this, yachts' batteries also have to store a lot of current and then give it up as fully as possible to the many consumer points on the yacht over a longish period. If you use car batteries (which were not designed for the job, and so are unsuitable) in this way it substantially reduces their life and efficiency. So far as I know, Hagen AG are one of the few battery firms to research the special needs of yachtsmen and develop a special battery with extra thick plates designed for a capacitive load. These multicraft batteries can, if necessary, be used for starting the boat's engine, but it is better to keep an ordinary car starter battery for this purpose. This, rather than just playing safe, is the main reason for having a proper starter battery available. The engine will either have to be fitted with two dynamos for charging the two batteries, or they will have to be charged simultaneously (in which case there *must* be a blocking diode to separate the circuits).

It is important to keep constantly in mind that the discharging of a battery follows rigid physical laws, and wishful thinking about what it can do is quite pointless. If a battery has a 72Ah capacity, not much more than 55Ah can be got out of it in practice, and if the refrigerator draws 5A every hour then the battery will be completely flattened in ten hours. Most electrical appliances will, in fact, be marked with their consumption in watts (W), and the ampere figure can easily be worked out from this using the formula:

$$\frac{watts}{volts} = amperes$$

If a yacht's navigation lights take 20W, they will need 1.7Ah if running on 12V. Using the regulation lights (two navigation lights and a stern light) consumption will total 5Ah, so with the battery mentioned a moment ago they definitely cannot be kept on for much more than 10 hours when sailing at night.

This would be no tragedy if it were possible, next day, to charge the completely flat battery straight away. But charging a battery is not just a matter of having a hefty generator that will push out the amps needed; the charging process must be slow and gentle if the battery is not to be damaged. Damage can be avoided only if the hourly rate of charge does not exceed one-tenth of the battery's capacity – or in other words:

> A completely flat battery needs to be charged for 10 hours.

The generator

In the past the generators fitted to boats' engines were almost exclusively direct-current dynamos; today, alternators producing AC electricity are becoming more and more common. The latter have the advantage of putting out much more current, and of producing it at low engine speeds. The second point is of minor interest for our purposes, since at cruising speed the engine will be running in the middle of its rev-range.

Modern generators can produce as much as 50A. The output will usually be marked on the generator in watts, eg. 400W (400W ÷ 12V = 35A approximately). With these 35A it would, of course, be possible to run quite a few power-hungry items of equipment. But as we can charge the battery with only one-tenth of its capacity per hour, the 35A output would not be much use to us unless we carried an enormous battery with a 350Ah capacity; on a small yacht this would be impossible, if only because of the weight. And this is where we find ourselves caught in a vicious circle: modern generators have a high output, but there is not much we can do with the current they produce. If the boat were rather larger, large enough for the extra weight not to matter, my main concern would be to be sure of carrying the highest possible battery capacity. An example will make clear why:

Yacht A		Yacht B	
generator	400W	generator	400W
daily consumption	35Ah	daily consumption	35Ah
battery capacity	70Ah	battery capacity	350Ah
engine needs to run		engine needs to run	
5 hours a day		1 hour a day	

Every generator is fitted with a *regulator*, which ensures automatically that the battery is not having too much current pumped into it. The regulator will usually, after an initial period, reduce the charging current to a few amperes. This is right for a car (for which the set-up has in fact been designed), but will not make much sense if the boat carries a big battery; so it is a good idea to fit a regulator on which the charging current can be adjusted by hand. The regulator circuit shown here (designed by Hietschold and Dillmann) can be made up by any electrician at a modest cost – the parts come to £5 or so – and will allow the skipper to adjust the charging

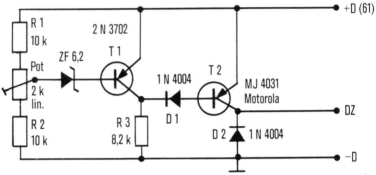

With this regulator, the generator charges at full power until the preset cell voltage is reached: so a high charging current can be used without damaging the battery.

voltage and, consequently, the maximum charging current.

The terminals on most alternators are stamped with the markings '+D', 'DF' and '−D', but if there is any doubt (or you come across an alternator carrying different markings) you *must* consult a qualified electrician: a wrong connection, even one lasting only a couple of seconds, can cause expensive damage to the insides of the alternator. A voltmeter and ammeter must still be connected to the battery, so that a check can be made on the charging process.

Donkey engine

If all you are wanting to do is charge the battery, it may seem rather uneconomical to run the big boat's engine, with its sizeable horsepower, and for this reason many yachts carry a special generator unit solely for charging the battery. The main drawbacks of doing so are:

1. The generator units suitable for our purposes (eg. the Honda ED 250) run on petrol, with its explosion risks.
2. All generator motors are intolerably noisy when used in small anchorages and harbours.
3. The fuel costs are hardly less than with a boat's main engine.
4. It means an extra engine that needs servicing.

Shore mains

Nowadays most marinas have electricity supply points at the quayside. This shore-based supply can be converted to 12V DC using a battery charger, for charging up the battery (but take care to use only a charger *with an isolating transformer*).

It is, of course, also possible to use the shore mains directly to supply ordinary household appliances. This calls for very special care, because generally speaking things on a yacht are not well earthed. If a skipper is tempted to rely overmuch on shore mains, he should remember that mains voltage differs in different countries. Europe has an almost universal 220V at 50Hz, while the Americans use almost exclusively a less dangerous supply of 110V at 60Hz.

If there is no shore mains supply available and yet we still, exceptionally, need a 220V supply on board, 12V DC can be converted into 220V AC by using a transistorised inverter. Modern inverters operate with a very low current loss, and up to 500W.

Attempts have long been made to generate current without having to use the engine, or a noisy generator unit; all the experiments using wind-driven devices and freewheeling propellers in the water have more or less failed. They do work, after a fashion, but the output is usually inadequate. The same must be said of solar cells; a set of these will derive only 6W of energy from the sun.

An inexpensive meter should be kept on board (they can be bought for as little as £5) to check the electrical system as a whole, and not just the individual appliances. As non-experts, yachtsmen will tend to use the meter solely as a continuity tester or as a voltmeter. In the former case, it is switched to the ohmmeter, or resistance-measuring, setting; a full-scale deflection of the needle will then indicate either that a lead is sound and unbroken, or that there is a short-circuit between two wires where there should not be one (lamp-bulbs can be checked with the meter, which will show continuity if the bulb is sound). When you want to check the battery voltage, the instrument is set to a rather higher voltage range than you actually need (eg. to 20V for checking a 12V battery); then the negative probe (usually black and marked with a minus sign) is applied to the negative terminal of the battery, and the red positive probe to the '+' battery terminal. The dry batteries needed for torches, radios, etc. can also be checked in this way; as soon as a 1.5V cell is showing only 1.4V, throw it away.

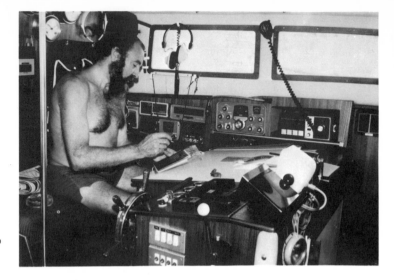

Electronics galore – fun to have, so long as it all works.

Electronics aboard

Echo depth-sounder

This is the most important piece of electronic gear; a useful aid to navigation, and in particular almost essential when anchoring. The depth-sounder reading will tell you how much chain or warp to lay out, and let you estimate the swinging circle accurately in advance. There is only one area where, despite popular opinion, it does little to help – it will hardly prevent you running aground, because dangerous shoals are often so steep-to that no advance warning is given on the sounder. For navigation purposes, a sounder should have several ranges, and a top range of 100m and more would be ideal. Echo sounders have various indicating arrangements, including flashing lights, pointers and digital displays. The last-named are most convenient to read, but the light indicator is clearer since it makes it possible to recognise spurious echoes from fish, air-bubbles and the like. The accuracy of these instruments is, for all practical purposes, extraordinarily good, and very much better than the hand lead. They use only a negligible amount of current. A chart depth-recorder is not, I think, much use on a cruising yacht, especially since the trace is not true-to-scale and therefore cannot

76

be used directly to provide position lines. An alarm that gives an audible warning automatically at a preset depth is, however, very useful. The depth below the water-line at which the transducer unit is installed must be allowed for in all readings. The transducer must not be painted over, and growths of barnacles should never be removed with a sharp metal tool.

Modern echo-sounder/log, with digital display and an adjustable sound warning device.

Nowadays these are usually combined in a single instrument. Once they have been calibrated over a measured distance (something that is all too seldom done) they are accurate and reliable. The underwater unit is often a small plastic rotor, and frequently there is no mechanical transmission; in this case, the instrument works rather like the price indicator on a garage petrol pump, where in a similar fashion the plastic impeller spinning round in the flow of petrol behind the sight-glass gives magnetic pulses that are converted electronically into a reading in gallons. In our case, of course, the reading is in knots. To give an accurate reading, the impeller or rotor has to be kept spotlessly clean, so it must be possible to retract the transducer inboard to remove fouling, even with the boat afloat. The amount of current consumed may at first sight seem insignificant, but with continuous use during a long cruise it can be quite considerable. The well known Walker patent log uses no current. Though I have had trouble using it, it served the Hiscocks well during several round-the-world voyages, so the fault is undoubtedly mine.

Electronic log impeller: not a good design, because it is not retractable.

Wind speed indicator (anemometer)

Once upon a time, I believed that an experienced sailor should be able to judge wind speed fairly reliably. I have changed my mind since, because the estimate will, I have found, be influenced a great deal by personal mood (fear of a storm, loneliness and so on). In these circumstances, an objective reading from an instrument will make it easier to decide whether to heave to or take in a reef. Most anemometers are nothing more than a tiny dynamo driven by the wind via the spinning cup unit; the more wind there is, the more current is generated and the further the pointer moves round the dial. The anemometer draws no current at all from the battery.

Wind direction indicator

This is not needed on a cruising yacht, since the masthead burgee or the vane of the self-steering gear will do the same job. If you do fit one, make sure that it will not interfere with radio reception and need measures to overcome this.

This Windex mechanical wind-direction indicator is very popular.

Radar

A marvellous thing to have, if you have enough space, electrical power and money to afford it. The range will depend on how high up the antenna is installed, which is why on a ketch rig you usually find it in front of the mizzen crosstrees. There is no really suitable place on a sloop. Depending on the range, current consumption will be at least 10A, and a radar installation will cost you £2000 or more. Incidentally, radar not only makes up for poor visibility, but close to the coast can also serve for fixing your position. Concentric rings on the screen (with the boat at the centre-point) will show the distance from a target at a glance, and a rotating scale will provide the bearing. The difficulty about using radar as a navigating instrument is not, however, in operating method, but in identifying the object on which you are taking a bearing. Many landmarks that visually are very distinct give a very weak echo on the screen and this may lead to a confusing radar picture. For this reason there are radar charts for some areas, with landmarks depicted as they appear on a radar screen.

The right radio receiver

Marine accessories manufacturers tell us constantly that yacht radios need to be specially designed and built for use under the difficult conditions of a moist and salt-laden atmosphere. Because of the small numbers produced, such sets cost an astronomical amount compared to ordinary radio sets. From my own experience, however, I can assure you that ordinary receivers made by well-reputed firms, like those to be found in big stores, will do their job on a yacht every bit as well as special 'yacht radio receivers'. Obviously, you will not expose an ordinary radio to salt spray, such as a DF set made specifically for yachts might be able to cope with; but at the same time it should be realised that the latter will be made from exactly the same components (transistors, capacitors, and so on) as any other item of electronic equipment.

To start with, however, we should not take price into consideration, but look instead at what signals we want to be able to pick up when at sea, and what receivers there are on the market that will let us do so. A brief glance at the specifications on sales leaflets will then tell us at once which sets can be ruled out from the beginning.

The simplest approach, of course, would be to choose a receiver that has on its tuning scale all the radio frequencies we want. The 'frequency' is, put in basic terms, the number of radio waves received in a given time, and is measured in hertz (Hz); a hertz is one cycle of oscillation each second; radio waves start at a frequency of about 100 kilohertz (abbreviated to kHz). One kHz is equivalent to 1000 cycles a second, and 1000kHz are called 1 megahertz (MHz). Because the wavelength depends on the frequency, we can in broad terms arrange the tuning scale of a radio receiver in long, medium, intermediate and short waves. Ultra-short waves (above 30MHz) are used particularly by hi-fi enthusiasts because of the exceptionally good quality reproduction they give, but are of less interest to the yachtsman.

What transmissions are needed?
Weather reports

Special weather forecasts for shipping should be used whenever possible. The frequencies for these are shown in *Admiralty List of Radio Signals* where we find that in Europe all the weather forecasts broadcast in speech are transmitted in the intermediate-wave or 'marine' band between 1.6 and 3.8MHz, or on long-wave (eg. Niton Radio on 1834kHz, or BBC Radio 2 on 200kHz). On very long cruises, however, weather forecasts can also be picked up at higher frequencies (eg. Port Moresby is on 6.405MHz).

It is uncommon, however, for cruising areas to be as well provided with weather stations as the northern European waters, and by the time one has reached the Canary Islands or Azores there can be considerable difficulty because of not knowing the language. The FM 46 weather analysis system provides a marvellous opportunity, using very simple equipment, of getting a complete chart while at sea. A chart will sometimes be far more useful than a brief forecast. The principle of this weather chart transmission is explained on page 182, and the FM 46 code can be found in the *Admiralty List of Radio Signals, Vol 3.* In the Mediterranean, Malta Radio transmits FM 46 signals, while the North Sea and Channel are covered by Portishead Radio. Malta works on the following frequencies:

4.319MHz	8.594MHz	
6.495MHz	13.105MHz	16.988MHz

It is not enough, however, to have just one of these five frequencies available on your radio; the various frequencies differ markedly from one another in such things as range and propagation conditions. Certain frequencies are particularly good at night, while others are best for daytime reception. The higher frequencies, in general, have an especially wide range, but cannot be picked up inside a radius of, say, 100km from the transmitter; close to, the lower frequencies will then have to be used. Transmissions in Morse code, like the FM 46 transmissions, are impossible to receive without a BFO (beat-frequency oscillator); a transmitter does not send out any sound, merely energy switched on and off in accordance with the Morse dots and dashes. Without a BFO, the most one could do would be to watch the receiver's signal-meter needle flicking in time with the Morse signals: there would be no

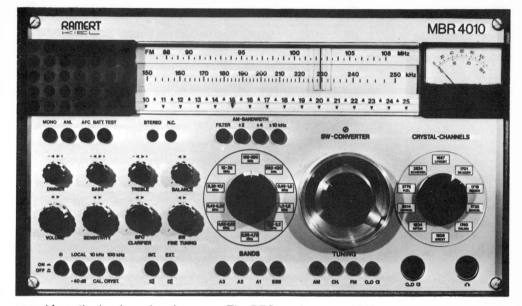

sound from the loudspeaker, however. The BFO produces a whistling note whenever transmitted energy is being picked up by the receiver.

The Ramert MBR 4010 – a top-class receiver specially designed and built for the long-distance cruising yachtsman.

In some overseas cruising areas there are no special weather reports for shipping at all, and you have to be glad to be able to get the ordinary weather forecasts (usually following the news broadcasts) intended for civilians: this is why the radio should have a medium-wave band as well.

Broadcast programmes

It is a matter of course, nowadays, that you are supplied with the latest news wherever you are in the world. Besides this facility, having background music can make a big difference to the mood on board when at sea. All these broadcast programmes are transmitted on medium wave, and can thus be picked up on any receiver.

Unfortunately, the range of medium waves is only 1000km at best, and when crossing the Atlantic the radio will fall silent after a couple of days unless it can receive shortwave stations (ie. above 5MHz) as well.

Radio direction-finding (RDF)

Radio beacons transmit solely on the navigation band, which is next to the long-wave band on the scale and stretches from 285 to 425kHz. Any receiver that covers these frequencies will allow radio fixes to be taken if you also have a directional DF antenna (see page 209). *Consol beacons* work on the same frequencies, and will give far more accurate fixes than the DF stations without the need for a rotating DF antenna. The dots and dashes transmitted by Consol beacons can however only be heard if the BFO is switched on (see page 216).

One-way radio traffic

Even if a yacht does not carry a transmitter, it is possible for friends and relatives at least to send messages to those on board. Coastal stations can read out telegrams addressed to vessels if the receiver has a marine band (ie. the wave-band used for shipping weather forecasts).

Time signals

If astronomical navigation is being used, with the need to know the time to the nearest second, the yacht's radio receiver must be able to pick up time signals. This is a far more accurate and usually a cheaper method than working with hideously expensive ship's chronometers. And, besides, the cheap quartz watches that are now fashionable are too inaccurate for navigational purposes after a couple of days of the wide temperature changes that are common at sea, unless they are constantly checked against a radio time signal. The time-signal frequencies are easy to remember: the principal transmitters work on 2.5MHz, 5MHz, 10MHz, 15MHz, 20MHz, 25MHz and 30MHz. Again, it would be a mistake to make do with a receiver that can get only, say, the 15MHz transmitter; my experience is that you are sure of being able to tune in to the time signal only if you can pick up *all* these frequencies. I have often found that from the wide choice of time-signal stations, there was only one on which you could hear the regular ticking of the signal.

Grundig Satellit – excellent value for money, it offers the cruising skipper a full range of facilities.

Colour plate: What cruising is all about – fabulous Hanavave Bay on Fatu Hiva (Marquesas Islands).

A versatile yacht radio will therefore cover the following frequencies:

Weather reports in Europe	marine band (1.6–3.8MHz)
Weather reports overseas	short-wave (4– about 10MHz)
FM 46 weather reports	short-wave (4–23MHz)
Broadcast stations in mainland Europe	medium-wave (535–1605kHz)
Broadcast stations overseas	short-wave (4–25MHz)
Radio direction-finding	long-wave navigation band (285–425kHz)
Time signals	short-wave (4–25MHz)

Even if a receiver does cover these frequencies and has a BFO, this does not mean that it is bound to be ideal for our purposes. If, for example, the scale was very narrow although in theory it had a wide range, we would not be able to tune into many stations, especially on the short-wave band. This is because every station takes up a certain width on the scale, usually about 10kHz. The range between 1000 and 3000kHz could therefore accommodate about 200 transmitting stations without these interfering with each other. Between 28 and 30MHz there would, from the electronic viewpoint, also be space for 200 stations; yet it will be obvious that it will scarcely be possible to tune in to 200 stations on such a tiny length of scale, even if we can find them. The transmitter frequency needs to 'drift' only slightly (because of temperature fluctuations or mechanical vibration), and the receiver will lose the signal immediately. So a high-quality receiver should, especially on the short-wave band, have as much 'spread' as possible, and for this reason the really top-class sets divide up the frequency range shown above over as many as 30 separate bands. Unhappily, many special yacht radios are very poorly provided for in this respect. The very least one should expect is a fine-tuning device, which provides a mechanical or electrical 'gearing-down' of the movement of the main tuning knob.

The ideal yacht radio should provide:

■ all frequencies from 150kHz to 30MHz

■ a short-wave range with enough spread for a transmitter station to be found at the first attempt

■ a BFO

■ an optical tuning indicator

- a connection for a DF antenna
- a choice of single-sideband or double-sideband operation. In a few years' time, practically all transmitters in the marine band will work with a single sideband, and this will make receivers extremely expensive. If needs be, however, these transmissions can be picked up by any receiver that has a BFO (a useful tip when doing this is to have the volume control turned down as far as possible).

Antenna This need not cause any real headaches: the wire back-stay, fitted with a porcelain insulator at top and bottom, is ample for reception purposes.

Yacht radios on the market

	Grundig Satellit	Hitachi Navigator 2	Ramert MBR	Sailor R 108	Sailor R 104
Bands	150–400kHz 540kHz–30MHz	150–410kHz 530kHz–4.5MHz	150kHz –22MHz	150–430kHz 495kHz–4.5MHz	170–525kHz 700kHz–4.2MHz 11 crystals 1.6–4.2MHz
All weather stations (Europe)	yes	yes	yes	yes	yes
All weather stations (overseas)	yes	no	yes	no	no
FM 46	yes	no	yes	no	no
Time signals	yes	no	yes – crystal settings	no	no
Radio direction-finding	with DF antenna	built-in antenna	with DF antenna	with DF antenna	with DF antenna
Consol	yes	yes	yes	yes	yes
Broadcast	yes	yes	yes	yes	yes
Home broadcast SW stations at long distance	yes	no	yes	no	no
SW tuning spread	fair	fair	good	good (marine band)	good (marine band)
Reliable station-finding without searching of SW band	no	no	yes – crystal settings	yes	yes – crystals on marine band
Convertible to SSB in future?	yes – but complicated	no	yes	no	already equipped
Price (approx)		£60		£220	
Suitable for coastal cruising	yes	yes	yes	yes	yes
Suitable for ocean cruising	yes	no	yes	no	no

Transmitters

Until only a short while ago yacht skippers had to resign themselves to the idea that a transmitter was out of the question for them. For one thing, yachts' electrical systems were not as reliable as they are today, and for another the older generation of transmitters used vacuum tubes, which took a lot of current. Nowadays, tubes are found only in the output stages of quite powerful transmitters, and even there they are soon going to have to give way to transistors. Yachtsmen tend to be bemused by the vast array of modern sets and systems on offer; few of them really know whether what they need is an 11m set, a marine-band transmitter, a single-sideband transmitter, an amateur-band installation or a VHF set. So I shall try to bring some sort of order into all this confusion.

The 11m set is the most tempting for the layman. This kind of walkie-talkie can be bought in many department stores for not much over £20; the sets are simple to operate, and their power consumption is literally negligible, because they get their 'juice' from built-in batteries. You must, of course, be careful to get the Post Office licence you need to use these sets; otherwise you will be running the risk of being prosecuted for pirate transmitting, which can be quite unpleasant. The authorities will allow only sets transmitting on a very limited power, and working in the 27MHz SW band. An external antenna is prohibited, and all that can be used is the built-in telescopic antenna. The performance of these walkie-talkies is correspondingly limited, and not even on the open sea can one count on a range of more than three nautical miles. All one can really do with them is to talk to another yacht (that has to be almost within sight), provided a time has been agreed beforehand.

An 11m walkie-talkie is child's-play to operate, but offers only a very limited range of possibilities.

Even in our European waters there is no official station monitoring traffic on the 11m band, so these sets are quite useless in an emergency. If you do carry one, you must realise that what you have got is a toy; a very pretty toy, but nothing more than that. Above all, no-one should imagine that they can use these sets to make a distress call; you will either be out of range of other walkie-talkie users, or the band will be so busy that there will be only a slim chance of making yourself heard.

Marine band sets are to be found on all smaller merchant ships, and within limits one can say that they have, by and large, proved very useful to the leisure-and-pleasure sailor as well over recent years. I must stress, straight away, that an official RT (speech) transmitting licence must be obtained from the Post Office before the equipment can be used on a ship. These transmitters operate on the intermediate-wave marine band, next to the MW band on the scale: one frequency in this band that everyone should know by heart is 2182KHz, the international distress and calling frequency. A yacht's batteries cannot be expected to give much more than 30W output, which will give a range of 30–50 nautical miles (record distances can, naturally, be covered from time to time, but this cannot be relied on). The main advantage of the marine band is that all coastal radio stations in the world are equipped with these frequencies, and that it will thus be possible to talk to any harbour in the world. There is also the possibility of being linked into the public telephone network (at a fee, of course) from aboard your yacht, via a coastal station. The 2182KHz distress frequency is monitored 24 hours a day throughout Europe, so that there is a good chance of getting help if you make a distress call on 2182. It is even possible to fit the set with an automatic alarm generator, which in the event of trouble will transmit a distress signal automatically until the batteries are exhausted.

It should be noted that most sets still work on the AM, or amplitude modulation, system, and here again a changeover to the single-sideband (SSB) system in the near future is planned.

A short-wave single sideband installation will be almost out of the question for our purposes if only because of the extremely high cost (up to £2300). The SSB transmitter works on various frequencies and is able to make contact with relay stations all round the world. Using an installation like this, I have been able to talk to a friend in Germany on his own telephone from an isolated anchorage near Bora-Bora, in the South Seas, and the quality of the line was not much worse than that on an ordinary long-distance call inside Germany. For a small yacht, however, the power consumption of several hundred watts would be too high, and the sets are in any case quite bulky. Here again, of course, an operator's licence from the Post Office would be required. Apart from that, it is a nice thing to have – if you can afford it.

VHF transmitters work on frequencies between 156 and 174MHz, and in the yachting world they seem likely in future to take the place of the present marine-band stations. Their advantages

VHF radio telephone set

are self-evident: they use less current, have almost the same range as MB transmitters, are unaffected by atmospheric interference, are more compact, do not need costly and complicated antenna installations, and are relatively cheap at around £450. A VHF network has been built up around the European coasts, so that in the North Sea and Baltic it is almost always possible to make contact. Moreover, a constant radio watch is kept on Channel 16 (distress and calling frequency). Practically all large ships have a VHF set on the bridge, so that even from the middle of the ocean it may be possible, with the help of one of the Big Boys and via the ship-to-ship channel, to send a message home. An RT operator's licence is again required.

An **amateur band transmitter** is, in my opinion, the best of all. The gear will cost around £400–500, and will usually be of ultra-modern design (with single-sideband). Some transmitters already have a transistorised output stage, so that power consumption is reduced to an absolute minimum.

This compact set allows conversations worldwide. It uses very little current, but a generator set is a useful adjunct.

The amateur has access to all the amateur ('ham') radio bands, and can choose any frequency he likes inside these. The characteristics of the various bands are so varied that one can guarantee being able to make a contact. The ham bands most preferred are the 15 and 20m bands; on these, the skipper will be able to talk directly from continent to continent with no trouble at all. They do have one snag, in that there is a 'dead area' (of a few hundred km) around the transmitter; but this is no problem for the ham, who simply switches over to the 80m band which, though it will not give him long-range contacts, works extremely well at short distances. The equipment is very small and compact – the latest transistorised transmitters are hardly bigger than a cigar box. The backstay, fitted with insulators, is quite satisfactory as a transmitting antenna, and has allowed me to get through from New Guinea to Wuppertal.

The fly in the ointment is getting the radio amateur's licence, which is much harder to qualify for than the RT operator's licence. Obviously, an amateur-band set can only be used to contact other radio hams, so making a distress call to a coastal radio station will not be possible. However, it will be only a matter of a few minutes before a distress call is picked up by an amateur *somewhere* ashore, and this fellow ham will then be able to set the wheels in motion by making an ordinary telephone call. A radio amateur would, in any case, hardly be likely to go away on a long voyage without arranging a regular schedule of link-ups with other amateurs. He will be able to report his position daily, so that if the worst does happen the most likely location of the accident will be quite closely pinpointed. Conversations between amateurs are not, of course, subject to any fee (there is an all-in amateur licence fee of £5.50), but the amateur is not allowed to pass on messages to third parties, that is to say non-amateurs. In plain language, this means that one is not allowed to have a ham friend back at home called up to find out if everything is all right. Nevertheless, one never feels lonely, even far out in the middle of the ocean, with an amateur 'rig' to hand.

There are, in fact, a number of radio amateur groups who have made a speciality of organising regular contacts with 'maritime mobile' stations round the world (there is, for instance, the Micronesia Net and the South-East Asia Net). Full information about radio amateur licencing regulations and tests, and about special maritime mobile licences, can be obtained from the Home Office Radio Regulatory Department, Waterloo Bridge House, Waterloo Road, London SE1 (tel: 01-275 3154), while the club contact aspect of amateur radio is looked after by the Radio Society of Great Britain, 35 Doughty Street, London WC1 (tel: 01-837 8688).

Yacht handling

Ropes, wire ropes and knots

Ropes can be divided into the braided and the twisted or 'laid' types. Braided rope has the advantage of being a great deal more supple, but is also much more expensive. It is used mainly for sheets. Laid rope is used for mooring lines, for anchor warps, and for the main and jib halyards if wire rope is not used for these. There is one feature of synthetic ropes (those made from man-made fibres, like Terylene) that has to be allowed for, and that may be desirable or undesirable depending on the purpose for which they are being used. Every man-made fibre has a certain amount of stretch, and gets longer under strain: in extreme cases, the increase may be as much as 20 per cent. Keep this always in mind, for a 20m warp may suddenly become a 24m warp! For this reason such rope can never be used for shrouds and forestays and backstays. Prestretched rope has been developed for halyards; this is stretched during manufacture to (almost) the full length it will reach under conditions of maximum strain. Prestretched rope is not, however, suitable for mooring lines or anchor warps, because here stretch is a positive advantage; if a yacht is bucking against her anchor in a seaway, the elasticity of the rope will absorb the shock of the sharp tugging. Synthetic rope does not rot; but it does

Some recommended rope diameters (in mm) and breaking strains (kg approx)

boat's weight	sheets	spinnaker & running sail sheets	halyards	mooring lines & anchor warp	topping lift
up to	braided	braided	laid prestretched	laid	laid prestretched
1t	8(850)	8	8(1250)	10(2100)	6
3t	10(1400)	8	8(1250)	12(3000)	8
5t	10(1400)	10	10(1750)	14(4100)	8
8t	12(1900)	10	10(1750)	16(5300)	8
12t	12(1900)	12	12(2400)	20(8100)	10

become fatigued through being overstressed and through UV radiation, and loses strength as it gets stiffer. According to recommendations from the Liros ropemaking factory, who have been doing a lot of research on wear and tear in yachting, the constant load on ropes should be only one-fifth the rope's breaking strain. On cruising yachts, which are not going to be sailing a triangular course for just a couple of hours and where a couple of kilos extra weight make no difference, the ropework can therefore do with being of generous dimensions. One spin-off from space developments is Liros Kevlar ropes, which give five times the strength of steel wire of equivalent weight! Because they have the drawback of poor resistance to kinking, and hence are vulnerable to being knotted, they have only limite d uses in cruising though they can usefully be employed as mainsheets and spinnaker and running-sail sheets. Because of their slight stretch (60 per cent that of polyester rope) and enormous strength they are excellent as backstays and as emergency replacement stays or shrouds.

Every sailor must be able to deal with his own ropework. One seldom takes delivery of a boat completely equipped for cruising, and in any case a rope will sometimes need repairing or replacing. One also needs a few tools for dealing with rope work:

- marlinspike (left) The hollow type is much more suitable than the solid, and though these cannot be bought, most small toolmakers will be willing to bend and file a short length of copper tubing to the shape you need.
- whipping twine
- scissors, and matches or a cigarette-lighter

Ways of using a knotted whipping (see opposite page).

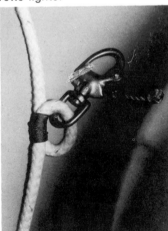

Every rope-end needs to be finished off so that it will not unreeve of its own accord. If necessary, the end of synthetic rope can be secured by heating the strands in a match-flame and then, when they have just reached finger temperature, briefly pressing them together so that they stick to each other. This stuck end may, however, very easily come apart under stress, and there is nothing to beat a proper *whipping*. I believe that the knotted whipping illustrated here is the best for use on a cruising sailboat, because it does not have to be stitched with a needle and palm, is child's play to produce without tools, and holds 100 per cent reliably. I used seizing like this to preserve my jibsheet, and the joint held throughout the whole 32000-mile trip round the world.

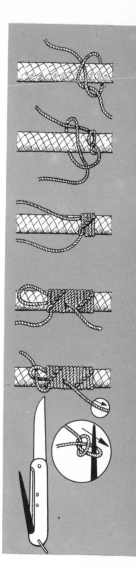

In this knotted whipping, all turns are taken close together in the same direction and are pulled tight individually (best done by using the marlinespike, as shown). About halfway along the planned length, the turns are taken over the bight of the other end, which is finally pulled through with the marlinespike to finish off.

Loose rope must always be kept coiled, making sure that it does not kink as loop after loop is turned on to the hand, and does not form figures-of-eight. If the rope does show a tendency to twist, this can easily be counteracted by giving it a half-turn between the finger and thumb. The coil can be finished off as shown in the photograph above right, or second from right.

However, a halyard actually holding up a sail, that may need to be cleared away within seconds, can best be finished off as shown below.

Working with ropes

Nowadays effective winches, pulleys and patent cleats mean that even a woman, with her lesser muscular strength in arm and wrist, will have no trouble in hoisting a sail up hard, and there is not a lot to comment on on this point. Even in light winds a jib sheet should never be cleated directly, without taking at least three turns round the drum of a snubbing winch; a sudden gust of wind would be bound to damage either the cleat or the sheet. There is no need for the surface of the winch-drum to be roughened, because the friction needed to prevent the sheet from slipping will come solely from the number of turns. Four turns on a drum will leave only 5 per cent of the strain on the sheet actually on your hands. It is not however wise to take as many as four turns on the drum when going about, because if we then haul in hand-over-hand on the loose jib sheet it will be certain to jam up on the winch drum. The normal rule is, therefore, to have only one turn on the winch immediately before going about, to haul in hand-over-hand and then immediately, just before the sail fills again, to take at least two more turns round the

Once there are enough turns on the drum, the sheet can be held like this in a jam cleat.

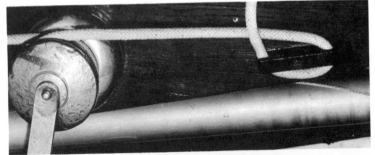

Left: the wrong way to start.

Centre: the final turn is wrong here.

Right: correct – with thin rope, this would need an extra cross-over turn.

winch. Very often there is then an ordinary cleat behind the winch. If this is not a patent jam-cleat (for which a single turn is enough to belay the sheet) the rope will have to be cleated with several figure-of-eight turns. Exactly the same knot is used for making fast a mooring line. The first turn provides enough friction on the cleat for it to be possible to hold the fall of the rope and control the boat. It can then be finished off with as many figure-of-eight turns as you like, ending up with a proper jamming turn.

You often read in books that in general a half-hitch, or jamming turn, is strictly taboo on a yacht other than for belaying a halyard holding one of the crew to the top of the mast. This idea is a carry-over from the days of natural-fibre ropes, when in rainy weather the jamming turn could indeed jam absolutely solid as the rope swelled, and would then need a hatchet to cut it apart. But in an age of synthetic ropes this is no longer something to worry about, especially when, as here, a jamming turn is being used merely to prevent the figure-of-eight turns on a cleat from working loose (ie. when there is no pull on the jamming turn whatsoever, even with the rope under full load).

This has dealt with the first knot you will need for working on and around a boat. There are umpteen books on the market showing how to tie hundreds of different knots; yet in fact only a few, quite simple knots are used on a yacht (far fewer than you need for passing a seamanship examination). These basic knots are, however, ones that every sailor ought to be able to tie in his sleep.

Knots

A proper seaman's knot will not come undone by itself, but can easily be untied at any time.

This is why the *granny knot* really is taboo on a yacht. It can come untied by itself, yet once it is jammed really tight you can break your fingernails trying to get it undone.

Left: granny knot

Centre: reef knot

Right: slip knot

The *reef knot*, on the other hand, is right for joining two (similar) ropes. It can be used wherever a landlubber would tend to use a granny, eg. for lashing down the mainsail. There is no use whatsoever aboard for the *slip knot*, other than perhaps for a practical joke with someone's hammock! It must never be confused with the reef knot, which finishes up with both the ends of the rope on the same side. A derivation of the reef knot is the *sheet bend*. If this were based on the slip knot, I would not trust it; and yet many quite sound books do illustrate it tied this way. In fact, a simple sheet-

Left: sheet-bend (started like a reef knot).

Right: double sheet-bend.

bend is in any case hardly ever used, the *double sheetbend* being a very popular way of joining two lengths of rope of different thickness. I do not however put too much trust in this knot if it is to be under a varying strain, unless it is further secured with a half-hitch. There is in fact a far simpler way of joining two ropes together: two linked *bowlines*.

The bowline, more than any other, is the truly universal knot that no sailor can manage without. Its essential feature is that the loop it

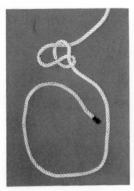
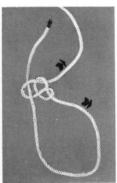
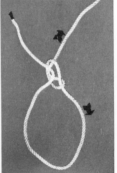
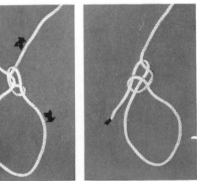

Bowline, 'American-style'.

forms will not tighten of its own accord. American yachtsmen (and mountaineers) have an ultra-simple way of making this knot, easier even than the well known aid to memory about the rabbit 'coming out of his hole, round the tree and back down the hole'. Depending on the size of loop wanted, you push the end of the rope through a

96

marline-spike hitch (see page 93) in place of the marline-spike, and then pull the end away from the loop to form the bowline. This universal knot is used particularly for making a boat fast.

A *clove hitch* should not be used for mooring a yacht; on a large yacht it is ideal for securing fenders to the boat's rail.

One thing to be remembered about all these knots is that any knot reduces the breaking strength of the rope, by about 40 per cent. If things are getting rough in a storm, it is therefore better to

Clove hitch – not for making fast!

make mooring lines fast to a bollard by using a *round turn and two half-hitches*, as the reduction in strength will then be kept down to only 25 per cent or so. Last of all comes the simplest knot of all – the *figure-of-eight*. This is a stopper knot, put at the end of every sheet to prevent the rope running out through the block.

Blocks

When the pull on a rope has to change direction, the rope will have to pass through a block; nowadays those used for ropework are made almost exclusively from a Tufnol type of plastics material.

Left: round turn and two half-hitches.

Right: figure-of-eight

Plastic sleeving protects mooring lines.

This American 'Nauti-Press' can handle stainless steel wire up to 6mm – a most useful tool to have on board. *(North Service)*

They are virtually maintenance-free, but must be wide enough to give the rope a clear run; if rope rubs against the cheeks of the block, it will have a fairly limited life. Sheets or other ropes that run through a block always at the same point along their length will need some form of protection, especially on long voyages. Beef suet, obtainable from any butcher, is excellent for this if rubbed thoroughly into the rope at the vulnerable points; the process should be repeated every 2000 miles or so. Ropes that pass over a sharp edge (eg: mooring lines) are best protected by a simple tough plastic sleeve.

Wire rope

Over recent years the sailor has come to enjoy more and more the boon of stainless steel, though this miracle unfortunately has to be paid for at quite a handsome price. Nevertheless, the advantages far outweigh the extra cost, because whereas in the past steel wire had to be painted with a protective coating, there is virtually nothing that needs doing to stainless steel halyards. It is however impossible to work on this kind of wire yourself; in particular, it is too brittle to be spliced. Terminals can be put on with the tools available on board if you use screw-on terminals of the kind made by Norseman; these need only pliers and a small vice. Following the instructions provided, it is no great problem to fix an eye to the end of a wire halyard. The threads can be dabbed with one of the modern epoxide adhesives to stop the screw from coming undone by itself.

Stainless steel wire is vulnerable to kinking, so when the genoa is being hoisted the wire halyard should be guided with one hand to make sure that the last few turns on the winch come at an empty part of the drum; otherwise, an underlying turn of wire rope can easily be pinched and crushed.

Watch carefully when first using new wire halyards. If snagged strands appear from the outset, this is a sign either that the sheave over which the halyard runs is jamming, or that the sheave diameter is too small. Sheaves carrying wire rope must have at least the following diameters:

Wire diameter	Sheave diameter
5mm	7cm
6mm	8cm
7mm	10cm
8mm	13cm

The skipper

The skipper is absolute master of his ship, old-fashioned though this phrase may sound. There is no democracy on board where matters of manoeuvring or steering the ship are concerned. The need for this is obvious if you compare skippering a ship with driving a car. In a car, the driver has all the necessary controls within his reach, and is using his own two hands and his own two feet to control the vehicle. On a yacht, above a certain size, the situation is totally different. The controls are not within reach of any one person, but spread out all over the 7m or more of the boat's length. The crew members have to perform the tasks that the car-driver demands of his own feet and hands. If the driver wants the car to go faster, for instance, he presses on the accelerator with the toes of his right foot. Translating this into sailboat terms, the mainsheet needs to be hauled in tighter; and if the skipper is not able to handle the mainsheet himself, the job has to be done by a crew member – and as near to immediately as possible. Raising queries, or even 'suggesting a better idea', is absolutely out of the question. The essential cooperation between skipper and crew can be guaranteed only if the crew follow the skipper's orders to the letter, and understand them fully. So it is not mere clinging to tradition, and harking back to the past, to insist on clear and easily-understood orders being used for the job of running a yacht. It is best to keep to the phrases that have been used on all sailing ships for centuries. In theory it is quite possible to work out your own language of commands, but there are sound reasons for discouraging this even on yachts that basically always have the same crew, it is quite likely that occasionally there may be a friend or guest aboard for a trip; this person will only be able to lend a hand with the work if he knows the commands used. Should help from ashore be needed, it is again a big help if the standard set of commands are used, because they will be familiar to anyone who has to do with sailing.

The loudness with which commands are given has nothing to do with whether they sound pleasant to the ear or not, but is in general dictated solely by circumstances. Commands must always be loud enough to be understood without difficulty by everyone on board. To indicate that the commands have been understood it is important that the members of the crew for whom they are intended should acknowledge them by 'repeating back'. The fact that the orders have been carried out is also always reported, against the (admittedly unlikely) case of the skipper not having noticed that his instructions have been followed.

Since the skipper is the only one giving orders, the crew must never respond to instructions from some onlooker ashore eager to help; and a skipper must never let someone else take over the giving of orders so that he no longer has full control of the ship handling.

Examples of the most commonly used commands are listed below. It will be obvious from their nature whether repeating-back is needed to indicate that they have been carried out (eg. 'Cast off stern rope' – 'Stern rope cast off').

Commands

Mooring commands
'Cast off stern rope'
'Head spring ready to slip'
'Stand by after spring'
'Head rope ashore'
'Put out springs'
'Make fast aft'

Steering commands
'Hard astarboard' (boat turns to starboard)
'Put about'
'Luff up'
'Bear away'
'Steer 220°'
'Steer for the harbour entrance', etc.

Sail commands
'Stand by to hand the main'
'Bring down jib'
'Take up topping lift'
'Harden in mainsheet' (only when close-hauled)
'Haul up jib'
'Slacken off mainsheet'
'Haul in jibsheet' (this sheet is not hauled in hard, but to suit the sail setting wanted)
'Back the jib'
'Stand by to gybe – gybe-oh!'
'Ready about – lee-oh!'

Anchor commands
'Stand by to drop anchor'
'Let go anchor'
'Stand by to weigh anchor'
'Bring anchor up-and-down'
'Haul in anchor'

Generally the skipper will have time to prepare the crew and the boat for the impending manoeuvre. It is better to start much too soon than too late, and in any case it is useful to explain everything to the crew beforehand. No manoeuvre should be started on until the skipper is clear in his mind what he plans to do: a good skipper will have the whole thing plotted out exactly in his mind's eye.

The **size of the crew** is generally not crucial for carrying out a given manoeuvre successfully. Things will naturally go more smoothly if there are more skilled hands available, but practically all operations can be undertaken with a very small crew. Usually a cruising yacht has a man and wife as the 'normal' crew, with perhaps another couple joining them on a longish cruise. An exception to this will be a chartered yacht where – for reasons of cost – there will almost always be more people on board.

A special problem is presented by the willing but totally inexperienced 'swimming-party guest'. Never try, come-what-may, to involve them in working the ship if it is possible to cope with the normal crew alone. These unhappy folk usually stand around getting in everybody's way, or at the very least in the skipper's line-of-sight, and the best place for them when something is going on is below decks. They should certainly never be trusted with any job, if the success of making fast or casting off depends on it.

Nearly all the manoeuvres discussed in the following pages can be coped with quite easily by a small crew, eg. the skipper and one crew member. In these circumstances it is up to the skipper to plan matters so that the various operations can be carried out one after the other. If a yacht is coming into harbour, for instance, it may look very dashing if the fenders needed for docking are put out at the very last moment; yet there is nothing to be ashamed of about the skipper having his one and only crew member tying the fenders to the rail before the boat comes in through the harbour entrance.

The following basic principle applies to every boat-handling manoeuvre:

There must always be time to think through a manoeuvre; then – once the skipper is quite clear about the sequence of operations – carry it out with firmness and confidence.

To be avoided at all costs is a manoeuvre approached with the attitude 'Let's try it this way – it'll come right in a minute'.

Boat-handling in harbour

On a mooring

A cruising yacht must never, never be made fast to the quay in the way one would tie up a dinghy. If a yacht of any real weight is made fast by a bow painter alone, as would be perfectly reasonable with a dinghy, the slightest offshore breeze will, if there is a long mooring line, make her pick up forward way, of her own accord, and ram the quayside.

As a basic rule a yacht should always – provided there is enough

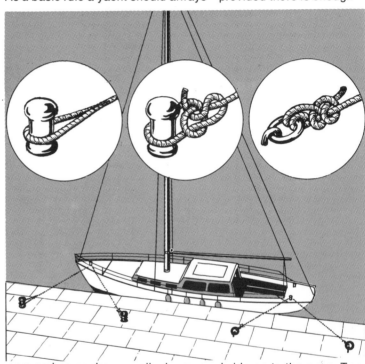

Yacht moored correctly with four lines, and fenders only where needed.

room and no onshore swell – be moored side-on to the quay. Two mooring lines (a head rope and a stern rope) are not enough for this, since the yacht will then always pivot slightly about her widest point: two further lines are needed – the head and after springs.

The strongest rope available on board should be used for mooring lines. Each line should have its own cleat (as strong a one as possible), and the rope made fast to it by taking several figure-of-eight turns and finishing up with a jamming turn. At the shore end, a mooring line should whenever possible (ie. where there is a bollard) be made fast with a bowline. The advantage of this is that any willing stranger ashore will be capable of dropping the loop over the bollard.

There is a golden rule that governs all manoeuvres carried out with the help of a mooring line (which means almost all harbour manoeuvres):

All lines should be tended from on board, not from ashore.

Lines should not be kept too taut. If the boat is moored in tidal waters, lines will need to be adjusted from time to time, to allow for the changing state of tide and to prevent the boat from hanging on her ropes. In harbours with a very marked rise-and-fall, it is advisable to try to moor to a floating pontoon, or to make fast alongside a commercial craft that is not in use.

A yacht should never be moored alongside a quay without fenders, for the slightest movement of the water (eg. when another boat passes in the harbour, causing a wash) will damage the vulnerable outer skin. A sufficient number of fenders must be put between the hull and the quay wall, and positioned only where they are actually needed, ie. midway along the boat's length. If the yacht is moored properly, with head and stern ropes and head and after springs, no fenders will be needed at the bow and stern quarters. A common sight in harbours is a row of fenders stretching from stem to stern, and it usually betrays either the beginner or the unknowledgeable.

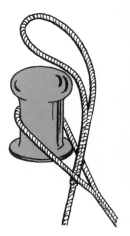

If there are other lines already on a bollard, this will not interfere with anyone wanting to cast off.

Lying alongside other yachts is not all that different from lying alongside the quay wall; the main rule here is that the longest boat must lie on the inside, next to the wall. If the boat between you and

the shore should happen not to be substantially larger, then you will need to put out your own head and stern ropes. It goes without saying that a skipper will ask permission before lying alongside other yachts, as well as permission to go ashore across their decks. A basic rule, when doing so, is always to go across the foredeck, so that your neighbours' privacy is disturbed as little as possible.

Manoeuvring under engine

Once upon a time it was a matter of pride to every sailor to carry out every mooring manoeuvre under sail. In today's densely-packed harbours this is not really appropriate, and the first consideration must be safety. Since picking up a mooring under sail alone is more complicated, more time-consuming and less certain than doing so under engine, it is not good seamanship to sail around in a crowded anchorage unless the lack of an auxiliary engine forces you to do so.
The golden rule is:

> Whether under sail or under engine, the boat should during every manoeuvre carry as little way as possible.

This is the best way of keeping control of what is going on. The minimum speed will be governed by the yacht's manoeuvrability, ie. the ability still to answer to the rudder. In smooth water and calm air this will, for the average yacht, mean a speed of around one knot. In a breeze, the boat may sometimes need to be moving a good deal faster, so that the bow is not pushed off by the wind.

Before trying to manoeuvre under engine it is essential to know one basic fact about the propeller fitted, irrespective of whether you are using an inboard or outboard engine. When a propeller turns in the water, it not only drives the boat forward but also has a tendency (depending on which way it is turning) to push the boat's stern to one side or the other. This 'kick-effect' comes from the fact that the propeller blades find the water at the top considerably easier to push aside (and thus offering less resistance to the blades) than the water lower down, below the axis of the propeller. The kick-effect is easier to understand if one imagines the propeller turning against solid ground.

Right-handed propeller – kicks the stern to the right.

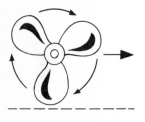

104

A propeller turning clockwise (looked at from astern) thus has a tendency to push the stern of the boat to starboard; an anticlockwise, or left-handed prop will have exactly the opposite effect. A right-handed prop becomes a left-handed one when running astern, so the same propeller that pushes the stern off to starboard when going ahead will push it to port when moving astern, until the boat picks up way and the kick-effect is lost. The slower the boat's speed, ahead or astern, the greater the kick-effect will be; with many boats the effect is scarcely noticeable at the tiller or wheel at 1½ knots or more.

Rule: Never try to manoeuvre a boat under engine until you have found out whether it has a right-handed or a left-handed propeller.

Getting away from a quay

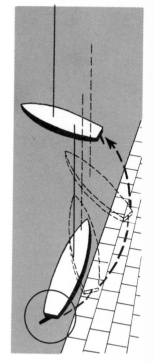

Before starting to think about getting away from the quayside under engine, you need to understand clearly just how a boat moves. Up to now, we have been comparing our yacht to a car; but here the comparison can no longer be maintained, for there is a fundamental difference in the ways a boat and a car move and steer. The car's steering works on the front wheels, while the boat – under sail or under engine – has steering that acts at the stern. An example will show clearly what effect this has:

If the helmsman puts the rudder hard to port (ie. so that the boat moves to port), the first thing to happen is that the boat's stern moves to starboard. If the space into which the stern would move with the rudder at this setting is not free (because another yacht, or the quay itself, is in the way), the turn simply cannot be made. This must be kept constantly in mind when coming alongside or moving away from a mooring.

If the yacht is lying with her starboard side to the quay, it is thus impossible simply to turn to port. Every casting-off manoeuvre must be aimed at first creating enough distance between the vessel and the shore to allow a turn to be made; and when making the turn, the helmsman has to keep a very close watch on his stern.

Getting away from the quayside with a small yacht is no problem because it is always possible to make enough space, by simply pushing off with the hands, feet or – better – a boathook, to motor

Putting the rudder hard to port will clout the stern against the quay wall.

away without scraping the quay wall. The most effective way of shoving a bigger yacht off is to do so at the bow or stern quarter; trying to shove off midships will have little success.

With a biggish yacht (more than 6t), or when the wind is onshore, shoving off by hand will always be more difficult, and this is where the help of the auxiliary has to be called in. The kick-effect of the propeller is at its greatest when the boat has no way through the water, and this fact can be put to use for moving away from the quay wall. Let us assume that the yacht has a left-handed propeller (normal in almost all cases nowadays) and is lying with her starboard side to the quay, and that there is no wind.

An offshore breeze makes getting away very simple, because the wind does the work of pushing the boat off from the quay wall; even with large boats, where shoving off by hand is barely feasible, the wind can do the work unaided. An onshore breeze, on the other hand, will make it more difficult to move off from the quay, and a strong onshore wind can make even the manoeuvre described below impossible.

> *Rule:* Always take the wind into account when manoeuvring, whether under sail or under engine.

When boat and crew are ready to cast off, *additional* long warps are passed from the boat ashore, round bollards and back aboard. It is best at once to have warps like this 'held ready to slip' (see diagram alongside) where the mooring lines are under strain. The mooring lines can then be brought aboard, leaving the boat held solely by the warps.

The point of doing this is that it makes it possible during the

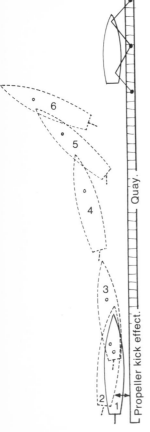

Left-handed propeller, quay to starboard (the ideal situation).

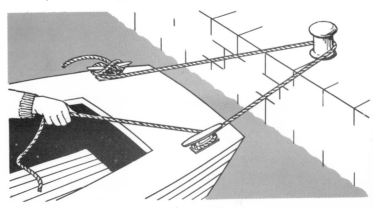

The mooring line is held checked, ready to let slip.

manoeuvre to tend the warps from *on board*, and not to have to rely on the friendliness of passers-by ashore (who can be guaranteed to drop the lines in the drink at just the wrong moment!). There should be no loops, not even a knot, at the ends of the long warps, otherwise they may fail to run free when slipped.

Once the engine is running, the skipper gives the order 'Stand by to cast off', and all other mooring lines are brought aboard. The important task now is to get the stern clear of the quay wall. In the case we are considering (ie. with a left-handed propeller and the quay wall to starboard) this will happen automatically, because when (after shoving off) the order 'slow ahead' is given, the boat will not gather way at once and the kick-effect of the propeller will 'paddle' the stern clear of the quay. As soon as the boat is far enough away from the quayside, the skipper gives a little more throttle and the boat gently moves forward.

The wrong thing to do at this point is to put the rudder hard to port, because since the distance from the quay is still not all that great the stern will then inevitably swing round and crash up against the wall. An extremely large and gentle turning radius is needed when getting away.

Take great care if the quay is not free for a long distance ahead (eg. if there is another, beamy boat moored further along).

Increase speed only when you are certain that the boat can move away clear of the quay and any other obstacles, and out into the harbour.

In the circumstances just described the kick-effect of the propeller helps the skipper when casting off, and the same would be true with a right-handed propeller when lying port side to the quay. In the opposite circumstances (eg. left-handed screw and quay to port) it is impossible to cast off in this way. Even bearing off from the quayside all the time would not give all that much space, because the rudder might then need to be put to starboard and finally hard to starboard, and the only result would be to scrape along the length of the quay. In this case, the boat must be brought clear of the quay by first moving astern, so that the kick from the left-handed prop pushes the stern out to starboard. When doing this, have fenders ready at the bows, to prevent damage as the

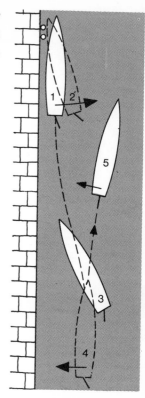

Left-handed propeller – quay to port.

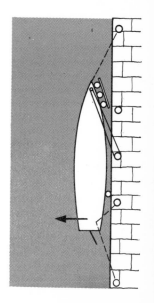

During the manoeuvre described on the next page ('springing the boat'), careful use of fenders at the bow is essential. With the wall to starboard, put the rudder hard to starboard!

107

bow quarter touches the wall. A sail boat pivots about a point roughly level with the mast, so when the stern moves outwards the bows will swing inwards, and vice-versa. It will take a while (two or three boat's lengths) for the boat to be far enough away from the wall to risk putting the rudder over to starboard and slowly moving forward and away from the quay.

Because we can turn away from the quayside only very gently, there has to be quite a lot of space ahead or astern along the quay. Unfortunately, conditions in a harbour are very seldom that good, and usually a yacht will be in amongst others. The very simple and effective way of getting away here will then be:

Casting off by springing the boat

Here the head spring is replaced with a spring 'held ready to slip'. It is important to have the bow well fendered, and the spring warp held as far forward as possible. When all other mooring lines have been taken in, engage the engine in forward gear (running slowly, as in all mooring manoeuvres) and run gently ahead against the head spring. Since this is attached at the bows, these will be turned towards the quay by the pressure of the boat against the spring. If the quay wall is to starboard, the rudder is put hard over to starboard, as if you want to turn into the wall. As soon as the head spring is taut, with the fender cushioning the bow safely against the quay wall, the engine can be put to half-speed ahead; the stern will turn away from the quay quite smartly, and even against a strong wind the boat can be brought to an angle of 45° to the quay wall. Bring the engine back to tickover, and then gently engage reverse. The stern will be far enough away from the quay for the yacht to move slowly astern, and once the bows are clear of the wall the head spring can be slipped and brought aboard. Enough space will have been gained to back off the quay and, once completely clear, to go ahead and out of the harbour.

Rule: Never change from 'half-speed ahead' to 'half-speed astern' – and certainly never from 'full-speed ahead' to 'full-speed astern'

You should always, coming from 'ahead', pause a few seconds in neutral before engaging 'astern'. The reason is that if you go straight from forward to reverse gear the strain on the shaft and

Springing clear.

gearbox will be harsh enough to break them. This danger is much less with a hydraulic system.

Generally, casting off mooring lines that are under strain will take two persons. When the man on shore is ready to take the loop of the bowline off a bollard, it helps enormously if another person on board *slackens off the line*, so that the loop can be freed from the bollard with no danger of getting the fingers crushed or the like. The command is merely 'Cast off stern rope' – a well-drilled crew will know that this includes first slackening off the line.

Crew tending the mooring lines should invariably report the carrying out of instructions, so that when the skipper orders 'Cast off stern rope' he gets the confirmation 'Stern rope cast off'.

Even on a small sail boat the skipper's task will be made much easier if he always has full information about how things stand without having to check every item for himself.

When tending mooring lines, always take a turn round a cleat. If there is strain on a rope that is merely being held in the hand, it will be impossible to give it exactly the amount of slack needed and then cleat it again. Moreover, even a girl member of the crew will, with the line passed round a cleat, be able to hold quite a large boat in check with one hand, and prevent the line from running out.

Always pass mooring lines round a cleat, never straight to the hand.

Coming alongside under engine

The one golden rule for all boat-handling under engine is:

> never do things in a hurry!

Spend time finding the place where you are going to moor, and checking exactly what the layout is. It does no harm to motor past the jetty a couple of times in succession to make sure that there really is enough space alongside the wall, and that the mooring is not soon going to have to be given up to a home-coming fishing-boat. It is good manners to ask other yachts about the harbour and its peculiarities, and especially about the mooring you have chosen. Obviously a good skipper will have checked well beforehand in the appropriate *Pilot* and other reference books he carries aboard, to find out as much as he can about the harbour; the fact of immediately finding an ideal mooring alongside the quay, of just the right size, in an otherwise jam-packed harbour should be enough to arouse suspicions! While cruising round the harbour to find a mooring, the crew should not be busy doing some other job (nor even, indeed, smartening themselves up to go ashore!) nor should they just stand around on deck – they should sit down somewhere where they will obstruct the skipper's view as little as possible (which is also why all sails should be cleared away).

Once a suitable mooring has been located, thought must be given to exactly how to come alongside. Remember that every boat has a 'best side', invariably the side opposite that towards which the propeller turns (eg. the starboard side with a left-handed propeller).

If you have decided that, having a left-handed prop, you are going to moor starboard side to the quay, tell the crew this: a well-trained crew will then, without having to be told, put out fenders to starboard and get the four mooring lines (stern and head ropes, head and after springs) ready on that side. The ropes must be prepared so that the ends (tied in a bowline) can be passed across at a moment's notice. The bowline should have too large a loop rather than too small – so take a good look at the bollards beforehand!

A properly-trained crew will do all this automatically as soon as the skipper calls out 'Ready with lines and fenders to starboard!', and it is helpful if the crew report their readiness one after the other – 'Stern rope ready', 'Head rope ready', and so on. If the crew is only a small one, eg. the skipper and his wife, it is enough for the crew to shout 'Lines and fenders ready to starboard'.

When coming alongside with the 'best side' to the quay (ie. to starboard, with a left-handed screw), fenders must be put out at the bow quarter. At the start of the operation the skipper will have taken way off the boat until there is just enough to give proper steerage.

If the bollard is too big for the loop you have made ready, this is the quick way to put matters right.

With a wind blowing, the skipper will generally realise if he is going too slow from the fact that the bows are being pushed off by the wind – in other words, the wind is having more effect than the rudder. If the boat is fitted with an electronic speedometer that can show quite small changes in speed through the water, it will be easier to use this as a guide once a certain amount of experience has been gained.

When coming alongside, the yacht will approach the quay slowly at an angle of about 30°, and it will help the skipper if a crew member in the bows calls out the distance (in boat's-lengths). Depending on the weight of the boat, the engine will then be put into neutral (after a while it becomes possible to judge the right moment quite accurately); ideally, the boat should have scarcely any forward way left as the bows come up to the wall. In practice, however, this is hard to achieve, so at the right instant the engine will be put 'astern': this serves two purposes – firstly it takes way off the boat and brings it to a standstill, and secondly the kick of the propeller pushes the stern, which is still some way out, in towards the quay wall.

It is always better to carry out the manoeuvre so that you end up too far away from the quay and have to 'go round again', than to come in too fast and thump the jetty. Even with good fendering, the skin of the hull is likely to get badly scraped if this happens. If the manoeuvre has been carried out properly, it is no problem for a member of the crew to jump or climb ashore; the easiest place for doing this is always midships, because there he can hold on to the shrouds, and is closest to the quayside.

Important: the mooring lines should be got ashore as quickly as possible, especially if there is a strong wind, swell or current.

Mooring lines are thrown to the jetty, and every member of the crew must have practised throwing a line. It is easy to overestimate one's capabilities here, and even an experienced seaman will be unable to manage more than 20m: against the wind, his throw will be a good deal less than this.

It may be vitally important to be able to get a line ashore at the right moment.

The **technique of throwing a line** therefore needs to be practised from time to time. The rope is first gathered into a coil of about 10 turns; the first and second turns must never be bigger than the rest, because then the line will not straighten out in flight. About a third of the bunch is then taken into the throwing hand, leaving the remainder in the other hand which is held open. The inboard end of the rope must be belayed to a cleat, or held down with the foot, and care taken to see that the line will not catch in the shrouds or stays.

The heavy warps of large yachts cannot be thrown ashore, and a *heaving line* will have to be used. This consists of a fairly thin and

Come alongside at an angle of about 30°, applying rudder about ½ to ¼ boat's-length away from the quay, depending on her turning radius. Then put out stern rope, head rope and springs.

111

Left: this is expecting a lot of the helper ashore.

Centre: what is anyone expected to do with a dog's-dinner like this?

Right: this won't work – all loops need to be the same size.

supple rope with a heavy object at one end, such as a 'monkey's-fist' knot or a small bag of sand. Lines like these can be thrown over considerably greater distances, so it is a good idea even on small sail boats to have a heaving line ready to hand, correctly coiled (the Panama Canal shore workers are able to throw these lines more than 40m, 10 times out of 10!). Once the heaving line is ashore, the end of it can be bent to the mooring rope proper. The best method for this is to use two linked bowlines, or a double sheet-bend; the latter is quicker to make, but the bowline has the advantage of being 100 per cent reliable (if made properly), and the end of the mooring line will usually already have a bowline in it anyway.

Much better – this will straighten out in flight.

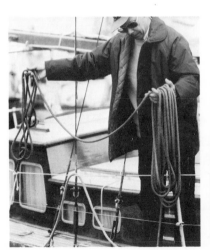

Manoeuvring in harbour under sail

Although it should be obvious to anyone, you see people time and again who are unaware of the fact that a sail boat cannot go backwards like a motor boat. In the motor boat, the reverse gear is used mainly not for going astern, but for bringing the boat to a halt. Under sail, this is impossible; a backed jib or mainsail (using a foreguy) will admittedly have some braking action, but the practical effect is so slight that it must never be relied on.

> Because of this, a yacht should never be brought alongside a quay by luffing up head to wind, if this means luffing towards the quay.

This manoeuvre, perfectly right and proper for dinghies and small craft, cannot be carried out with heavier yachts.

The fundamental difference is that a dinghy, being light, carries very little way, so that when you shoot up head to wind it comes to a standstill within a couple of lengths. What is more, a dinghy gets under way again quickly if you luff up short and have to haul in sheets and gain another few metres.

None of this applies to the keel boat. While all sailing textbooks teach you how to judge the distance when luffing up, it is essential to remember that if a luff is to achieve its purpose it needs to be accurate to within one metre at the most. This is easier with a dinghy, which may take some 7 to 10m to lose all way after luffing up, than with a heavy keel boat that can sometimes need 50m or more. If you have luffed up short with a heavy boat, it will be impossible to pick up way again by hardening the sheets, and the yacht will start to make lee-way – generally the jib will have most effect, so that the bows will pay off. If on the other hand you have over-carried by only one or two metres at the end of your luff, the boat's weight (often several tons) will make it impossible to fend off with hands or feet. The kinetic energy present is roughly the same as that of a slowly-moving and laden truck, so if there is even a minor misjudgement of the distance the boat needs to carry, serious damage is likely to be done to the bows.

The art of coming alongside a jetty with a sail boat lies in getting the sails down at exactly the right time (just like choosing the right moment to switch off the engine), and then – since there is no sternway – using mooring lines taken ashore during the operation to take off the rest of the way.

All these manoeuvres, right up to the final stage just described, are possible with a small crew.

> *Rule:* Never try to bring a slow, heavy yacht alongside the quay while there is still any sail set. A slackened-off main and even a flapping jib will still give an unwelcome amount of drive if there is much wind about. With the wind aft it will in any case be impossible to slacken off the mainsheet sufficiently.
>
> *Rule:* During all mooring and casting-off the mainsail can be set only when the boat is head to wind, or nearly so. The foresail, on the other hand, can and should be set and handed on any point of sailing.

Before the skipper even considers coming alongside under sail, he must know exactly what the quay is like, and what the wind conditions are *actually at the quayside*. Once again, therefore, it is advisable to cruise quietly round the harbour a couple of times, sizing up the situation. Special attention should be given to the position (and diameter!) of mooring bollards. Will it be possible to put out fenders to be certain of their cushioning the boat against the quay wall and preventing damage? If not, that mooring place must be ruled out, because the use of fenders has to be relied on whenever mooring under sail. Finally, the skipper must be sure that it will be possible to get a line ashore: is the jetty too high for a man to be able to step ashore? If there is someone on the quayside who looks confidence-inspiring, he can be asked to help by taking your line. If you have enough hands aboard, it may be a good idea to send someone ashore in the dinghy, or to sail slowly by close in to the jetty so that he can jump ashore and be ready to take your lines the next time round.

> Especially when mooring under sail, it is essential for preparations (fenders and lines) to be made beforehand, and for the sequence of operations to be clearly thought out.

The skipper should give the crew the order 'Ready with lines and fenders to come alongside to starboard' in a quiet, measured tone anything up to half-an-hour ahead.

114

The mooring manoeuvre will be handled differently depending on the wind direction relative to the jetty.

Coming alongside under sail with an offshore wind

Provided the quayside is uncluttered with other boats, there is little that can go wrong with this manoeuvre. If you do not manage to get lines ashore, the wind will push the yacht away from the wall, and as soon as there is enough clear space the sails can be reset and a fresh approach made.

Important: The mainsail can be handed only with the boat head to wind, or nearly so. Logically, therefore, coming alongside with an offshore wind should be done so that the boat approaches the jetty parallel to it (ie. with the wind on the beam) and about four boat's-lengths away – depending on size – and then shoots up head to wind; the skipper, having previously called 'Ready to drop main' and had the

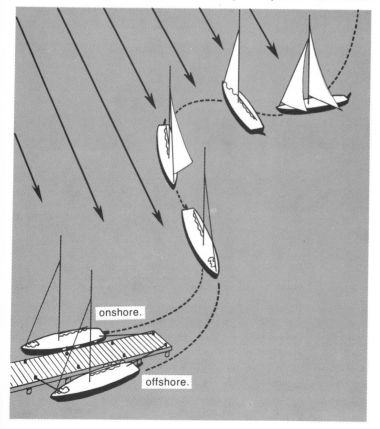

onshore.

offshore.

Coming alongside under sail with an offshore or onshore breeze: when the yacht has reached the jetty, all sail should be down.

The mainsail can be handed only when head to wind, and the remaining way then takes the yacht up to the jetty.

answer 'Main ready to drop', will then be certain that the mainsail will in fact come down immediately he gives the command. The main should, ideally, be dropped the instant the yacht's bows come up into wind. The jib, too, must come down at the same time or a few seconds later, because with the wind on the beam even the jib alone will give far too much way for coming alongside safely.

Here, again, the yacht's speed should be just enough for her to answer to the rudder, and no more; this means that with very little

As soon as a man is ashore, get the stern rope out to take way off the boat.

Colour plates:
Top: yachts from all over the world in Papeete, moored with bow anchor and stern to the quay wall.
Bottom: ready to hoist the mainsail.

wind the approach to the jetty will be at about 1 knot, under bare poles.

The operation can be made easier (especially if you have only a small crew) by getting the jib down well beforehand, though this will depend on how the boat handles under main alone.

The boat then approaches the jetty, just as when manoeuvring under engine, at an angle of about 30°. The operation should be attempted only if there are at least two boat's-lengths of free space along the jetty.

The remaining way is in this case killed not by putting the engine astern, but by using the *stern rope*. The fenders therefore need to be put

116

out midships and at the stern quarter. Special attention must always be paid to tending the stern rope, since this is all there will be to bring the yacht to a standstill.

If there is only a two-man crew, one of these must, as smartly as possible, jump ashore, run back with the stern rope and drop the end over a bollard. As soon as the boat is roughly parallel to the jetty the tiller can be safely left so that the stern rope, which is now the only thing that matters, can be tended. Using this, the boat is brought gently to a standstill; the line must always be held with a turn round a stout cleat, and *never* held simply in the hand. The stern will bump up against the quay wall, so a fender will be needed. Once the way is off the boat, the stern rope is quickly made fast and the other three lines got ashore.

> *Rule:* Always bring the boat to a standstill using the line opposite to the direction of the boat's movement.

If the head rope were used to try to stop forward way, the bows would inevitably ram into the jetty.

If someone is available to deal with the stern rope, opposite rudder can be applied as the stern rope comes under strain so as to counteract the movement of the stern inwards towards the wall (eg. when coming alongside to starboard, the rudder is put hard to starboard as if you were trying to steer into the wall).

As soon as there is strain on the stern rope, be ready with fenders at the stern and apply opposite rudder.

Coming alongside under sail with an onshore wind

Here again the rule is that the main can be brought down only when head to wind, or nearly so. Any yacht is – other than when hard on the wind – quite easy to manoeuvre under jib alone, so the skipper can have the main handed in plenty of time to approach the jetty with only the jib set.

Remember: the jib can be lowered on any point of sailing.

Once again, the skipper should ensure, by ordering 'Ready to lower jib' and having this instruction acknowledged, that he has full control of the ship at all times.

The quay will be approached at the usual angle of 20–30°. There must be at the very least two boat's-lengths clear to run alongside the jetty while way is taken off with the stern rope.

If you find you are approaching the quay too fast, let the jib spill wind before bringing it down at the right moment.

Caution: it is not easy to break off this manoeuvre and start again. As way is lost, the wind will have more and more effect, and will push the boat closer to the quay wall: so the approach should not be too slow. Getting the lines ashore, and then using them to stop the boat's way, *must* go quickly and smoothly.

Don't forget the stern fenders! As the strain comes on the stern rope, the stern will always swing in towards the wall.

Coming alongside with wind parallel to the quay

This is done in exactly the same way as with an offshore wind, heading into wind whenever possible. A strong following wind can push a yacht along at 3–4 knots even without any sail set, which is much too fast for coming alongside.

The mooring manoeuvres I have been describing can be carrried out with the smallest possible crew (even single-handed) so long as the skipper has thought the sequence through carefully and the various operations can be carried out one after the other and not all at the same time.

> *Rule:* The longer the yacht, the more difficult it is to come along-side under sail. More than a certain size, you should moor under sail only if there is no other choice.

A yacht should be manoeuvred under sail in a harbour only if:

- there is no other way (eg. if the auxiliary is out of order),
- it is not going to inconvenience anybody, and
- the skipper is quite confident of carrying out the manoeuvre successfully.

A yacht sailing round in a crowded anchorage out of control is every sailor's nightmare. The skipper must allow for every eventuality – for example, the friendly soul on the quayside who has taken your mooring line may not know what to do with it, and will just hold it in his hand instead of dropping the loop over a bollard. In which case, of course, it will be impossible to bring the boat to a halt.

If the engine is out of action and there is the slightest doubt about being able to carry out a manoeuvre under sail safely and reliably, there is one very simple and safe way of mooring without doing anyone any damage: this is to drop anchor out in the harbour and then, at leisure, to tow the boat to the intended mooring with the tender, or with the help of other yachtsmen. For the single-handed skipper this is often the only really safe thing to do.

120

Getting away under sail

Getting away under sail –
fenders at the stern, and
stern rope held ready to let
slip.

Just as it is almost always possible, if needs be, to get on to your mooring under sail by first anchoring further out and then warping your boat in to the quayside, you can in just the same way get away from a mooring if you are shorthanded by first taking a long anchor warp out in the dinghy, and then pulling yourself off with this. It then becomes the everyday operation of weighing anchor (see page 133).

For sailing away from a jetty with an offshore breeze, all you need do is to set the jib, take the springs and head rope on board, and finally cast off the stern rope. The wind will automatically push the boat away from the quayside. Once clear of the jetty, luff up briefly to set the mainsail; the boat will then be fully manoeuvrable.

The same manoeuvre can be done with the wind aft and parallel to the jetty, though care must be taken not to scrape the stern quarter along the wall; take the boat away from the quayside at a very shallow angle, without putting the rudder hard over. If the wind is coming along the jetty but from ahead, the boat will first have to be turned end-for-end at the quayside; this is a simple operation if the effect of the wind is used to help. First, take a line from the bows, on the side away from the quay, outside all stays and shrouds and to the jetty at a point aft of the boat. Then push the bows out slightly from the wall; before long, the wind will be helping to turn the boat, and the movement must be kept under control with a long head rope. The latter is not cast off until it is at an angle where it is having no effect. The stern should be cushioned, and someone must move the fenders as the boat swings round.

When turning a yacht at the quayside, it must be kept under control by the mooring lines throughout.

The only manoeuvre that cannot be undertaken by a very small crew is getting away under sail with an onshore wind. First, a long warp is laid out round a bollard well ahead (at least two boat's-lengths) with one end made fast at the stern and the other leading to the foredeck; then as many crew members as can be mustered haul on the warp to impart enough way to the boat for her to be steered – clear of the wall – head to wind so that the main can be set. If the boat is not far enough clear of the jetty at this moment, she will be forced back on to it by the wind before gathering enough way. It will be obvious that this manoeuvre is impracticable with more than a certain size of yacht.

Once again, however, it is perfectly possible to lay out an anchor away from the jetty, haul yourself out to it, and then up anchor and sail away.

Always remember: A yacht under sail has no 'reverse gear', and no 'brakes'. The mainsail can only be set and handed while hard on the wind or head to wind, while the jib can be set and handed on all points of sailing.

Anchoring – the right way

Equipment

Quite wrongly, scant attention often is given to equipping a yacht with sound ground tackle. Circumstances can arise where the whole safety of the ship, and her crew, will depend on having a good anchor. Carrying one anchor and one warp on a cruiser is certainly far from sufficient, if only because you never know in

advance what kind of holding ground you will be dealing with –
sand, gravel, ooze, mud or even, sometimes, hard rock.

There is no universal anchor that will hold equally well on all
kinds of bottom, and over the last 20 or 30 years a wide range of
different types have been designed. A mere handful of these have
proved suitable:

- the fisherman or Admiralty-pattern anchor
- the plough or CQR
- the Danforth anchor.

The fisherman anchor

This is nowadays becoming more and more unpopular, mainly
because it is so heavy (though this weight is needed if it is to hold
properly). On the other hand, its pointed flukes give it the incalculable advantage over the others of digging-in more quickly. And
this, after all, is the basic criterion for judging an anchor. The best
of anchors, with the greatest holding power, is useless if it fails to
dig into a hard seabed. Against this excellent digging-in capacity,
we have to trade-off a comparatively poor holding power (relative
to the weight), and this is why a fisherman anchor always needs to

The fisherman anchor is
the best all-rounder.

be a good deal heavier than the other two types if it is to do its job of holding the yacht securely in a storm, or even a strong wind.

It is, of course, impossible for an anchor to be too heavy, bearing in mind its holding power; yet there will be natural limits set by whether you have an anchor winch, or by the crew available. I recommend the following weights for a fisherman anchor:

boat's weight	anchor weight (approx.)
up to 2t	20kg
up to 4t	25kg
up to 7t	30kg
up to 10t	45kg
up to 20t	60kg

The CQR or plough anchor

The CQR holds well, provided it is heavy enough to dig in.

This was long hailed as the last word in anchors by British yachtsmen, headed by Eric Hiscock. The enthusiasm has waned somewhat now that a number of appreciable snags have become apparent. Only from a certain weight upwards can you be quite certain of a CQR anchor digging in. A great many tables that set out a certain boat's weight against a certain recommended anchor weight in almost linear progression tend to forget one important factor that does not alter with the size of the vessel – the nature of the bottom. A small anchor of, say, 3kg would certainly be able to hold a dinghy securely in a storm – but it would first have to get a hold; and because of its light weight it would be unable to do so even in mud that was in any way hard. The CQR has such a broad surface (giving it its enormous holding power) that this in fact causes the difficulty, by preventing it from digging in. On my world trip I had a 35lb CQR which held superbly once it had sunk down into the bottom; but all too often it just skidded across the surface. American yachtsmen realised the shortcomings of the CQR anchor a long time ago, and they frequently fill in the hollow underside of the plough with lead to make it heavier. A CQR anchor is, therefore, advisable only above 45lb (ie. about 23kg).

Yet once a CQR has dug itself in it can perform real miracles of holding power. In Hurricane Bebe the 13m yacht *Shebessa* was lying to two 60lb CQR anchors, and taking a 150-knot wind straight on the nose; her anchors held – and afterwards they had to be hosed out from 4m down in the mud by divers using high-pressure gear!

124

This is an extremely popular type, mainly because of its light weight, and has a holding power far superior to all other designs. Indeed, above a certain size (30kg or so) there are sometimes problems in getting a Danforth to break out, and for this reason I would always recommend a buoyed tripping line.

Recommended weights for a Danforth anchor are:

boat's weight	anchor weight (approx.)
up to 2t	10kg
up to 4t	13kg
up to 6t	15kg
up to 10t	20kg
up to 20t	30kg

Unfortunately, the Danforth has one big drawback – on a rocky

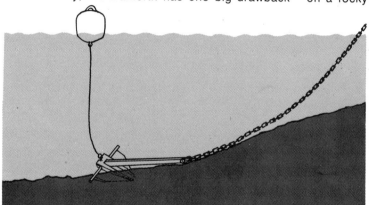

The Danforth can hold so well that a buoyed tripping line is a wise precaution.

bottom, where we can rely on a fisherman anchor, it becomes quite useless.

Having used all three types of anchor during our world cruise, I would recommend only the fisherman and the Danforth for use on a cruising yacht.

Warp or chain?

The only real answer is 'both!' The advantage of a warp is that a skipper is very often in conditions where he has to put out a second anchor. While it is impossible to carry a heavy anchor and chain in the dinghy further than 5–8m away from the mother craft, even in strong winds it will be quite possible to take a light Danforth anchor and a length of warp up to weather in the dinghy. In dire necessity, an anchor can even be attached to some form of buoyancy and 'floated out'.

125

On the other hand chain does have overwhelming advantages, so a yacht's standard tackle should always include a length of anchor chain. Recommended chain sizes are:

boat's weight	chain size (diameter)
up to 4t	6mm
up to 8t	8mm
up to 10t	10mm
up to 15t	12mm

The main disadvantage of the chain is of course its weight, which becomes far more of a nuisance on small, light yachts. Fifty metres of 8mm chain (which is the least you ought to carry) will come to about 100kg. It should be obvious that this concentrated weight ought not to be stowed where it will have the worst effect, that is to say right up in the very tip of the bows, just behind the stem. And yet in so many designs this very place has been chosen for the chain locker. A GRP boat will need a separate chain locker (of wood) so that when the boat is pounding in a seaway the couple of hundred-weight of chain does not slam directly against the hull wall; this is equivalent to dropping the same weight from a height of 2 or 3m. If the chain locker is located a little further aft, however, and the chain is lead into the locker at an angle shallower than 70°, it will undoubtedly not stow itself properly. Chain can in fact be

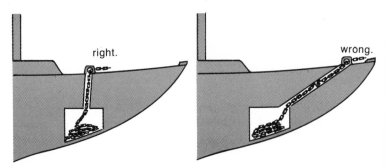

right.

wrong.

relied on to self-stow only if it leads down vertically, and there is plenty of space for it.

The great virtue of chain is its absolute invulnerability to *chafing*; the sharp edge of a rock underwater can finish a rope warp off in a matter of minutes.

To combat this danger, it is common to use a warp with a 5–10m length of chain shackled to it, known as a 'ground chain'. To avoid all chance of the warp chafing, it can be supported by one or two buoys to lift it clear of rocks past the end of the ground chain.

Using a ground chain is, however, no more than a compromise, and loses the main advantage of chain, the fact that its weight cushions the snatching load placed on the ground tackle when a wave lifts the yacht just when the anchor is under strain. Modern synthetic ropes now have a fair amount of elasticity, however, so the snatching is far less dangerous than it used to be in the days of manila warps, which had hardly any stretch.

The following diameters can be recommended for anchor warps, which should be at least as heavy as the boat's mooring lines:

boat up to 4t	approx. 12mm diameter
boat up to 8t	approx. 16mm diameter
boat up to 15t	approx. 22mm diameter

The anchor winch

On a boat up to about 6t an anchor winch is a rather pointless piece of gear to have, as anchors weighing up to 25kg can be handled by hand even by someone not very athletic. Any anchor winch that works on the well known force-x-distance principle will – if it is powerful enough for the job – be extremely slow in operation. When weighing anchor, you do not normally begin by hauling the boat up to the anchor by hand – you move up to it under engine, or even sometimes under sail. As the scope is shortened, the warp or chain is hauled in rapidly hand-over-hand, and a winch will be much too slow to do this. The power of the winch will be needed only for a very brief moment, as the anchor is actually broken out: and it is from then on that the real disadvantage of using a winch for hauling up the anchor is felt. This is a critical time during which the yacht is almost unmanageable, and is exactly when you want to get the anchor up and out of the water as fast as possible. Hands and arms are a much better means of doing this than a slow, plodding winch.

One can cope quite easily with breaking out the anchor, even without the help of a winch, in the following way: the anchor chain is hauled as near straight-up-and-down as possible, and you then wait for a wave to lift the bows. Only a few centimetres will be needed, and the force exerted is enormous. If the anchor has still not broken free after a minute or two, the crew is sent forward to haul the warp or chain up as tight as possible, and then everyone's weight is moved aft into the cockpit. In 99 cases out of 100 this will

A pawl ratchet will prevent the chain links from slipping back.

break the anchor out, and if this does not happen it shows that the anchor or chain is fouled on an obstacle (eg. a rock or a mooring-chain).

Far more important on a small cruising yacht are bow fittings that are big enough for the job, with a sturdy cleating arrangement. The ideal solution for this is a chain-pawl, which allows the chain to be hauled in but locks against the links in the opposite direction.

Everything that has just been said no longer applies, of course, once you have an anchor weighing over 30kg. Then you have to have an anchor winch, which if possible should be an electric or hydraulically-driven type. Since such winches exert enormous power they are, when hand-operated, much slower than the small winches used for 8mm chain. If a yacht has been properly designed, powering the winches should be no problem, as during

On the left, an electric anchor winch; with the one on the right, a short lever is inserted and rocked back and forth to raise the anchor – very slowly.

nearly all anchoring operations the engine will be running in any case, and can supply power for the winch without the need for a heavy drain on the battery.

Anchoring

Anchoring, like manoeuvring in harbour, needs to be carefully thought out in advance. Any warnings given in *Pilots* and other reference books must be strictly observed, while remembering on the other hand that an anchor symbol on a chart does not necessarily mean that the anchorage is suitable for yachts. Charts and nautical reference books are produced mainly with large, merchant ships in mind – and these can stand much more wind and,

128

especially, a much heavier swell.

The skipper should start by checking from the chart what sort of holding ground he will be dealing with. A rocky bottom should be avoided whenever possible. There are two kinds of anchorage in cruising – the 100 per cent ones, where a yacht will have no problems at all even in foul weather, and those that are sheltered only when the wind is in certain directions. With the latter, the skipper must plan very early on what he is going to do if the wind unexpectedly goes round to the 'wrong' direction; he can never rely on this not happening, so he must be able to get away from the anchorage if it does. If it is not going to be possible to clear out, the anchorage is unsuitable, and should certainly not be chosen for an overnight stop.

Just as when coming alongside in a harbour, the skipper should cruise gently round the bay a couple of times, if possible enquiring from other boats at anchor what things are like, before deciding to anchor himself. Invariably he should pass over the intended spot and check the depth with the echo-sounder, so that there is enough chain or warp ready to give the scope he wants.

The rule of thumb 'three times as much chain as there is water' invites trouble! At most, it works satisfactorily in good weather and ideal holding conditions. But if a skipper is sensible and responsible, good seamanship will prompt him to take every likelihood into account before dropping anchor, including that of the weather turning bad. In general, all you can say is that the longer the warp or chain, the safer the yacht is likely to be on her mooring. Provided there is enough space to swing, there is no reason at all why you should not put out a 5:1 or even 10:1 scope. Whatever the depth, it is sensible to have at least 25m of chain or warp out, since this will greatly reduce the risk of snatching at the anchor.

Even **under engine**, you should fetch up head to wind over the spot where you are going to anchor. The anchor must not be let go immediately the yacht comes to a standstill: wait with the engine in neutral until the wind starts to push the bows off, and then let go. At this stage, pay out only enough chain for there to be no direct pull on the anchor (one of the basic rules of sailing is 'take your time'!). If this amount is out, and the bows are being pulled back towards the anchor, this is an indication that the anchor has found a hold. Since the engine will in any case still be running, it is then sound seamanship to 'dig the anchor in'. Engage 'slow astern' until there is strain on the chain, and then go through 'half speed astern' and into 'full astern'. One constantly sees yachtsmen who avoid doing this because they are afraid of ripping the anchor out, which when you think about it is rather silly – if the anchor is unable to hold the yacht with the chain at full stretch and engine 'full astern', it is pretty surely going to break out in a strong wind, with a swell to match and the boat snatching savagely at her anchor. Even if I have anchored under sail alone, I invariably go through this drill with the engine, just to make sure.

Under sail, the procedure for preparing to anchor will be the same, ie. you sail round a few times and check the depth of water where you are planning to anchor. Then get the jib down, so that there is plenty of room to work on the foredeck. The anchoring point is approached in exactly the same way one is taught for the 'man overboard' manoeuvre; fishermen who at one time had to work under sail inside crowded harbours without an engine have taught me the following method, which I find by far the best for anchoring or picking up a buoy. It is unknown, or is not taught, in sailing schools since you dare not use it in a dinghy because of the danger of capsizing. The trick consists of sailing downwind, without a jib (ie. very slowly), and at the right moment killing this small amount of way by rounding up hard into wind. The manoeuvre has the advantage of coming off successfully straight away, even with an unfamiliar boat, if you come downwind 1 to 1½ boat's lengths to one side of the intended anchoring spot or buoy and then turn up into wind just as the helmsman comes level with the buoy. In all probability the buoy will then end up just under the stem. I have done this many times, under widely differing conditions and with many different boats, and have always been astounded by the accuracy with which quite heavy craft can be brought up short at exactly the right spot.

You then, once again, wait for the wind to force the bows off before letting go the anchor. Wait until you are certain that the anchor is holding before handing the mainsail; if you get the main down too soon, the yacht will be without power to manoeuvre if something goes wrong.

Let me repeat: it is good seamanship, even when you have anchored under sail, to use the engine to dig the anchor well in.

Since cruising yachts generally anchor close in to shore, taking a

boat at standstill.

one boat's-length

Coming up to a buoy, fisherman-style: approach always downwind (3); at one boat's-length off to one side put helm hard down as the helmsman comes abreast (4). The boat will turn up and stop dead.

bearing on landmarks will not be much of a guard against dragging anchor unnoticed, since a shifting transit could just as well be due to the boat swinging. I always think it is highly advisable to lay out a second anchor, using the dinghy. It takes only a few minutes to row out with a second, lighter anchor shackled to a warp, whereas if the weather deteriorates it can become a gruelling job to do in the middle of the night, with a wind blowing and a sea piling up. I lie to two anchors as a matter of routine; it means five minutes extra, fairly easy work – and a sound night's sleep even if the wind starts to howl through the rigging at two in the morning. If the available swinging circle is limited, two anchors are going to be needed in any case.

When putting out two anchors *for safety*, when bad weather is likely, both need to be out in the direction from which the storm is expected, with the warps making an angle of 30–45° with each other at the bows. It is unrealistic to think you can judge the length of the chains or warps so that both anchors take an equal strain: in really stormy weather the bow will tug alternately first at one anchor and then at the other. The point of having a second anchor is then not to halve the load, but to provide a second line of defence: if one anchor fails to hold, there is still the other to fall back on.

Mooring and kedging on a middled cable

Though this is described in virtually every sailing textbook, I have never in my whole sailing career actually come across it in use. The

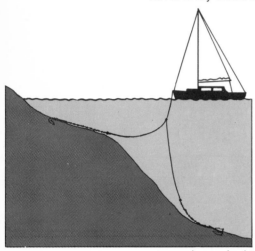

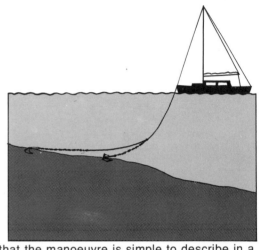

Left: mooring.

Right: kedge-mooring.

reason is no doubt that the manoeuvre is simple to describe in a book but extremely difficult to carry out in reality. It is in fact a good deal easier to lay out a second anchor than to have two anchors on one and the same chain. When we were in Suva (Fiji) and got a hurricane warning, it was interesting to see how the yachtsmen there at the time – experienced cruising men, one and all – prepared their ground tackle to cope with impending trouble. Not one of them chose to use a kedge, nor even to run a weight down the anchor chain on a sliding shackle (another method you often find recommended in textbooks). All the yachts veered as long a chain or warp as they could on all their anchors. *Bebinka*, for example, had 100m (!) of chain out in 4m of water, with what they considered

A properly-fixed cleat.

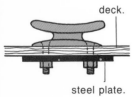

deck.

steel plate.

to be her most reliable anchor – a Danforth – shackled to the end of it. All over that very wide bay there was not a single yacht with less than three anchors out, and *Skylark* was in fact riding to four. After the 150-knot hurricane winds had swept across the bay, almost all yachts found that the weakest point had been not so much anchors and warps as, in most cases, the deck cleats. One boat had all her cleats carried away, and was lost. This is proof that a chain is as strong as its weakest link – which in this case was where it was cleated to the boat. It is plain commonsense that a part of the ship as important as this should not be just screwed to the deck; yet this is done even by some quite reputable shipyards. Every owner should therefore check this point on his own boat.

Weighing anchor

Simple though this operation is under engine, doing it successfully under sail often depends on a number of imponderables. For there to be no problem at all, you really need enough room to be able to sail away in any direction – and nowadays this is seldom the case. Usually, a yacht has to sail away on one particular tack.

Carried out properly, the manoeuvre will come off smoothly if the anchor has got a good hold (another reason for always digging it in with the engine). Start by setting the mainsail; the jib will only get in the way of work on the foredeck, though to be prudent it should be bent to the halyard and held to the rail with tiers. The mainsheet must be slackened off so that the boat will not start to sail until you want her to. 'Sailing the anchor out' is suitable only if there have been difficulties in getting the anchor to break out; and even then in a crowded anchorage, where the boat will have to be sailed away on one particular tack, it would be a highly dangerous thing to try, because the anchor would probably come free at just the wrong moment – ie. with its final tug setting the bows in the wrong direction. If there is only one tack you can sail away on, haul the boat up to the anchor very gently; when the bows are nearly over the anchor, keep a very close watch on it, because it may break out straight away – at the wrong instant – so that chain has to be paid out again at once. The anchor must come up only when the boat is pointing in exactly the right direction for sailing away from the mooring. You can ensure this by rigging a foreguy to back the main to the side on which you want to leave. A backed jib will be of little help here, because with the anchor chain up-and-down the pivot point is right at the bows, where the jib would apply its force.

In light winds it may take several minutes for the boat to swing round and point in the right direction. Only when you are quite certain that you need only haul in the main sheet for the mainsail to fill, can the order be given to 'up anchor'.

This is when close cooperation between skipper and foredeck is needed, since from his position at the tiller the helmsman will be unable to see just when the anchor comes free; yet this is the crucial moment, so the man at the anchor winch will have to call out 'anchor free'! With the main backed, the boat will slowly make sternboard, and the helmsman will have to reverse the rudder to help her turn. If, for example, you want to sail away to port, the rudder will have to be put hard to starboard while the boat is moving astern. When the main is sheeted in, the helmsman will have to watch carefully to change over the rudder as the boat starts to move ahead. The anchor must, of course, be brought aboard as quickly as possible, and safety comes before the cleanliness of the

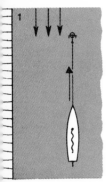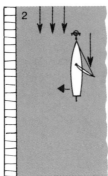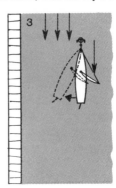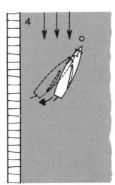

1. haul on chain until up-and-down;
2. take boom out with foreguy;
3. break out anchor;
4. when making sternboard, watch rudder setting and sheet in mainsail.

foredeck.

The risk in this manoeuvre lies in the anchor breaking out prematurely. As you can never be certain of this, it is advisable when there is a danger from nearby boats in a cramped anchorage to first kedge the boat out to a more favourable spot from where it will be possible to sail away without worrying about which side of the bow the anchor breaks free.

The Italian-style mooring that is so common in Mediterranean ports has several disadvantages: to be sure that a swell will not slam the stern against the jetty there always has to be a certain

Moored Italian-style, stern-to.

When stern-to a gangway is necessary.

minimum space left aft, and this makes getting ashore an awkward business unless you rig a gangway. Moored this way, you have to be absolutely sure of the anchor holding. At all costs it must not drag in a strong onshore wind, for this would at once mean ramming the wall – and serious damage to the stern and rudder. So the anchor definitely needs digging well in with the engine at full power; a well-dug-in anchor should be able to stand up to the engine running full astern for a couple of minutes.

Mooring Italian-style can, besides, be so difficult because of the mediocre handling of most sailing craft going astern (besides earning derisive grins from quayside onlookers) that it may in many cases be better to drop the anchor in the right place and then take a long warp ashore with the dinghy. Once made fast, the engine can then be switched off and the boat hauled in calmly using the power of the sheet-winches.

When weighing anchor from this position, good seamanship demands that the boat be kept under full command as long as possible: so the stern ropes are replaced with long warps held round a cleat, and these are slowly paid out as the boat is hauled up to her anchor. If the wind is on the beam, care must be taken to keep enough tension on the anchor chain and stern warp to avoid being blown on to another boat.

If you have the misfortune to bring up someone else's chain with your own anchor, lift it until you can get a hold on it with a boathook or lash it temporarily to your bows. If you have in fact pulled out another boat's anchor, you should obviously not just drop it back in the water – the skipper of the craft concerned must be warned of what has happened, and of course given a hand to relay his anchor.

Under way

Motoring

When cruising under sail the engine will not be used on its own all that often on the open sea. Motoring is uncomfortable without a steadying sail except when the swell completely dies away after a long period of no wind.

With a well-found sailing yacht, the speed the boat will be able to keep up with the engine at cruising revs will in any case be less than under full sail in a good wind. But what sort of engine speed is cruising revs? There are two factors that govern this on a sailing craft. We are not of course interested, like commercial shipping, in the profitability of the ship, nor in maximum operating range, and we shall hardly ever come near to using up all our fuel. Merchant ships, and our motorboat brethren, determine their cruising engine speed by how far a certain amount of fuel will take them, but we have no need to gauge this exactly by consumption trials over a measured mile, and so on. Basically, we run an engine so that it gives a good performance and still has a little power in hand. If it is the right size for the boat, this means running at about 70–80 per cent of its maximum speed; if full throttle gives a reading of 2500 rev/min, for instance, we shall cruise at around 1750–2000 revs. We shall soon discover that the difference in speed between 2000 and 2500 rev/min is not all that great if the power-to-weight ratio of the engine is over 3hp/t.

Secondly, there is the criterion of quiet running. Diesel engines, which are commonly used in yachts, are extremely noisy compared to petrol engines. The worst are the single-cylinder types, while there are 4 and even 6-cylinder diesels that cause hardly any problem at all. Unfortunately, however, single and twin-cylinder models predominate in boats of our size (up to about 11m overall). Flexible mountings, which have been almost universal in small boats in recent years, do solve many of the problems, but even with these there are some speeds at which the engine runs very lumpily and out of balance, while at others barely more than a slight vibration can be felt. The trick, therefore, is to set the engine speed around the figure mentioned earlier (about 75 per cent of maximum revs) at a point where it gives smooth running.

Running on the engine out at sea can be very unpleasant. The sea is seldom flat calm, and usually the previous wind will have left something of a swell. This makes the boat roll, which not only gets on our nerves but has a bad effect on the engine as well; it can even lead to breakdowns if the dirt or condensation water in the fuel tank is stirred up and ends up blocking the filter. Many engine mountings are designed to cope with a vertical load, and react to lateral forces caused by the boat rolling by allowing severe vibration. To limit rolling to some extent, set the mainsail and keep it sheeted in hard. Setting the jib or genoa will only make things worse because they cannot be sheeted in hard and brought amidships, and the most they would do is slow the boat down. Nevertheless, the flapping of the mainsail can be quite infuriating, and some improvement can be obtained if the main is reefed a few turns so that the belly is tautened. If you don't mind the effort of sailchanging, the same effect can be obtained by setting the try-sail.

If there is plenty of wind about, there is really only one justification for running the engine on a sailing yacht, and that is if you are finding it impossible to point high enough under sail alone; help from the engine will let the boat come a little closer to the wind. But if you point so high that the sail is *only just* filling, then it is not in fact producing any real drive, and it would be better to bear off a few degrees. A glance at the speedometer will show the best course to steer.

With a lot of wind and a lively boat this method must not be used, because with the boat heeling hard it may well happen that the engine does not get enough oil for its vital lubrication needs. One ought really to be able to expect allowance to have been made for this in engines produced for yachts, but unhappily this is not so. An angle of more than 20° – if maintained for any length of time – must be avoided at all costs, and will undoubtedly wreck the engine. Heeling at more than 20° for a moment or two – eg. in a swell, or when the boat is rolling without a steadying sail – can however just be coped with. These conditions are allowed for only on the bigger engines, like the 6-cylinder diesel by Caterpillar which has two oil pumps built in for this very reason.

A properly-installed engine should be able to run all day long without stopping, but a careful and *constant* watch must be kept on the oil pressure and engine temperature.

With water-cooled engines, especially those cooled by seawater alone, the temperature gauge must be checked at least every 10 minutes. Engines cooled by seawater should not run hotter than 60°, otherwise chalk and salt crystals will separate out and block the narrow water passages in the engine; this would cause the temperature to soar very quickly.

It may occasionally happen that the intake valve for the cooling water gets stopped up with fish or flotsam or plastic bags. If the outlet for the seawater-cooled exhaust is above the waterline, an alert helmsman will notice that something is wrong at once, from the rather duller sound. A glance at the temperature gauge will then show him that the temperature is going up fast, within a matter of seconds. The throttle must be shut back at once, and the engine then switched off a few seconds later (an engine should never be stopped while on full load). If the cooling-water intake is blocked, the engine cannot be used, even in an emergency.

If the engine is kept running for long periods, bear in mind that some types need an oil-change at fairly short intervals (eg. 50 hours).

Boats need to be well ventilated throughout when the engine is being used. If possible, all hatches should be kept open; if some of the crew need to sleep during this time, they can best do so in the forepeak, with the hatch open. An engine must, of course, in any case be installed so that none of the exhaust gases can get below decks, but I would still urge extreme caution. Even a slight degree of carbon monoxide poisoning, which may not even be noticed at the time, can lead to a quite serious fall-off in physical capacity. Severe headaches, nausea and loss of appetite are among the telltale signs, and can greatly reduce the crew's efficiency. With a following wind exhaust gases may get blown down the companion-way, and though this may not represent a danger to life the disagreeable symptoms just listed may occur during long periods of motoring.

If the helmsman hears a 'funny noise' in the engine, it should always be shut off immediately, after a few seconds at tickover.

Under sail out at sea

On the wind

There is a saying that 'only idiots and racing helmsmen beat to windward', and the reasons are obvious. Not only does the sea slam hard against the boat, but the relative wind is a great deal stronger too. If the true wind is blowing at, say, Force 4 and a yacht is beating hard at 6 knots, then the wind speed indicator on board will show Force 5 on the Beaufort scale; running before the wind, however, it will measure only Force 3, and this explains why weather conditions tend to be underestimated by a crew with the wind aft. On the wind, the constant heeling of the boat also heightens the subjective feeling of discomfort. Strain on the boat and her rigging will be many times greater when beating than on other points of sailing under the same weather conditions. The wave form has a lot to do with this, because when going to windward a boat is having to climb up the steeper, lee side of the waves.

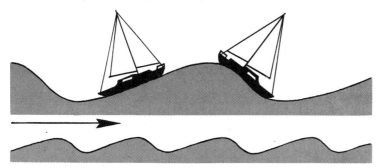

Because of the wind, the lee of a wave is steeper; heading into the wind is far more wearing than running before it.

So skippers usually feel that out at sea it pays to wait for the wind to go round, rather than plug on into it. On a long passage it is often a good idea, in such circumstances, to give the crew a rest and heave to until the required course can be steered direct.

The wind will seldom be coming so directly from the desired heading as to make it difficult to decide whether a port or starboard tack is more favourable. To check this, all you need do is to put the yacht on port tack and read off the compass course, and then do the same on starboard tack (making allowance, of course, for the current).

I know from experience that there is a temptation to carry too much canvas on the wind. If the boat on the wind has so much weather helm that the helmsman feels a hard pressure on the tiller, it usually means that the main needs reefing. There will be hardly any speed lost by doing so, while the boat will answer better to the helm, heel less and most of all give a far more comfortable ride. Because of the relatively greater wind strengths when beating, the genoa will need to be changed for the jib much sooner after reefing the mainsail than, for example, when reaching or running. On most yachts it would however be unwise not to have reefed the main down somewhat before changing foresails; reducing foresail area alone will only produce more weather helm.

On the wind, the foresail must be sheeted in as hard as possible. When close-hauled you will of course no longer be steering a compass course, merely trying to point as high as you can. Because the wind always swings to and fro about its general direction, wind changes will have to be compensated for at the tiller, and nowadays this task – once the art of a skilled helmsman – is made easier by highly sensitive electronic wind-direction indicators. If you like to spend the money, you can even fit the yacht with waterproof cockpit instruments that show the optimum course to steer to the wind. While this gear may be a must on a racing yacht, where giving up a few metres to windward can mean the difference between victory and defeat, a cruising yacht can manage quite well without. Then, however, all the helmsman can do is to sit down to lee and watch the foresail all the time. The foresail luff will tell him quicker than anything else whether he is pointing too high and the sail is not drawing properly, or whether he is giving away a few degrees. As a rule the foresail will start to collapse slightly about halfway up the forestay, the clearest sign that the jib is no longer drawing and that the helmsman should bear away at once. Having done so, he can feel his way back up to the wind until he again sees this slight trembling at the luff of the jib. If the sails are set correctly, and have not yet lost their shape, the leech should not tremble at all; if it does, it suggests that the sail is not sheeted in hard enough.

A self-steering gear works extremely well when close-hauled, though it is nonsense to say that it does the job better than a good helmsman. A helmsman can react immediately at the very instant the bow starts to point too high, while self-steering gear will by its very nature not react until the boat is already too high on to the wind.

If the yacht is in a lumpy sea she may crash down repeatedly into a trough, and lose almost all way; the bows will then be pushed off before the boat gathers speed again. If. this happens a lot, it is a sign that you are pointing too high and in fact making very little ground by doing so. It is far better helmsmanship to bear off enough for the seas not to bring the boat up dead.

The higher the sea, the more you need to bear away.

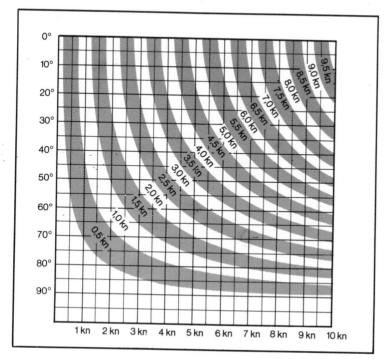

The graph shows the effective speed (indicated by the curves) made towards a destination at a given speed through the water, when a direct course cannot be laid. Example: a boat's speed of 7 knots at 50° to destination will give a speed of 4½ knots toward the latter.

In any case there is little to be gained from 'pinching'. As you can see from the chart, it is better to do 6 knots at 50° to the wind than 5 knots at 45°; you will make almost half-a-knot better speed to windward, and have a more comfortable ride into the bargain.

On a reach

It should never be forgotten that a boat must be sailed so that trouble is as unlikely as possible; safety comes first, last and always. A major source of accidents on board is the boom sweeping across. The risk is least when close-hauled, when the boom stays almost amidships and the wind pressure is at its highest; even if the wind were suddenly to drop the boom would do little harm in a rolling swell. On all other points of sailing, however, it needs to be secured with a foreguy, or 'preventer'; this is simply a line led from the end of the boom as far forward as possible. On a reach, the main is slackened off a little further than it needs, the preventer is made fast up in the bows, and the mainsheet is then hauled in a little tighter. The foreguy serves two purposes: first, it stops the boom from swinging across in a swell if the wind should drop. Even if the boom slamming across with the wind broad on the beam does not endanger the shrouds, it can still cause damage by the sudden tug on the mainsheet attachment. And secondly, it prevents the boom (and with it the sail) from lifting, which can only improve the set of the mainsail. The same job is done by a *boom downhaul*, or kicking-strap; but this is not often found on a cruising yacht, as it involves quite a complicated arrangement if there is roller reefing.

Kicking strap; impractical with roller reefing.

Following this principle of running minimum risk, as little work as possible should be done up on the foredeck. This is where there is the greatest likelihood of falling overboard – something that simply must not be allowed to happen. There is a simple way to avoid having to tend the foreguy from up in the bows: a long line is taken from the rear end of the boom, through a block in the bows and back to the cockpit on the side opposite the boom, where it can be made fast to the sheet winch (which will not be in use on this tack). Someone will have to go forward to set up the guy in the first place, but from then on the sail setting can be adjusted from the cockpit. It is not a bad idea, in fact, to rig two permanent foreguys through a double block in the bows; then, when going about, it is merely a matter of changing one foreguy for the other as the boom passes amidships.

The helmsman will have to take care, when running free with a strongish wind, not to luff up to the gusts; he should resist this

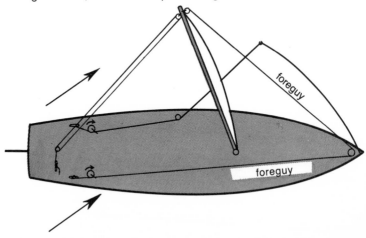

This foreguy can be controlled from the cockpit.

tendency on the part of the boat by putting a firmer pressure on the tiller before the luff starts. If the pressure needed on the tiller begins to feel excessive, this is again an indication that the mainsail ought to have a reef taken in. A well-designed boat hardly ever shows lee helm. The best way of counteracting weather helm is always to reduce the area of the mainsail.

Though a foresail set without the main is not very effective on the wind, because the boat will be unable to point at all well, it is possible with a freshening wind to hand the mainsail altogether if reefing has made no real improvement to the pressure on the tiller.

Rule: it is always better to reef the mainsail, or hand it altogether, before changing to a smaller foresail.

Running or broad-reaching

When a helmsman on a reach bears away even further, so that the boat makes an angle of 30° to the true wind direction, the foresail begins to be shrouded by the main. The jib starts to tremble, and for the helmsman this means two things:

- the jib is ineffective, having ceased to draw, and might just as well be taken down.
- the boat is getting close to the dangerous downwind point of sailing, where the helmsman has to guard against a jib all-standing (which in a strong wind could snap the mast).

If we now haul down the jib, the logical thing to do, we can at once see the weakness of the fore-and-aft rig. When running with the wind free, where because of the lighter apparent wind we want to carry as much sail as possible, we in fact have only half of it available. It may seem an obvious answer to take the jib out on the opposite side; but here it will fill only if it is boomed out, and in any case will not draw properly unless we bear away even further. There is only a very narrow range over which both sails will draw fully without the dirty wind from the main spilling into the jib, and because self-steering gear normally hunts to and fro it is hardly likely to be able to hold this course.

If we do not want to sail along using only half of our sail area (ie. the main or the jib)'and thus making considerably less speed, we need to set a far more efficient rig when before the wind. There are two ways of doing this.

The spinnaker was invented by racing yachtsmen who wanted to make as much speed as possible over their opponents on the downwind leg. Because a spinnaker is never used when on the wind, only when broad-reaching and running (where the apparent wind is less strong), it usually has an extremely large area compared to other sails. Setting a spinnaker is not simple, so hoisting and handing the sail should be practised in light winds as often as needed – a twisted 'wineglass' spinnaker can lead to a whole series of nasty moments, especially when it cannot be got down in a rising wind. Once a spinnaker is set, the helmsman needs to keep a constant watch on it. If it starts to collapse, the sheet needs to be twitched to fill it again, or the helm put up. Only very small spinnakers will be stable enough not to need continuous tending.

Neptune 26 cruising yacht under main and spinnaker.

If a spinnaker collapses completely, the wrong thing to do is to

come up head to wind – you need to turn *down*wind. The fact that the spinnaker needs constant watching makes it unsuitable for use with self-steering gear, which while it may alter the tiller is unable to pull on the sheets as well. On long passages the spinnaker is in any case not a great deal of use: unless you rig a complicated backhaul-cum-deflector arrangement, the spinnaker pole is going to exert considerable pressure on the forestay on a broad reach; and a leather cuff protects only the pole from damage. When running, the lower edge of the spinnaker becomes frayed on the forestay (the sailmaker can double the lower edge to prevent it being worn right through).

Twin jibs. Over recent years these *running sails* have become more and more popular. Originally an invention mothered by necessity – people wanted a rig that would free them from the drudgery of continual steering – running jibs are today standard equipment for long passages with the wind aft. The system comprises two jibs of identical cut, each of which is boomed out with a pole.

Twin headsails are best set on stays.

Until only a few years ago there were no windvane gears, and the only way of achieving self-steering was to run the two jib-sheets to the tiller, so that this was moved by the sails themselves. Running sails were said to give their best self-steering effect only if the tack of both sails was not right forward at the bow fitting, but just in front of the mast; and the best airflow conditions would be obtained if the feet of the two sails were one-quarter of the keel length apart. Another point of argument was whether running sails should be set flying or hanked to a stay (the latter brings the further complication of rigging separate stays before the sails can be set). It was thought that self-steering would be improved by keeping the clews of the running sails forward of their tacks.

Considerations like these no longer apply now that self-steering is coped with quite efficiently by windvane gear, and the only point about running sails that still matters is that they should be able to work over as wide a range as possible. I find that the same tack attachment point as is used for the jib and genoa serves perfectly well for twin running sails. Setting and handing them is made considerably easier by the fact that they are not set flying, but are hanked to the normal forestays. If the boat has only one forestay, this is no disadvantage if the hanks for the running sails are clipped on to the stay alternately and both sails are hoisted on a single jib halyard (since they then both have to be set at the same time a strong halyard winch is needed; hoisting them by hand would be impossible).

When steering manually, normal running sails can be used over a range of up to 30° to the true wind. This will not work with a self-steering gear, because even with a good design the boat will 'snake', and when getting to the limit course (30° to the wind) the yacht will stray from the *possible* range and one of the sails can easily be taken aback. The big drawback of running sails is that setting and handing them takes a good deal of time and trouble. Allowance has to be made for this when sailing a downwind course when – especially at night – you may find yourself on a collision course with a big commercial vessel and unable to alter course by more than 30° because of the twin jibs. This may explain, too, why running sails have become really popular only with the out-and-out blue water yachtsmen, who spend weeks on end alone in the middle of the ocean.

This spinnaker was left flying too long. The remnants could only be cut away from the shrouds in harbour.

Sail changing

Foresails can be handed and set on all points of sailing; yet you still see many yachts unaccountably heading up into wind to do the job. The boat loses way, and in a seaway starts pitching up and down. The foredeck gets wet, and the crew has difficulty in keeping a firm footing. And with the pressure off the mainsail the boom starts slatting to and fro, to add to the problems. Things are very different if you bear away to change a foresail; the relative wind is less, and the foresail starts to flap slightly because it is being shielded by the mainsail. The jib-sheet can be grasped with one hand, close to the clew, while the other hand releases the halyard. It is no great disaster if part of the foresail falls over the rail and into the water: since the boat is running downwind, the foredeck stays dry and the movement is gentle, so the piston hanks can be quietly unclipped and the jib stowed. With a good halyard winch there should be no problem in hoisting the new sail, either. If there is no winch, come up into the wind briefly so that the hanks are not pressing hard against the forestay as the sail is being run up.

There is no real reason why the advantages of a quiet movement

On a large yacht, the watch below will have to help with sail-changing.

of the boat and less relative wind on a downwind course should not also be enjoyed when handing the mainsail. The only thing that stands in the way of this is the sail battens in the mainsail, and these have no real job to do on a cruising yacht, anyway. Before the boom is hauled in tight, to prevent it swinging, it will of course need to be taken up with the topping lift. Naturally the mainsail, which is being pressed slightly against the mast by the wind, will not come down by itself on this point of sailing, but mainsails of up to 30 square metres can quite easily be hauled down by one person if the mast track and slides are in good condition; penetrating oil applied to them before the start of each passage will work wonders. Here, again, there should be no problem in hoisting the main using the halyard winch; the last bit of tension can, if necessary, be 'swigged up' by coming head to wind for a moment or two. It is even possible to set a sail fitted with battens this way, provided care is taken not to let the battens catch in the spreaders: a second member of the crew can haul the leech midships, so that the battens clear this danger point as the sail goes up. When manoeuvring in harbours, the main should only ever be set and handed while head to wind.

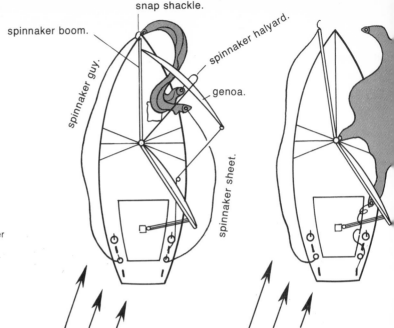

spinnaker boom.

snap shackle.

spinnaker halyard.

spinnaker guy.

genoa.

spinnaker sheet.

Left: preparing a spinnaker so that it can be hoisted without problems.

Right: to hand the spinnaker, the snap shackle is released, and the pressure empties outwards.

Centre and right: only this shackle will do when there is a heavy strain on the sheet.

Left: with a shackle like this, the sheet will hang up.

Setting a spinnaker only presents problems if the wind catches this (usually enormous) sail before it is completely hoisted. For cruising yachts with a small crew, the method adopted by Berend Beilken on his one-tonner *Optimist* a few years ago for setting and handing the spinny works extremely well. The sail is stowed in its bag with the head and the two clews uppermost, and the sailbag is lashed to one of the foredeck stanchions close to the genoa. The halyard is taken down in front of the genoa and clipped to the spinnaker, while the spinnaker sheet is likewise taken to the clew beneath the genoa. The second clew is taken beneath the foresail and around the stay to the spinnaker pole (already lifted) which can rest quietly against the forestay. At this point one has to use one of those horribly expensive snap shackles which can be released when under load. The spinnaker is then hoisted with the halyard, but will not fill since it remains blanketed until the genoa is dropped.

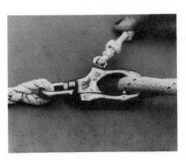

To *bring in the spinnaker*, you simply break open the snap shackle at the end of the spinnaker pole, whereupon the sail streams out in the wind like a flag. With one man easing away the halyard, it can be pulled into the cockpit by means of the sheet in the shadow of the mainsail, and then stowed back in its bag.

Reefing

Today almost all yachts have roller reefing. Only a few years ago cruising skippers looked on this device with some distrust because all too often it left them in the lurch on a long passage; but that was mainly in the days before nylon bearings. which now need hardly any maintenance. I used roller reefing on my world trip, and it worked perfectly throughout. Despite having nylon bearings I did lubricate the gear well at regular intervals, however, and I must admit that before starting on this major cruise I had slab reefing points put in the mainsail as well, just to be on the safe side.

The big advantage of *roller reefing* is that, just as we have been

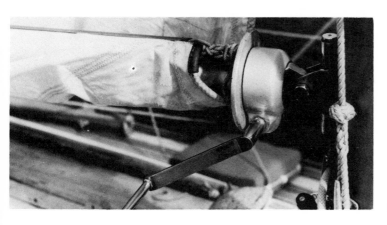

Roller reefing.

saying for setting and handing the mainsail, it allows the main to be reefed on any point of sailing. When six or seven rolls have been taken in, the rear end of the boom will (because of the cut of the sail) droop so much that it may touch the cabin roof when close-hauled. This can be prevented to some extent by rolling-in sail-battens or other objects, or by fitting wooden wedges to the boom (see drawing on page 19). There is no point in taking up the topping lift slightly, because the mainsail will then lose much of its effectiveness.

These problems do·not occur with *slab reefing*, but this does

149

Slab reefing – cannot go wrong.

have the drawback that the boom has to be brought midships to reef and all pressure taken off the sail – which is only possible by coming head to wind. Against this, there is the fact that it is absolutely reliable. Speaking personally, I would gladly always have both roller *and* slab reefing on any yacht of mine.

Safety at sea

Even if a cruising yacht has been built to provide every possible precaution, there is still a whole range of dangers that face any small ship at sea:

1. man overboard;
2. collision with another vessel;
3. going aground;
4. accident or illness on board;
5. foundering through being swamped;
6. fire;
7. being overwhelmed by a breaking sea;
8. collision with a whale.

Colour plate: Both mast lights in a straight line – too late to take avoiding action!

Though the risk of colliding with a whale comes at the end of this list of potential disasters, there are experienced skippers who fear this the most on the open sea. I myself know of a dozen yachts that have been victims of these otherwise good-mannered creatures; it is in fact most unlikely that a yacht would ever be attacked by a whale, and usually the gentle giants are seeking a collision just as little as we are. What is noticeable is that there are hardly ever any incidents between powered craft and whales; in the New Hebrides, where the waters abound with whales and where the fishermen take their motorboats out every morning, no-one knows of a fishing boat ever being rammed by a whale. It seems certain to me that the whale is kept at a distance by a loud engine noise. I would not dare follow the oft-repeated advice of keeping the echo-sounder switched on; I did this once in the middle of a school of porpoises, and the result was that the animals who had until then been moving around the boat quite dexterously became so confused by the ultrasonics that they crashed heavily against the hull. A deterrent measure which I tried over 15 000 miles, and which at least does no harm, is a length of flag halyard stretched between an underwater rudder fitting and the guardrail; throughout the voyage, no whale came near us. The flow of water past the line sets it vibrating and making a thrumming noise, and it *may* have been that this would warn a sleeping whale of my yacht's presence. But you do need to get used to the noise yourself when in your bunk!

Man overboard is a matter of *life or death*, whether you are close inshore or out at sea.

The chances of survival are slim or nil, depending on the sea and visibility and the water temperature. The much-practised 'man overboard' manoeuvre (which should be practised rather as a 'buoy overboard') should be attempted in this kind of emergency only if there is no engine, or the engine is unusable. If someone does go over the rail, here is what I would advise:

1. The helmsman puts the rudder over hard to bring the bows through the wind. This should be an automatic reaction, with no need to think.
2. Throw the man in the water a lifebelt; better still would be a lifebuoy, to mark the spot. Throw other floating objects over the side at short intervals, to mark the track back to the victim.
3. While the yacht is going about, the helmsman should be starting up the engine.

153

4. With the foresail backed, the yacht should lie more or less quietly broadside-on. As soon as the engine is running, get the sails down (no prizes for doing this tidily: but remember to take up the topping lift, and as soon as the mainsail is down, haul the boom down tight with the mainsheet).

5. Now approach the man under power. If there is a risk, because of the water temperature (under 16°C), of the victim quickly becoming unconscious or unable to move, a line must be got round him as quickly as possible. In most cases he will still be able to help himself for a short while, but it would be stupid to let him try to clamber back aboard up a swimmer's ladder. With numb fingers and waterlogged clothing he will stand no chance of doing so, and once exhausted it will usually be too late for him to be able to put a bowline round himself. With the water above 20°C, however, care and time should be taken to bring the casualty alongside at the broadest part of the boat, and up to weather – if he is down to lee, or anywhere near the stern, there is a great risk in a seaway of him being hit by a pitching boat. Watch out for the propeller, which can cause lethal injuries.

6. The greatest danger is over as soon as there is a line between the boat and the man in the water. Generally the victim will be in no state to get himself aboard. There is no single, surefire way of heaving a person back aboard; but under no circumstances should another person – even if secured with a line – jump into

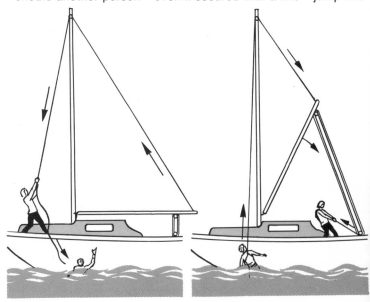

With outside halyards this will give a weakened casualty a chance.

the water to help. This would mean one important person less where you need him most. If the mast is fitted with stout winches, I would recommend using the main or jib halyard to haul the man aboard. The most effective method is to take the boom up as high as possible with the topping lift, use the fall of this to pass a loop round the man in the water, and then haul down on the boom with the multi-part tackle of the mainsheet to lift the casualty aboard (this will not, of course, work with halyards running inside the mast).

If the lifelines get in the way, they should be cut through without further ado – a man's life is at stake! Another method, though it needs a strong and practised crew, is to lift the person aboard using a small sail. The storm jib is fastened to the deck by the clew and tack, and the main or jib halyard is clipped to the head. As soon as the person has been floated over the sail laid flat on the water (with the help of a boathook), the head of the sail can be hoisted up. If it has been impossible to get a line round the casualty, this method may offer the only hope.

If visual contact with the casualty has been lost, it is an excellent idea to put the liferaft overboard as well. At Force 5 or 6, when foaming crests have already started to form, it can already be hard to make out a man in the water even if he is only a couple of hundred metres away; but probably he will be able to see you. The liferaft tossed overboard then gives him a further, slim chance of saving himself. The (slight) drift will make it pointless for him to swim after it, but will mark where he went overboard.

Rescue using a stormsail; the worse the weather, the more hands will be needed.

I would, besides, always use the liferaft if there is the least risk – because of a heavy sea – of injuring the man while bringing him aboard. In such a case he may be able to clamber into the raft which can then be secured to the yacht with a long line (100m or so) until the weather improves. So long as there is no lee shore close by, the casualty can stay in the raft for hours on end, or even a day or two, until he can be taken aboard when conditions get better, or with the help of bigger vessels called up to help.

155

Advice for the man in the water:

1. Don't panic – it halves your chance of survival.
2. If there is some form of buoyancy (lifebelt, etc.) close by, try to reach it and hold on to it.
3. On no account shed any articles of clothing.
4. Don't wave, don't shout, don't tread water. Float on your back, face downwind.
5. If there is a whistle on your lifejacket, give a blast every 30 seconds.
6. Pray!

Constant wearing of **safety harness** is the only certain way of avoiding the disastrous situation of having a man overboard. This may be feasible on a short passage, but will be impractical on a voyage lasting any time. Nevertheless, one can get into the good habit (like wearing a seatbelt in a car) of never venturing on to the most accident-prone part of the boat – the foredeck – without a harness. In bad weather it should be obvious that no-one must leave the cockpit without a safety harness, and if there is the slightest chance of seas coming into the cockpit everyone in the cockpit should be clipped-on as well. Opinions differ about the design of safety harness, and a good compromise seems to be harness without straps passing between the legs (these have proved not to be essential); this kind is a good deal more comfortable, which means it is far more likely to be worn.

It is an excellent idea to have the harness incorporated in the oilskins. With the harness integral with the jacket, there is no need

Below left: the ideal solution, a jacket with built-in safety harness and lifejacket.

Below right: here the safety harness is hooked on to a slide running along a rail, avoiding dangerous changeovers from one clipping point to the next.

for braces and the like; a single movement is enough to ensure that the wearer is firmly hooked to the guardrail.

Every seagoing craft should carry a **buoy with a light;** in an emergency, a floating pocket-lamp would serve the same purpose. If you do carry one, make sure before starting each trip that it still works, and that the batteries are not flat. If someone goes overboard at night, this inexpensive safety aid will offer the only chance of ever finding him again; which is why such a light-buoy needs to be thrown out as quickly as possible. As soon as it is out, the casualty must try to get close to it.

Lifejackets must work reliably for the unconscious, and for this reason most modern lifejackets are designed to turn an unconscious wearer on to his back, with the chin held up above water by the collar so that he can breathe. Lifejackets may be made from solid buoyancy material, or be inflatable; the latter are more and more popular because they can be stowed easily, and may be either semi- or fully-automatic. In the semi-automatic type, a compressed-air or CO_2 cartridge has to be released by hand and will then inflate the jacket fully within seconds. The fully-automatic type inflate by themselves, solely from the fact of the jacket being in

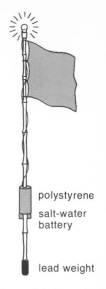

polystyrene

salt-water battery

lead weight

Rescue light buoy – can be home-made.

Fully-automatic lifejacket, unobtrusive when worn under oilskins.

the water; modern designs are so good that they are hardly ever triggered off by heavy rain, or by a wave breaking over the cockpit. A lifejacket that has to be blown up by mouth is not going to do much for you if you get knocked out as you go overboard, or become unconscious while in the water, so my choice would be either a solid-buoyancy type or a fully-automatic lifejacket.

The same applies to lifejackets as to safety harness – you ought really to wear one all the time, yet you cannot seriously expect anyone to do so. A jacket must of course be worn whenever the crew is exposed to risk, eg. in heavy weather or in fog (when a collision with another boat is possible). If you are having to abandon ship, or are being taken off by another vessel, you would obviously wear a jacket.

Every lifejacket should carry a whistle and a light, the latter powered by a small battery activated by salt water. Lifejackets must be checked thoroughly once a year, especially if they are the fully-automatic kind, and if the CO_2 cartridge shows the slightest sign of rust a fresh one must be fitted. In fact it is much better to discard the relatively-cheap cartridge after twelve months without waiting for visible danger-signs to appear.

A similar replacement policy should also apply to the **flares** carried on board. Every flare should have an expiry date marked on it, and you must never rely on rockets and flares that are out-of-date. The most effective kind are of course the more expensive type of signal rocket fitted with a little parachute. These climb to 70m or so and then stay aloft for a good deal longer, increasing the chances of being spotted. If a disaster does happen you should naturally not fire off your precious rockets and flares in the first hectic moments when there is no likelihood of people seeing them, but wait until you think there is a real chance of attracting attention; then, one or two rockets will help guide rescuers to the spot.

There should be a **signal (Verey) pistol** ready to hand on the bridge deck of every cruising yacht, though the legal rules governing its use must be followed very strictly.

Warning: a loaded Verey pistol is a lethal weapon, so the greatest care is needed! The pistol can be used not only to fire a 'red' in case of distress, but also provides an excellent means of attracting attention when there is risk of collision. A white cartridge fired towards the approaching vessel will usually bring a swift reaction.

The **liferaft** is essential equipment for every cruising yacht. It must never be carried below decks, but must be kept within reach of the cockpit. On very small yachts, it will have to be stowed in the pushpit – but otherwise the cockpit is the right place.

Note: the inflation of a liferaft always has to be triggered off, and it will not inflate automatically when thrown into the water. The ripcord has to be pulled from its casing and given a final tug to

Five-person liferaft.

operate the firing pin for the CO_2 cylinder. The raft will then unfold within a few seconds, and inflate by itself. Inflation must therefore *never* be started off with the liferaft on deck, because it could all too easily inflate and jam inside the shrouds, making it impossible to get it into the water. A hissing noise will be heard for some time after the raft has been inflated, indicating that the relief valve is letting out excess pressure. The raft will carry a folding knife for severing the rope that will still link the raft to the yacht. As supplied, liferafts carry very little water – usually only one day's ration – and hardly ever any food stores, and are thus unsuitable for carrying on an Atlantic crossing in this state. Without water a man will last 40 hours at most, whereas if he is lucky (and healthy to start with) he can manage for up to a month without food. Water takes up space, so it is hardly practical to pack extra water supplies in the raft.

What you can do is to ask the manufacturers (who will gladly

159

comply) to pack the following in the raft:

- a plastic bag or solar distilling device (eg. the Mark 3 Solar Still)
- sleeping-bags made from silver foil
- a small net with a very fine mesh
- some fishing-tackle.

The plastic sheeting will allow fresh water to be collected when the sun is shining – the bag is merely spread out over some articles of clothing soaked in salt water, and then condensation collects on the plastic as droplets of fresh water. The sleeping bags are used to protect the body from the sun's rays, thus preventing fluid loss.

The fine-meshed net is used to scoop up plankton from the water; this is a good source of nutrients. All you need for fishing is a few hooks, a spinner, or shiny piece of metal, to lure predatory fish, and 20m of fishing line. These extras will pack easily into any liferaft, and greatly increase the chances of survival. especially in remote waters. What will really help lighten worries, however, is a big plastic jerrycan full of clean drinking water taken on to the raft as you board it, and a jerrycan like this should really be kept ready close to the liferaft at all times.

Left: inside a locker is not the right place for the bilge-pump.

Right: an excellent arrangement, the pump can be operated from the tiller with a handle without having to open the locker.

Bilge pumps are, of course, part of a ship's safety gear. Pipes to and from the pump should be of tubing stiffened with a wire spiral, so that they cannot become flattened. Ordinary plastic hosepipe, which may have been quite satisfactory in cold North Sea waters, can easily become so soft in the heat of the tropics or the Mediterranean that it collapses on itself, particularly on the suction side of

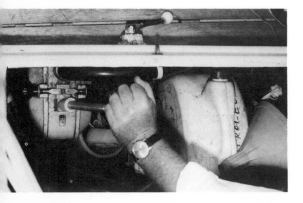

160

the pump. Normally, a modern yacht will be watertight enough for the bilge pumps seldom to be needed, so they must be checked regularly to make sure they still work. A well-equipped yacht will have two completely independent high-capacity pumps: it must be possible to operate one of these from the cockpit without having to open a locker or the like to do so. It is best to have the pump close to the helmsman, so that he can lend a hand with the pumping in an emergency. When it is a matter of survival, however, a simple bucket is by far the most effective way of getting rid of unwanted water.

Fire on board must never be underestimated as a real danger: even if you carry no gas or petrol, a fire can still start somewhere. Remember that a fire needs oxygen to be able to burn: if there is a fire in the engine compartment, don't remove the engine cover, because this will feed the flames with the air they need. Try to turn the boat round so that the wind drives the flames away from the boat as much as possible.

There should obviously be at least two BCF-type fire extinguishers aboard, one kept in the cabin and the other ready to hand in the cockpit locker. They need regular maintenance. Remember that ordinary extinguishers have not been designed for service on a yacht, so they must be protected from salt spray. If the paint on an extinguisher peels off and rust starts to form beneath it, it is a source of danger because of the pressure inside it, and must be got rid of as soon as possible.

Avoiding collisions

Dr Gerd Meyer-Uhl

The biggest danger facing a small yacht at sea is commercial shipping. To ensure safety for shipping traffic, new international rules for the prevention of collisions at sea have been compiled, and came into force on 15 July 1977. They apply on the high seas and on adjacent navigable waters in the absence of any special rules promulgated by local authorities. Every skipper leaving harbour must know the rules of the road, and in particular the collision avoidance rules, because failure to obey these, or uncertainty about them, can have fatal results – quite apart from someone being liable for damages that can amount to hundreds of thousands through doing the wrong thing (eg. forcing a vessel that has priority to change course suddenly so that it goes aground).

A constant bearing means a collision course

The time needed for two craft approaching each other to arrive at the same point can be calculated from the speed of the other ship plus that of your own, allowing for the distance. The speed of a big commercial ship may be from 15 to 30 knots, while yachts our size will probably be doing between 5 and 10 knots. This can often leave us the frighteningly short time of some 5–15 minutes for the all-important job of checking the bearing of a ship that has hove into sight and deciding whether to alter or hold our course. In daylight, even without taking a bearing, it is not all that difficult to make out what course another vessel is on – the bow-wave, the superstructure and so on make it fairly simple to gauge size, direction and speed. At night, if the white lights of an approaching steamer (the aft light is always the higher) or her navigation lights do not show clearly that the two tracks are taking the ships apart, the bearing must be checked with a hand-bearing compass with an illuminated scale (note down the bearing and time, accurate to the minute).

If the bearing does not change – if the reading stays the same · – then there is a danger of collision.

Who gives way?

Nowadays no sailing craft can place too much reliance on Rule 18(a)(iv) of the Collision Regulations, which give it priority over a power-driven vessel; the fact is that large ships, because of their size and speed, are often incapable of taking avoiding action. A 100 000t tanker may need three nautical miles to come to a halt, with her engines going full astern. If the rudder is put hard to starboard, she will take two minutes, and more than a mile, to turn 20° off her original track. What is more, the yacht skipper cannot be absolutely sure – particularly in areas where shipping is not used to meeting small craft – that he has even been seen. Automatic pilots and radar all too often mean that the bridge may be left unmanned for short but vital periods. Bearing all this in mind, the obviously sensible principle to follow is to get out of the path of any large ship, even if we do strictly have right of way.

Steering and sailing rules

a) Two sailing vessels

1. When each has the wind on a different side, starboard tack has priority over port tack (position of the mainsail is decisive).
2. When both have the wind on the same side, the leeward boat has priority over the windward boat. In cases of doubt, however, a leeward boat on port tack must keep clear.

b) Two power-driven vessels

1. *Head-on* (ie. the masts of both are in line, or at night both sidelights are visible straight ahead): alter course to starboard.
2. *Crossing:* the vessel to starboard has right of way.

c) Power-driven vessel and sailing vessel

The sailing vessel has right of way, but must not hinder a power-driven vessel in a narrow channel.

d) A stand-on vessel

(ie. one having right-of-way) must maintain her course and speed. If, however, the action of the give-way vessel nevertheless results in a danger of collision, the stand-on vessel too must manoeuvre to avoid collision.

e) Overtaking vessel

Must keep clear, and remains responsible for doing so until past and clear.

f) Responsibility of vessels towards each other

Vessels must keep clear of others, in the following sequence of priority:

Overtaking vessel

Power-driven vessel under way

Sailing vessel under way

Fishing boat

Vessel constrained by her draft

Vessel restricted in ability to manoeuvre, and hampered vessel.

These Sailing Rules are closely linked with Rule 34 (*Manoeuvring and Warning Signals*). Admittedly this applies only to power-driven craft, and sound signals are given by these only sparingly – especially in dense traffic – to avoid confusion; but the appropriate sound signals *must* be given simultaneously with the change in course if there is any risk of collision (possibly combining each blast with a white flash of light, of equal duration, visible for at least five miles).

Manoeuvring and Warning Signals

	Power driven vessels within sight, in a narrow channel or fairway.		
·	I am altering course to starboard*	— — ·	I am overtaking to starboard.
· ·	I am altering course to port*	— — · ·	I am overtaking to port
· · ·	I am going astern*	— · — ·	agreement
· · · · ·	in doubt (wake-up signal)*	——	in a bend when view is obstructed

*combined with light signals if appropriate

For the sailing skipper, to whom power-driven craft are supposed to give way under the Rules, the reality of the situation when at sea is rather worrying. On the one hand he is required, having the right of way, to maintain his course and speed; but on the other he can never be absolutely certain that the other ship on a collision course has actually seen him and will give way as it is supposed to. My advice to a cruising yachtsman would therefore be – especially when there is very little traffic – to move out of the other vessel's way so early on that the question of right of way does not arise, because a constant bearing never occurs.

Sound advice to the yacht skipper:

1. Always keep a good lookout.
2. Use your binoculars in plenty of time.
3. Check frequently that your lights are working properly, and watch the state of charge of the batteries.
4. Check the course and speed of large ships carefully.
5. Always assume that a large ship has not seen you.
6. Keep a Verey pistol, with white cartridges, close at hand, for calling another ship's attention to your right of way.
7. Change course in plenty of time, and by at least 45°. Never alter course to go across another vessel's bows, always under her stern.
8. Cross shipping lanes by the shortest path possible.
9. If your green sidelight faces the other ship's green sidelight, or the two red sidelights face each other, there is no danger of collision.
10. If the lower of the two white steaming-lights of a power-driven craft seen to your starboard is to the *right*, there is no danger of collision (and likewise if the lower steaming-light is to the left when seen to port).

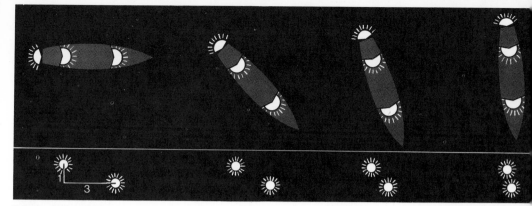

This is all the skipper sees

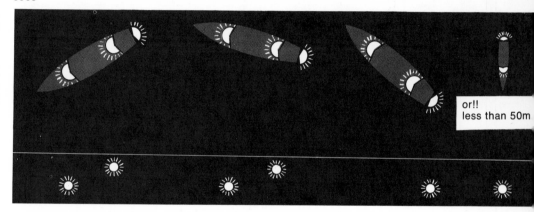

or!!
less than 50m

How to tell what kind of vessel the other is

Between sunset and sunrise the compulsory lights that vessels have to carry make identification possible. Because of this, other lights shown by craft must not hinder recognition, prevent a lookout being kept or be likely to be confused with the regulation lights.

The diagrams on page 169 give a general survey of these lights and their range. In the case of a power-driven vessel it can readily be seen that the two *sidelights* and the *stern light* together cover a sector of 360°. The stern light (like the towing light of a tug) has a sector of exactly 135°, within which the sidelights, logically enough, cannot be seen. All following vessels inside this sector are classed as overtaking vessels. Only a vessel approaching from dead ahead sees both sidelights at the same time. The prescribed ranges are in practice often not achieved, especially by smaller craft; sailing vessels in particular when heeled are difficult to make out. Experi-

If the sidelights cannot be seen, the masthead steaming lights will often show the course of another ship.

165

ence shows that all white lights are more readily seen than the red and green sidelights.

For very small vessels under 20m the Regulations allow combined sidelights, with the red and green in a single housing. A sailing man will always opt for these rather than separate lights, because he has to be sparing with his electricity and can save some 20W every hour in this way. The same is true of tricolour lamps, which have the stern light in the same housing as well. The Regulations now allow these for sail boats under 12m in length when not under engine. When anchored in harbour and using the dinghy, you must have a hand-torch, since the tender comes under 'vessels under oars' which the Regulations now require to have a white light ready to hand, Rule 25(d)(ii). The recognition lights for fishing vessels will only be encountered in fishing grounds; elsewhere, fishing boats display the same lights as other power or sailing vessels.

Anchor lights, or 'riding' lights, have to be shown by all vessels without exception. Cruising skippers especially I would urge to use anchor lights in strange harbours, even if they think they are well protected alongside the quay or on a mooring. They will not only be obeying the rules, but safeguarding themselves as well.

There are very few signals for the time between sunrise and sunset. One of these, the cone shape pointing down shows that a sailing boat is under engine and does not have a sailing vessel's right of way under the rules. A cone pointing up, as well as an hourglass shape or basket, tells us that a fishing vessel is working with a net extending horizontally more than 150m. A diamond shape marks each vessel – towing and towed – of a tow-train longer than 200m. A black cylinder is shown by a vessel constrained by her draft. Black balls 60cm in diameter have the following meanings:

1 ball	= vessel at anchor
2 balls one above the other	= vessel not under command
3 balls one above the other	= vessel aground
2 or 3 balls, one each at	
foremast head & foreyard ends	= minesweeper
ball-diamond-ball	= vessel restricted in ability
	to manoeuvre
plus 2 balls on obstructed	
and 2 diamonds on passing	
side	= dredger

In fog – sound signals and actions

Just as a keen sailor is unlikely to avoid a first encounter with foul weather, he is certain somewhere or other to be caught out in fog. Though there may be weather warnings, and though no sensible skipper would leave a harbour with fog coming down, banks of fog can form too suddenly and unexpectedly for no-one ever to find himself in a pea-souper.

Fog, and reduced visibility in general, greatly increase the risk of collision at sea, especially for a small craft; and paradoxically enough, the spread of radar has made the danger worse for them. Fog brings three new dangers:

1. the high speeds at which modern big ships travel;
2. the danger of a small vessel not being seen on a radar screen (if the bridge officer turns the gain down to cut out sea clutter on his screen, the weak echo from a yacht's radar reflector may be cut out as well)
3. the difficulty of locating a sound accurately.

Though in restricted visibility every vessel is supposed to proceed at a safe speed, and indeed to stop engines if it hears a fog-signal ahead and then navigate cautiously until the danger is past, and though this of course also applies to vessels equipped with radar, there is a big gap between the letter of the law and what is done in practice. Big ships run to a predetermined schedule, and there have been many court cases showing that the guilty master was ploughing ahead through fog at 18 knots. Big ships are able quite happily to keep up full speed with a Force 8 blowing and poor visibility, and this is why the rules on how to act in reduced visibility are so important. They apply to all vessels, just as every vessel is required to make sound signals. It will be easy to tell a large ship, with its deep-noted siren, from smaller craft with their whistles and foghorns. It must be said, incidentally, that nearly all the foghorns one finds on sale in yacht chandlers are unsuitable for practical use. In fog they become inaudible within a few metres, especially with the engines of a large freighter thumping away in the background. The only devices that are really effective are the piston foghorns that used to be carried by the old sailing ships, and which nowadays one very occasionally sees on sale only in antique shops.

Note: the deeper the note the greater the audible range

Radar reflector gets in the way least below the crosstrees.

It can very often be difficult to work out just where a sound is coming from. Banks of fog produce echoes and alter the loudness, deceiving the eyes and ears (which quickly become tired). There are rules born of experience that need keeping firmly in mind. One assumes that a good skipper will, if he has not in fact worked out the ship's position accurately before the fog started, at least have a checkable dead-reckoning position. From here on he must pay the closest attention to his dead-reckoning, because the only aids he will have are compass, log, depth-sounder, chart and, perhaps, a tidal stream atlas. All he can do is:

- give sound signals
- check the radar reflector
- post a man to listen out in the bows
- maintain silence on board
- sail clear if in a shipping lane
- make the whole crew don lifejackets

Sound signals in reduced visibility:

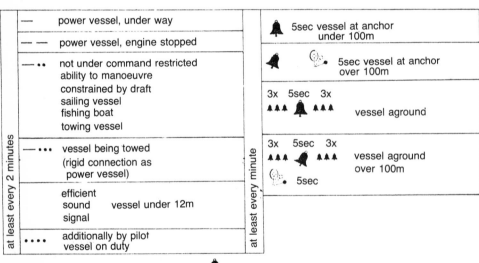

at least every 2 minutes		
—	power vessel, under way	
— —	power vessel, engine stopped	
— ••	not under command restricted ability to manoeuvre constrained by draft sailing vessel fishing boat towing vessel	
— •••	vessel being towed (rigid connection as power vessel)	
	efficient sound signal	vessel under 12m
••••	additionally by pilot vessel on duty	

5sec vessel at anchor under 100m

5sec vessel at anchor over 100m

3x 5sec 3x   vessel aground

3x 5sec 3x   vessel aground over 100m
5sec

- • short blast of 1sec duration   bell
- —· long blast of 4–6sec duration   gong

Colour table: The new version of the Rules came into force during 1977. For the cruising skipper this involves two important innovations.
1. a towing vessel must show a *yellow* 'towing light' above the normal stern light.
2. a sailing vessel under 12m may carry a tricolour light at the masthead instead of the previous lights. With a 25W bulb this gives a range of 2 nautical miles.

essel's length	>50 m	12 - 50 m	<12 m	<7 m
ghts		Range in nm		
asthead light	6	5: <20 m–3	2	—
delight	3	2: <20 m - Comb	1	—
ernlight	3	2	2	—
owing light	3	2	2	—
l-round light hite, red, een, yellow	3	2	2	—

	Power vessel under 7m length and 7 knots maximum speed		
			Sidelights if possible, otherwise white all-round
	Sailing vessels must carry side and sternlights depending on size	Tricolour light permitted	As before if possible, or light to hand
	Vessel under oars may show sailing vessel lights, otherwise light to hand		

Symbol for all-round light

Symbol for masthead light

Symbol for flashing light

ower vessel nder way ★) 50m can how 1 asthead ght	Air-cushion vessel under way ★) <50m can show 1 masthead light	Towing vessel <200m under way ★) ★★★)	Towing vessel >200m under way ★) ★★★)	Sailing vessel under way ★) may show	Pilot on duty 1. at anchor appropriate anchor light 2. under way ★)	Trawler under way★)	Fishing vessel moving through water ★)
nd masthead ght aft and igher	As before	Vertically one above other	As before				

Not under ommand, when moving through water ★)	Restr. ability to manoeuvre, when moving through water ★)	Constrained by draft ★★)	Towing vessel unable to change course while towing > 200m	Power vessel restr. manoeuvrability, dredging or carrying out underwater work ★★)	Vessel under tow
					Sidelights and sternlight

Minesweeper ★★)	Vessel at anchor > 50m > 100m must switch on decklights	Vessel at anchor <50m	Vessel aground anchor lights acc. size plus	Sailing vessel < 12m may show tricolour light	Sailing vessel < 7m light to hand instead of side- & sternlights or tricolour light	Power vessel <7m not faster than 7 knots
	Stern					

★) plus side- & sternlights according to length

★★) plus masthead & sternlight with sidelights acc. length when moving through water

★★★) plus yellow towing light above sternlight

Distress signals

These are signals that every skipper must know by heart; there must be not the slightest doubt or loss of time if they are seen, or have to be given. They are the distress signals listed in Annex IV to the *Collision Regulations*, totalling 14 in number, and should be used only in immediate danger when help is needed at once. A broken mast which does not endanger the crew's life, for example, or running out of fuel, would not justify giving a distress signal.

Apart from raising and lowering the arms to the side, which is effective only over short distances, the following signals should be committed to memory:

1. Sound signals

(a) a gun or other explosive signal at intervals of about a minute (not really suitable for small craft).

(b) continuous sounding of a fog signal.

2. Rockets

(a) rockets or shells with red stars.

(b) red parachute flares, or red handheld flares. (These are the most suitable and effective signals for small cruising yachts. Under ideal conditions they can be seen for 5 miles by day, and up to 20 miles by night. They should be kept in a waterproof packing, and replaced from time to time.)

3. Radio

(a) radiotelegraphy: SOS in Morse · · · — — — · · ·

(b) radiotelegraphy alarm signal: 12 Morse dashes of 4 seconds each within a minute.

(c) radiotelephony: the word 'Mayday' on 2182kHz.

(d) radiotelephony alarm signal: 30sec–1min of two alternating sounds.

(e) radio signals from a distress radio beacon.

Since many yachts today have radiotelephony gear, radio distress calls are becoming more and more common.

4. Flag signals

(a) international code flags NC.

(b) square flag with a ball shape (use a fender) above or below it.

5. Fire

(a) flames (from a tar barrel, oil barrel, etc.)

(b) smoke signal giving off orange smoke (suitable for small craft).

Because these rules are so important, all the distress signals should be checked through and explained thoroughly to the crew.

distress flag signal NC

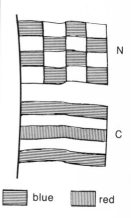

blue   red

What to do in a storm

To get things straight from the start, severe storms are most unusual in our latitudes and during the time of year when we are usually sailing. A sail boat has very little chance of surviving a Force 12 hurricane, with ocean seas to match, which is why Eric Hiscock has very rightly said that the fight for survival starts as early as Force 9. One thing one should be clear about: if the wind speed indicator on board is showing an average reading of, say, Force 6 and the pointer now and then runs up to Force 8 in a gust, this does not mean there is a Force 8 storm blowing – you are in Force 6 strong breeze, and no more.

In a storm the big problem is a lee shore, and as far as possible you should never allow yourself to get into this situation. A Force 8 storm and a lee shore a few miles away can easily mean a wreck, and things could hardly be worse out in the middle of the ocean. Make no mistake about it – it is quite impossible to sail against a Force 8 wind, let alone make way against it under engine. Even if you could carry sail you would not make one metre to windward, especially with a heavy sea running; which is why when sailing close to a coast one should always listen attentively to the weather forecasts.

Out at sea, on the other hand, a storm need not present insuperable problems. Above Force 8 one cannot heave-to with any safety, of course, and then there is only one real answer – to run before the wind, if necessary under bare poles. The boat's speed must not be under-estimated, however; at Force 8 a 6-tonner under bare poles can be doing 4 or 5 knots, which means 100 miles in a 24-hour period. If the wind gets even stronger, so that the seas rolling up astern look more and more menacing and the yacht starts surfing down the wave fronts more and more often, something must be done to take some of the speed off. At one time a sea anchor used to be recommended for these circums- tances, but today there is general agreement in the sailing world that a sea anchor is in fact quite useless. It is wishful thinking to believe you can lie to it as you can to a fixed anchor. As the wind resistance of a yacht's bows is in any case greater than that of the stern, she will only lie head to wind for a few moments at a time before the bows are pushed to one side again by the storm and the very thing that ought to be avoided in a storm happens – the boat broaches to, and ends up sideways on to wind and waves. But a sea anchor is not the right way of keeping the stern into the wind either. For one thing it has to have quite a large diameter to be effective, making it almost impossible to handle in a storm: and for another there is the risk of it holding the stern back *too* firmly, so that the ability to steer is lost. The same purpose can be served by much simpler means, such as trailing warps astern: if these do not provide enough resistance, they can be streamed in loops. If you want to run safely before the wind, a speed about 20 per cent less than hull speed would seem the best compromise. Some people advise carrying as much canvas as you can when running before the wind; I wouldn't listen to them, because I would fear for my mast, and for the boat itself. Cases have indeed been known of yachts shooting down the side of a mountainous wave and practically tripping over their own keel because of their enormous downhill speed. If you had ever stood on the deck of the 15m *Sandefjord* you would find it hard to understand how such a solid, beamy boat (nearly 5m) could ever pitch forward end-over-end. Yet that is what happened to her in the monstrous seas of the Roaring Forties, with the loss of one of her crew.

Years ago, Bernard Moitessier put forward the view that you should take a curling sea aft, but at an angle of about 20°, and not stream anything astern. He was virtually alone in this, and in fact a few years later he told me that he had not adopted this technique during his later round-the-world voyage. It is true, of course, that on passage from Tahiti to Alicante, Moitessier weathered some very severe storms; but this is surely not enough to prove that his method is the only right one.

Storm warning! All objects on deck that are not solidly bolted down must be made fast; this applies in particular to the dinghy. If the storm seems inevitable, it is best to get the mainsail completely off the boom at once. All lashings (those holding the anchor, for instance) should be checked. If you are in the slightest way vulnerable to seasickness, take preventive tablets in plenty of time, a couple of hours before the bad weather starts. At moments like this you will undoubtedly not have much appetite, but coping with heavy weather takes a lot out of people, so you do need something to eat.

A big Thermos flask to keep a supply of preheated food handy can prove invaluable in circumstances like this.

If at all possible, an accurate fix should be taken before the storm starts. If members of the crew can be spared, they should not be employed on pointless tasks but sent below to try to build up a reserve of sleep. It goes without saying that lifejackets and safety harness must be worn at all times in stormy weather. If it is so rough that broaching-to would be really dangerous, the self-steering gear must not be used for running before the wind; even though it seriously depletes the crew, there must always be a man on the tiller (clipped on by his harness) to prevent broaching-to.

No sailing man really enjoys bad weather, and the people you hear at the club bar carrying on about how they would 'love to experience a real storm, just once' are, to be blunt, stupid. If one is honest about it, you are scared all the time during a storm, though you may admit it to yourself as little as possible. There is the point, too, that at night or with a dark-grey, menacing sky the weather always looks a lot worse than it actually is. When I went through a mistral storm in the Gulf of Lyons in sunshine, under a blue sky, it was much less impressive than a mere Force 6 wind off the Azores with the rain lashing down in my face.

Remember that there have been very few cases of yachts not surviving a storm; there have been far more instances of crews abandoning yachts in a panic, which were then found a few days later, floating along deserted but otherwise perfectly safe and sound. So long as you are not being driven towards a lee shore, there is really not a lot to worry about.

The boat is stronger than you are!

Wind · Weather · Waves

To think, as many sailing folk tend to do, that it is pointless paying attention to weather forecasting because even professional forecasters often get it wrong, is short-sighted. We need to know, for the safety of our ship, how strong the wind is going to be and from which direction it will be blowing.

Wind

The air pressure conditions provide a relatively simple explanation for almost everything to do with the wind. As we know, the earth is surrounded by a 'skin' of air, only about 20km thick. Naturally, air has weight, even though a very slight one. The height of the column of air exerts a pressure on the earth's surface of about $1kg/cm^2$.

This **air pressure** is of course not the same everywhere, and depends a good deal on temperature. When two adjoining areas have different air pressures, the air will naturally try to flow from the high-pressure area into the one with low pressure. This flow of air powers our sails, and we call it the wind; the bigger the pressure difference, the faster the air will flow into the low-pressure area.

Wind strength

Today this is quoted internationally as the speed of air masses, given in knots. For sailors, the traditional Beaufort wind scale is a practical system, and relates the wind force (from 1 to 12) to certain speed ranges in knots. The yachtsman can either measure wind speed with a meter, or estimate it. A measurement taken from a boat will of course only measure the apparent wind speed; this means that if we are sailing dead before the wind at 5 knots, we need to add 5 knots to the indicated wind speed to arrive at the true speed. If we want to read Beaufort wind strengths from an anemometer, we should not of course take peak readings, but an average of all those shown by the pointer. In a 40-knot wind the pointer may easily run up to 60 knots in the gusts without there in fact being a Force 11 blowing. This is why the claims of many weekend sailors need taking with a big pinch of salt. An old and experienced ship's officer once told me that the worst storm he had ever known reached Force 10; so when I hear many of my friends who seem to encounter Force 10s and 11s several times a year, my tendency to distrust is confirmed! Wind strength can be estimated from the sea conditions, but a little experience is needed. The following table will help:

The Beaufort Scale

Beaufort	Knots	Effect on open sea
0	0	sea like a mirror
1	1–3	ripples, without crests
2	4–6	small wavelets, already distinct
3	7–10	occasional white, breaking crests
4	11–15	fairly frequent white horses, breaking waves making constant sound
5	16–21	white horses everywhere; breaking waves can be heard as a murmur
6	22–27	breaking wavecrests leave sheets of white foam, spray begins to fly
7	28–33	white foam begins to stream out along direction of wind
8	34–40	foam lies out along wind direction in pronounced streaks
9	41–47	high waves with toppling crests of considerable length, sea begins to roll
10	48–55	spray interferes with vision, whole of sea appears white with foam
11	56–63	estimation of wind speed no longer possible
12	64+	hurricane, little chance of survival for a yacht

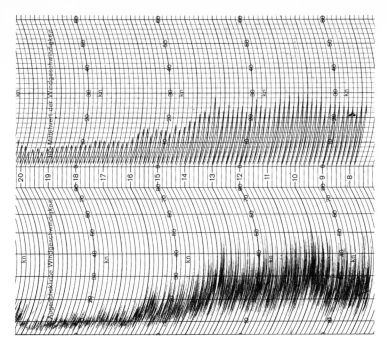

Top: The mean wind strength at 1000 hr was 30 knots = Force 7.
Bottom: maximum wind speed (in gusts and squalls) at 1000hr was 50 knots.

The wind strength can be gauged from the way the boat behaves. At Force 6 it is still possible to beat against the wind; at Force 7 this is a hard struggle, if indeed possible; at Force 8 you can just lie hove-to, while at Force 9 and over there is no question of sailing – man and ship are fighting to survive.

One of the most important instruments that must be carried is the *barometer*, which shows the air pressure at any moment (measured nowadays in millibars). The pointer should be adjusted, using the screw at the rear, to a current pressure reading obtainable by a telephone call to the local meteorological office; after that, if you want to find the pressure, a slight tap will free the needle and bring it to the right position. The slight jump the needle makes from its previous 'stuck' reading will show whether the pressure is rising or falling. It is important to realise that the pressure we measure on board at a given moment will not tell us much on its own; only a full weather report, or a weather map, will give a clear picture of how the weather is developing.

Pressure systems A weather map is far easier to read than most yachtsmen imagine. If you understand the three main components – pressure systems, isobars and fronts – they tell you a lot about the wind conditions in the various areas. All that a pressure system

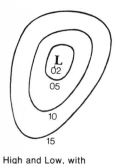

High and Low, with
associated isobars

is is an area having the lowest (or highest) pressure in the surroundings, and is thus described as a *'low'* or *'high'*. A low pressure
area is bound to be surrounded solely by areas of high pressure,
and vice versa.

If you were to take a large number of air pressure readings
around a low, you would find that the pressure rises at varying rates
as you move away from the centre; this can be shown diagramati-
cally by joining up all the points having the same pressure with
lines known as *isobars*. Naturally a separate line is not drawn for
each millibar of difference – isobars are drawn at intervals of 10 or
5mb (995, 1000, 1005mb and so on). On a weather map, for simplicity, these are written not as 1005 but merely '05', etc. If you
remember that isobars are merely lines joining all points with the
same pressure, it should be obvious that they never cross (there
cannot be a point with two pressures at the same time). Isobars
can, in practice, tell us a lot – indeed, just what the yachtsman
wants to know, which is the direction and strength of the wind.
Remember what we said a moment ago – that the greater the pressure difference, the stronger the wind? In isobar terms, this means
the closer they are together, the stronger the wind.

So long as the isobars are relatively straight, the wind strength

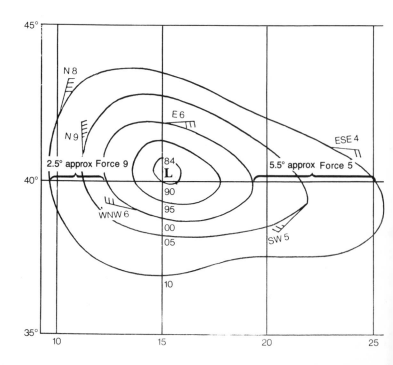

The wind blows
anti-clockwise in a Low

178

can be estimated by measuring the distance in degrees of latitude between two isobars representing a pressure difference of 10mb, at our position. If the isobars are very curved, deduct about Force 1 on the Beaufort scale.

Distance	Channel and North Sea area	Mediterranean
1°	Force 12	Force 12
2°	Force 8	Force 10
4°	Force 5	Force 6
8°	Force 3	Force 4
15°	Force 2	Force 3

Wind direction

Now let us see how to gauge the wind direction from the shape of the isobars. This is simple if you remember that air masses move from high-pressure areas towards the lows, flowing out of the high-pressure area clockwise and into the low-pressure area anti-clockwise (but vice versa in the Southern Hemisphere). The wind direction makes an angle of about 15° with the isobars.

A weather map naturally applies only to the time at which it was plotted. It is, however, easy to calculate, from the predicted direction and speed at which a pressure system is moving, what conditions are going to affect our area some time ahead. The less time has elapsed since the last information was gathered, the more accurate a forecast will be.

A barometer provides invaluable data for keeping an eye on what the weather is doing. It must be stressed again that the air pressure measured aboard at any one moment tells you next to nothing unless you look at the trend in your area over the past hours or days. To this end, the pressure should be noted in the logbook at frequent intervals. A useful thing to carry aboard is a barograph, which charts air pressure and makes it simplicity itself to see changes in pressure (eg. a low forming). Unfortunately a barograph carried in a small yacht is likely to be exposed to a lot of jolting and vibration, so this must be damped as much as possible when it is installed. Rubber feet and special 'oil damping' of the stylus arm may help, but are not always successful. Even if you carry a barograph, you still need a barometer because it will generally be a good deal more accurate.

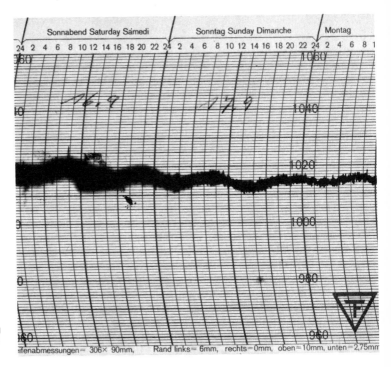

On 16 September there was only a Force 4 blowing – the oil damping was not working properly.

Weather forecasts

Always try to get the latest weather map before starting a passage. In many ports the harbourmaster can help. Under way, however, you will have to rely on your radio for forecasts, and when abroad you should check early and often on which transmitters give weather reports (assuming of course, you can understand the language). Times and frequencies for weather forecasts all over the world are given in the *Admiralty List of Radio Signals, Vol. 3* which (like *Vol. 2*) should be carried by every cruising yacht. If you do not follow the language being used for a weather forecast, try taping it on a cassette recorder and then play it back several times with the

180

help of a dictionary. The *List of Radio Signals, Vol. 3,* does in fact list the main meteorological expressions in English, French, Spanish and Russian.

Weather maps

When you are at sea, you can also try drawing your own weather map from data broadcast for the Channel, North Sea and Mediterranean areas. It must be said at once that this is not easy, and besides practice it also calls for some experience. An excellent introduction to plotting weather maps, and especially to constructing isobars, is given in the *Admiralty List of Radio Signals, Vol. 3.*

Using the knowledge gained from pages 178,179 and 184 the wind strength and direction can be worked out from a weather map.

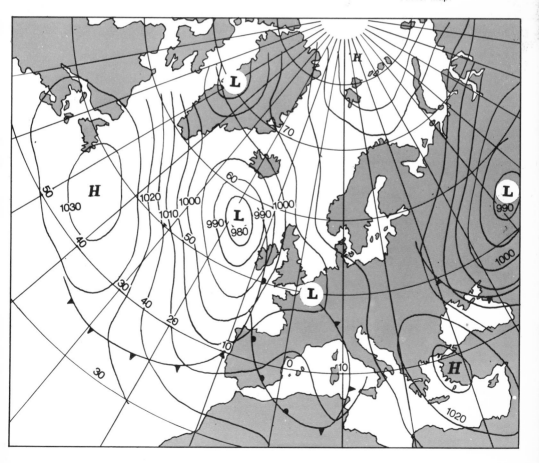

Weather maps on the FM 46 system There is another way of getting a weather map at sea (since most of us cannot afford either the money or the current consumption needed for automatic weather chart equipment); this is the FM 46 system, which is really intended for commercial shipping. It offers fantastic opportunities to yachtsmen as well, however, if one is willing to go to a little trouble. It will give us a weather map virtually certain of having none of the plotting errors that can otherwise so easily creep in. There is no need to know the language of the transmitter station, either, since the weather map is sent out solely in Morse code numbers. There is no need to be put off if – as is very likely – you do not know the Morse code, because the numbers are extremely simple to master:

1 = · – – – –		6 = – · · · ·
2 = · · – – –		7 = – – · · ·
3 = · · · – –		8 = – – – · ·
4 = · · · · –		9 = – – – – ·
5 = · · · · ·		0 = – – – – –

If you tune in at the right time to the right frequency (both are given in the *List of Radio Signals, Vol. 3*) to one of the FM 46 stations (eg. Malta Radio) your immediate reaction will probably be. disappointment, because the Morse is being sent much too fast to follow. What you need here is a tape recorder with several speeds; you record the signals at a high tape speed, and play them back at a slower one. Some of the numbers will then be immediately recognisable first go (not the whole transmission, of course, but you can replay the tape as often as you need). With a little patience, and plenty of time, I was able to copy out the entire transmission the first time I tried this. One point of possible confusion to watch for is that a single very long dash is often used instead of five dashes for the numeral '5'.

The figures are invariably sent in groups of five. Using the FM 46 code (which you will find both in the *Admiralty List of Radio Signals, Vol. 3,* and in the Meteorological Office's *Handbook of Weather Messages, Part 2*) it is then simple to plot the weather map, as the following example will illustrate:

Assume that you have copied down the following groups:

    1st group: 9 9 9 0 0

    2nd group: 8 1 1 1 3

    3rd group: 4 4 2 1 4

The *Admiralty List of Radio Signals* tells us the following about these three groups:

1. 9 9 9 0 0 = code group for pressure system
2. 8 P_t P_c P P

$\quad$ 8 = identification for pressure system

$\quad$ P_t = type of pressure system, where under '1' we find 'Low'

$\quad$ P_c = nature of pressure system, where under '1' we find 'filling'

$\quad$ PP = pressure in millibars, ie. '13' (= 1013 mb)

3. $L_aL_aL_oL_oK$

$\quad$ L_aL_a = latitude in degrees

$\quad$ L_oL_o = longitude in degrees

$\quad$ K in this case ('4') indicates full degrees

This may seem terribly complicated at first, but is really so simple that with a little practice you will be able to read the collection of figures in plain language. The figure groups mean:

1. pressure systems are about to be transmitted;
2. the first of these is a filling low-pressure system, with a pressure of 1013mb;
3. which is situated approximately at 44°N 21°W.

The entire weather map is transmitted in Morse in this way. The isobar transmission is similarly preceded by a code group meaning isobars, and is followed by a pressure and list of position data which we then merely join up to reproduce the complete isobar. The work involved is purely mechanical, and there is very little that you can do wrong.

The main advantage of having a weather map and a good forecast is that a change of wind direction is known about well in advance, so that you can plan to be on the right tack. They will also, of course, give you a better chance of dodging bad weather.

Weather maps only give the weather position in broad terms. Even if the weather map for our area shows only a Force 3 wind, it may well happen that we find ourselves caught in quite violent squalls, or even minor thunderstorms. As *fronts* pass through, the normal weather shown on the weather map may alter. Particularly

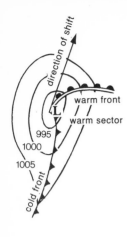

in the case of a cold front (ie. air masses – usually at the rear of a low – which are colder than their surroundings) there are likely to be heavy showers and violent squalls. As the front passes through, there may also be sudden changes of wind direction, recognisable in the weather map as isobar 'kinks'.

The wind expected can also be affected by local air-flow conditions. Close to land, especially, there are what are known as *land* and *sea breezes*, which arise because of the differential cooling or heating of the air layer over the land and that over the water. In general, air over the coast that has cooled during the night will warm up in the morning sunshine, and rise. This produces a locally-limited low pressure area, and colder air from over the sea flows in to balance it out. This is the sea breeze. It may be so strong as completely to mask the predominant wind direction in the area, so that someone sailing near the coast has a totally different wind to cope with. At night the opposite occurs, as the air mass over the land cools down again and sinks before flowing out over the sea. Generally speaking this land breeze is much weaker than the sea breeze. Particularly in the Mediterranean, where flat calms are very common in the summer, one can sometimes make useful progress using the sea breeze while another yacht only a couple of miles further out to sea is lying becalmed outside the range of either land or sea-breeze.

You may of course end up well away from your home cruising waters without a weather map or any other kind of meteorological report; in which case you have to work out what weather to expect as best you can with the means to hand. The possibilities are, it must be admitted, fairly limited: but you should at least have a clear idea of which way a high or low-pressure system lies, and with the help of the barometer (or even better, a barograph) you will be able to tell whether you are getting close to a high or low. There is a useful rule-of-thumb for this: standing with your back to the wind (in the northern hemisphere), you will have the high to your right and the low to your left.

It is some consolation to remember that the captains of the old square-riggers had to plan their voyages through the most rugged of sailing areas without weather reports, making use solely of what they could observe for themselves. A lot of the following tips come from the pages of a textbook for seamen, and are traditional sailor's weather wisdom.

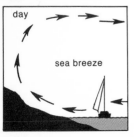

Weather lore

- Outside the tropics, a slowly rising glass always indicates the approach of a high-pressure system.
- Outside the tropics, a slowly falling glass almost always indicates an approaching low (though it may also show only a weakening of the high).
- If the sun rises brightly, or with a slightly reddish gleam, above the horizon and then disappears into cloud, expect wind and rain.
- If the sun sets in the evening bright and clear below the horizon or behind cumulus clouds with brightly-lit edges, there is good weather on the way.
- If the sun looks very large and shiny white as it sets, take in a reef in your mainsail.
- Dark clouds, or greenish-yellow light, at sunset herald bad weather.
- If the moon at night is pale and watery, expect rain; if it is red, expect wind; and if it shines sharp and silvery, expect good weather.
- If the sky is 'starry' and yet you can see only the brightest stars, make ready for wind and rain.
- A red sky at morning, with fiery colours, promises a day of rain with a lot of wind.
- If the evening sky stays red after sunset, there is good weather on the way so long as there is not a red glow to the east. A yellowish-red or copper-red evening sky promises wind and rain.
- Small cumulus clouds around midday mean fine, dry weather if the morning sky has been cloudless.
- Heavy clouds in the morning or evening sky bring bad weather.
- In general, unusual colours in the clouds, or striking cloud formations, are always a warning sign.
- If the wind freshens in the morning, there is good weather ahead, while a freshening evening wind means bad weather.
- If the wind suddenly changes direction after blowing from one point for a long time, this indicates a general change in the weather.
- 'When the rain's before the wind, halyards, sheets and braces mind; when the wind's before the rain, soon you may make sail

again.'

■ If you hear 'bacon-and-eggs sizzling' on your radio on the marine band or other kinds of atmospheric interference, especially during the daytime, a thunderstorm is on the way.

In the **tropics**, meaning mainly the tradewind areas, these weather rules have only a limited application. There, I have seen cloud formations that would strike fear and terror into a yachtsman in our home latitudes, yet there was seldom any deterioration in the weather. In the trades you do have to keep a close watch on changes in pressure; a typical pattern is an up and down movement over a range of not much more than 3mb, spread over the day. If the barometer strays substantially from this 3mb range, then the worst is likely – meaning a tropical hurricane. These are always deadly dangerous, with winds reaching 150 knots; a wind speed that in our latitudes is quite unimaginable.

Sea state

The kind of sea one is experiencing naturally has a major influence on the speed of the boat, and on the course one is able to steer. The sea state depends first and foremost on the wind and its strength. Waves are not in fact masses of water on the move: the

individual particles of water merely move up and down in time with the wave cadence. Nevertheless, a small boat will have considerable difficulty in making headway against waves, though this is mainly because it is constantly having to climb up the steeper, lee side of each of them.

The sea state depends on the wind; the stronger it blows, the higher the waves will be. It is quite possible for waves to be as high as a house, and in the North Atlantic seas of up to 16m have been measured. Even 20m waves are possible. This does not mean, however, that such giant waves are necessarily dangerous for a yacht: they usually have a length (200m and more) to match, and are only catastrophic if they break. By a wave breaking, I do not mean the crest toppling over, but the wave actually falling apart (as we see happening in surfing waves). Fortunately, this very seldom happens. A yacht would have virtually no chance – you have to remember that a giant wave like this would contain an unimaginable 30 000 tons of water. Seas become most uncomfortable if wind and current are opposed, when the waves pile up much steeper.

In these circumstances, a wave may sometimes break up. Off the east coast of South Africa, the Agulhas current sometimes runs at 4 knots, and the Admiralty chart for this area says soberly 'Caution: monster waves of more than 20m are possible in this area'. Before the First World War a big British warship of several thousand tons went down with all hands, evidently overcome by a freak wave of this kind, and several large merchant ships have been crippled or lost here in recent years.

The tides

It is of the utmost importance for a cruising skipper to know about the tides, ie. the times of *high* and *low water*. This is because:

■ Some shoal waters are so shallow that they are passable only at high water;
■ Currents along the coast are mainly determined by the tides. The local Sailing Directions will give details of current direction and strength at high and low water. Even in otherwise tideless waters there may be localised currents set up close to a coast which can be put to use (or avoided, if they are setting the wrong way).

In tidal waters you can put the varying depth of water to good use for carrying out repairs or maintenance on the hull. In many parts of the world shipyards are few and far between, and you count yourself lucky to find a tidal range that more or less matches the draught of your yacht; you can then let her dry out, and paint your hull between the tides.

Tides can be calculated in advance using *tide tables.* These are published each year, and the *Admiralty Tide Tables,* Vol. I, covers all European waters including the Mediterranean. The information provided makes it child's-play to find the time, and height, of high and low water:

578

PORTSMOUTH

Lat. 50° 48′ N.   Long. 1° 07′ W

HIGH & LOW WATER
1974

G.M.T. ADD 1 HOUR MARCH 17-OCTOBER 27 FOR B.S.T.

SEPTEMBER				OCTOBER				NOVEMBER				DECEMBER			
Time h. min	Ht. m	Time h. min	Ht. m.	Time h. min	Ht m	Time h. min.	Ht. m.	Time h. min.	Ht. m.	Time h. min	Ht m	Time h. min.	Ht. m	Time h. min.	Ht. m .
1 0415	1.0	16 0411	0.4	1 0415	0.9	16 0433	0.5	1 0453	0.9	16 0020	4.7	1 0510	0.9	16 0044	4.5
1118	4.5	1116	5.0	1115	4.6	1136	4.9	1152	4.7	0529	1.0	1211	4.7	0544	1.1
Su 1630	1.0	M 1633	0.6	Tu 1632	1.0	W 1653	0.6	F 1712	0.8	Sa 1232	4.7	Su 1733	0.7	M 1247	4.5
2324	4.4	2330	4.8	2324	4.5	2353	4.8	—	—	1749	0.9	—	—	1804	0.9
2 0445	0.9	17 0456	0.4	2 0448	0.9	17 0516	0.6	2 0012	4.6	17 0102	4.6	2 0040	4.7	17 0121	4.5
1147	4.5	1201	5.0	1146	4.6	1218	4.9	0531	0.9	0604	1.1	0553	0.9	0618	1.2
M 1702	1.0	Tu 1717	0.5	W 1704	0.9	Th 1734	0.7	Sa 1230	4.7	Su 1308	4.6	M 1255	4.7	Tu 1321	4.4
2354	4.4			2357	4.5	—	—	1750	0.8	1825	1.0	1817	0.7	1838	1.1
3 0516	0.9	18 0015	4.9	3 0521	0.8	18 0039	4.8	3 0055	4.6	18 0142	4.5	3 0129	4.7	18 0157	4.4
1218	4.5	0539	0.5	1219	4.6	0554	0.8	0610	0.9	0639	1.3	0637	0.9	0653	1.3
Tu 1734	0.9	W 1245	5.0	Th 1738	0.8	F 1257	4.8	Su 1311	4.6	M 1343	4.5	Tu 1341	4.6	W 1357	4.3
—	—	1759	0.6	—	—	1813	0.8	1831	0.8	1902	1.2	1904	0.8	1913	1.2
4 0025	4.4	19 0059	4.9	4 0033	4.5	19 0122	4.7	4 0140	4.5	19 0220	4.4	4 0218	4.6	19 0233	4.3
0548	0.8	0620	0.6	0556	0.8	0631	1.0	0650	1.0	0717	1.6	0725	1.1	0732	1.5
W 1251	4.5	Th 1326	4.9	F 1256	4.6	Sa 1334	4.7	M 1355	4.5	Tu 1421	4.3	W 1431	4.5	Th 1434	4.2
1806	0.9	1839	0.7	1813	0.8	1850	1.0	1914	0.9	1942	1.4	1952	0.9	1952	1.4

Extract from Tide Tables

The tide tables do not, of course, list every small port along the coast, but give certain selected ones known as *standard ports.* If you happen to be in one of the relatively few listed standard ports, things could not be easier: you merely look under the date in question, and read off the data you want.

In this instance, low water at Portsmouth on 1 September 1974 was at 0415hr GMT at 1m, with high water at 4.50m at 1118hr GMT. This means that if the chart shows an anchorage with 2m depth, there will be 6.50m of water at high water. Once you have the times and depths for high and low water, it is easy to find the depth of water for any other time, using the following nomogram prepared by Rudolf Braren:

188

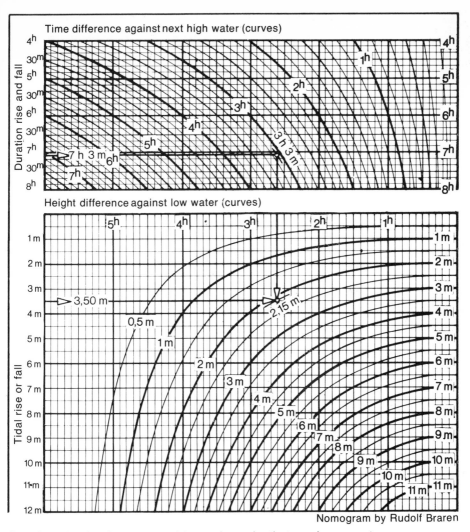

Time difference against next high water (curves)

Height difference against low water (curves)

Nomogram by Rudolf Braren

So what depth of water would you have in that anchorage at Portsmouth on 1 September 1974 at 0815hr GMT?

Entry in Tables:		Answer	
1. Duration of mean	11hr 18min	Height difference	
rise	− 04hr 15min	to low water	2.15m
	7hr 03min	Low water	+ 1.00m
2. Time difference to	11hr 18min	Chart datum	+ 2.00m
next high water	− 8hr 15min		5.15m
	3hr 03min		
3. Tidal rise	4.50m		
	− 1.00m		
	3.50m		

Tide curves are seldom so atypical that this nomogram (which is based on a regular curve) cannot be used. If this should be so, a curve will be found in the tide tables themselves from which the depth of water at any time can be found.

Naturally one is not always lucky enough to be in one of the standard ports for which the tables give exact figures. The tables however include a list of *secondary ports*, and show by how much the figures for these differ from the standard ports. If the port you are in is not in the tide tables at all, take the figures for the nearest secondary port.

The data given in tide tables relate to normal conditions; they may differ substantially in a storm. Calculations to the nearest few centimetres are not advisable in any case, and a safety margin of about 20cm should always be allowed.

Navigation

Navigation within sight of land

The whole art of navigation consists of finding the course that has to be steered to bring the boat to its destination safely and by the shortest path. To do this, you need to know your position at any given time as accurately as possible.

A position is always quoted as latitude followed by longitude; to make this possible, the globe has been covered with an imaginary network of coordinates.

Lines of latitude and longitude – the ship's position is 40° 20'N, 90°40'E.

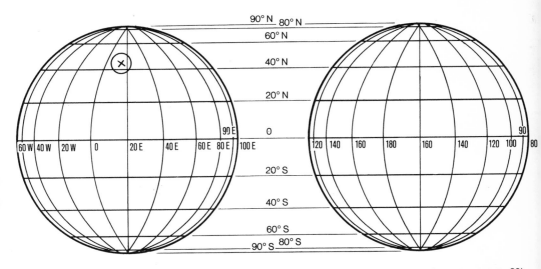

Degrees of latitude are measured northwards and southwards of the equator (0°), eg. '44°N' or '56°S'. The two poles are thus 90°.

Degrees of longitude are measured from the zero meridian, which runs north-south through Greenwich, and numbered east or west from this. Unlike latitude degrees, however, they go up to 180° of longitude, which runs north-south in the neighbourhood of Fiji. Longitude is quoted as, for instance, '44°W' or '166°E'.

A ship's position is measured on the chart using dividers, by simply taking the distance from its position to the nearest numbered degree of latitude in the dividers, and then reading off the

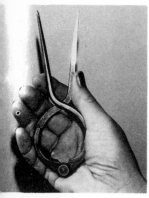

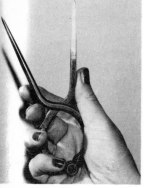

These dividers can be adjusted with one hand (leaving the other one to hold on with!)

latitude from the scale on the right or lefthand of the chart; longitude is likewise read off along the top or bottom edge. Because of the risk of injury, and because your charts would end up ripped to shreds, never use ordinary schoolboy's compasses. There are special chart dividers, and I prefer the kind illustrated here which can be adjusted with one hand while the boat is rolling about. Never leave them lying on the chart table – as the boat heels they can easily go flying across the cabin and do someone an injury!

Exercise 1

What are the coordinates of the following five points on the accompanying exercise chart (in a pocket inside the back cover)?

(a) beacon with a range of 17 nautical miles at Capo Circeo

(b) aircraft radio-beacon on the island of Ponza

(c) summit of Vesuvius

(d) flashing light with a range of 9 nautical miles at the mouth of the River Volturno

(e) red flashing light with a range of 7 nautical miles at Amalfi

(Answers to the exercises are given on page 305ff.)

Each degree of latitude is exactly 60 nautical miles, so every minute of latitude is equal to one mile. A nautical, or sea mile is 6080ft (longer than a land mile); all navigation is done exclusively in nautical miles (nm). If a vessel covers 1nm an hour, it is said to be doing 1 knot. If you want to measure distances on a chart, there is no need to go all over it hunting for the scale – just take the distance in your dividers and then lay these against the latitude scale along the right hand or left hand edge of the chart to get a direct reading of the distance.

Important! Only *latitude* minutes are a nautical mile long: *never* use the longitude degree scale at the top and bottom for measuring distance.

To transfer the spherical shape of the earth to a flat chart, a certain amount of juggling has had to be done, with the result that on the chart (though not in reality) the width of a degree of latitude increases as you get nearer to the pole. For this reason, distances should be measured against the latitude scale as near level with your position as possible. On ordinary coastal charts the disparity is scarcely noticeable, but on small-scale passage charts covering a wider area it would be quite possible for errors to creep in.

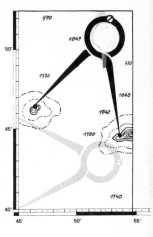

Exercise 2

How many miles is it from the end of the jetty at Terracina (41°17.0′N 13°15.6′E) to Punta Imperatore (40°42.6′N 13°51.2′E)?

The compass

Every cruising yacht must carry at least one compass. The compass card, graduated from 0 to 360, is in fact a freely-rotating magnetic needle, which as we know from our physics lessons always swings to point north. On yachts it is essential for this compass card to move with as little friction as possible so that it can

Left: spherical-bowl compass alongside companionway – cannot be used for taking bearings.

Centre: fully-gimballed Sestrel-Moore compass fitted at eye level, available with sighting attachment.

Right: spherical compass at the wheel – watch out for deviation.

swing to point north continuously while the boat is rolling about. This is best achieved by having a spherical bowl filled with fluid to give a damping effect, or by having the compass fully gimballed.

Compass variation

Though we said a moment ago that the compass needle points north, this is not entirely true. The earth's magnetic field has its own north and south poles, and these do not coincide exactly with the earth's poles. Magnetic lines of force run – not in straight lines – between these magnetic poles, and the compass needle (or north-south axis of the compass card) always swings to be parallel to

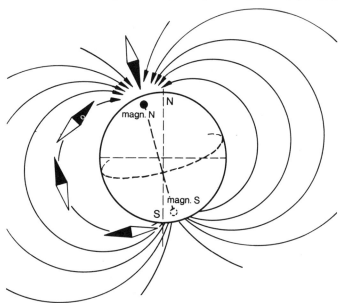

The compass needle does not point to true north, but lines itself up parallel to the lines of magnetic force.

them. So it does not, strictly, point north. The amount by which the compass differs from geographical north is known to sailors as 'variation', and on every chart this is indicated as 'westerly' (with a minus sign) or 'easterly' (plus sign).

Exercise 3

How great was the variation in 1975 for the Bay of Naples, making allowance for annual change?

To find out what course the helmsman needs to steer from one point to another, you first measure the *chart course*, or *true course*. For this you need a *triangular protractor*, the long edge of which is

194

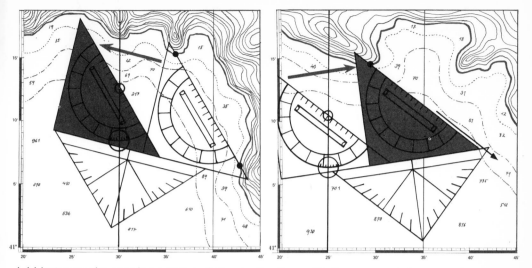

laid between the starting point and the destination, with the apex
pointing towards you if possible. A second triangular protractor is
then placed against the short side of the first, and the latter is slid
along until the zero point of the protractor comes over any meridian
(printed line of longitude). The true course can then be read off
where the meridian cuts the protractor scale; two courses are possible, depending on which direction you want to take. If you need to
plot a given true course on the chart, the whole procedure is simply
carried out in reverse – the protractor is placed with the zero point
on a meridian and with the latter cutting the protractor scale at the
required angle, and is then slid along another protractor until its
long side lines up with your point of departure.

Left: measuring a true
course:
1. place long side of
triangular protractor
against both points – 2.
using another protractor,
shift along until protractor
zero point comes over a meridian
(degree of longitude), then
read off course (large
circle).

Right: plotting a course:
1. place protractor on chart
with zero point and desired
course on a meridian – 2.
shift protractor along,
using another protractor,
until long side cuts the
point of departure – 3.
draw in course line.

At first you may be tempted to measure or draw a course using
just one triangular protractor; this is admittedly possible if the protractor is slid across the chart very carefully and patiently, but it
invites errors and takes longer to do.

Apart from triangular protractors there are other instruments for
laying off a course, such as parallel-rules (two linked rules which
are 'walked' across the chart); but two protractors, used as
described, are less likely to slip inadvertently and cause error. You
have now measured the true course on the chart between starting
point and destination; but because of variation you cannot steer
this course on the compass without applying a correction. Here I do
urge you not to bother your head too much about the mathematics
of the whole business; treat it as a purely mechanical operation, by
following this simple rule generally applicable to navigation:

This rule of thumb should be among every navigator's mental 'tools'. There are other mnemonics, but this is simple to remember. If, to take an example, the true (or chart) course is 261° and the variation is 11.2°W, the magnetic course will then be:

Course	261° T
Var.	11.2° W
	————
Course	272.2° M

Exercise 4

What magnetic course should be steered in 1975, from Capo Tiberio (40°33′.5N 14°14′.7E) to Capo Miseno (40°46′.6N 14°05′.4E)?

Exercise 5

What will be our position at 0900hr if we left Punta Madonna (40°53′.7N 12°58′.2E) at 0800hr sailing a compass course of 074° at 5 knots?

Deviation

Your compass is not only governed by the earth's magnetic field, which is a very strong one, but is also affected by any metal in its immediate vicinity. This effect is called *deviation* and will naturally be much greater in a steel-hulled yacht than in a GRP hull. Even in the latter there may be considerable deviation, however, if the compass is sited near the engine or alongside electronic gear. Metal objects in the helmsman's pocket can also cause deviation. Buying a very expensive compass will do nothing to guard against this deviation, even though some advertisers suggest it will.

A compass must not be used until its deviation has been measured exactly, so that it can (like variation) be taken into account when converting a true to a compass course or vice versa. Deviation is not a constant value: it alters *depending on which way the boat is pointing*. For this reason, it has to be measured for each heading and the results recorded on a *deviation card*. All you need for 'swinging the compass' is a quiet anchorage and a dinghy for turning the yacht round, a distant landmark on which to take bearings, and a sighting attachment on the compass with which you can take a bearing on this landmark. If you have a spherical-bowl compass, you will need a pelorus (see next page).

The mnemonic when converting *magnetic* to *compass* is:

'deviation west compass best
deviation east compass least'

Deviation card To prepare one for your own yacht, you swing her in a circle round her anchor, using a dinghy attached to the stern. One man watches the compass heading, and calls out 'now!' every 10°; a second man, using the sighting attachment on the compass, takes a bearing on the landmark. If an occasional bearing is missed because the mast or other obstruction is in the way this does not matter greatly: you begin by plotting a deviation curve, which will allow any missing readings to be interpolated. The deviation for each bearing is then worked out with the following simple formula:

Ideal position for the compass – no pelorus needed.

Chart (true) bearing of landmark
± variation
± compass bearing

= deviation

The calculated deviation values can then be plotted as a curve on the grid shown here; it will be easy to reconstruct any bearings that were missed out, and any mistakes will be obvious at once.

The curve is drawn mainly to detect measurement errors or to be able to interpolate missing bearings.

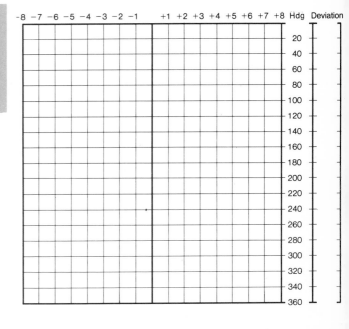

Exercise 6

Our yacht is lying to a buoy in the harbour entrance at Castellamare at 40°41′.8N, 14°28′.4E. Having swung the yacht once, taking bearings on the summit of Vesuvius every 10° (as possible), our notepad lists the following values:

Bearing of Vesuvius by chart 344° T
var   9° W
353° M

Yachts Head Compass	Bearing Compass	Magnetic Bearing	Dev	Yachts Head Compass	Bearing Compass	Magnetic Bearing	Dev
010°	353°	351°	2°E	190°	353°	355°	2°W
020°	353°	350°	3°E	200°	353°	350°	3°E
030°	353°	350°	3°E	210°	353°	349°	4°E
040°	353°	349°	4°E	220°	353°	348°	5°E
050°	353°	349°	4°E	230°	353°	347°	6°E
060°	353°	353°	0°	240°	353°	348°	5°E
070°	353°	Miss	—	250°	353°	349°	4°E
080°	353°	351°	2°E	260°	353°	350°	3°E
090°	353°	352°	1°E	270°	353°	353°	0°
100°	353°	353°	0°	280°	353°	354°	1°W
110°	353°	354°	1°W	290°	353°	355°	2°W
120°	353°	354°	1°W	300°	353°	355°	2°W
130°	353°	355°	2°W	310°	353°	356°	3°W
140°	353°	355°	2°W	320°	353°	356°	3°W
150°	353°	354°	1°W	330°	353°	356°	3°W
160°	353°	354°	1°W	340°	353°	355°	2°W
170°	353°	353°	0°	350°	353°	Miss	—
180°	353°	352°	1°E	360°	353°	352°	1°E

What shape is the deviation curve? and what deviation card would be obtained from the above figures?

If it is impossible to take a bearing direct from your compass (because it is of the spherical type, or inconveniently positioned) you will have to use a *pelorus*, a kind of dummy compass. At the moment of taking the bearing, the compass heading has to be noted. To arrive at the compass bearing, the simple formula is:

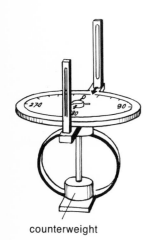

counterweight

bearing + compass heading = compass bearing
(if over 360°, take 360 away)

198

If the deviation values are all below 15°, the yacht's compass can be used in conjunction with the deviation card. Above 15°, compensation will be needed (usual with a steel hull) and this must be left to an expert. If a compass is well installed in a GRP yacht, the deviation should not be much over 5°. Deviation alters from time to time, and needs checking at the start of each season. When chartering a yacht, never start the voyage without first checking the deviation.

When calculating the true or compass course, deviation must be allowed for just like variation, using the rule above.

On GRP boats a *hand-bearing compass* can be used on deck at any time to fix your position without worrying about deviation, because this (held up high) will be far enough away from anything causing a deflection. An extremely handy and parallax-free little hand-bearing compass, much praised in the trade press, is the Mini-compass (see illustration), which can be worn hanging round the neck. People who wear spectacles must be careful, because many of the frames can cause deviation! Don't use a hand-bearing compass near the main compass, which is itself a strong magnet.

Mini Compass with built-in Beta-light. Held close to the eye when sighting.

Exercise 7

Having worked out our deviation card (Exercise 6), we want to motor from Castellamare di Stabia (40°42′.4N 14°28′.4E) to Punta Sn Pancrazio (40°42′.0N 13°57′.3E) on the south foreland of Ischia. What compass course do we give the helmsman to steer?

Leeway

It will be obvious that especially when on the wind the yacht will not only travel in the direction of her course, but also make a certain amount of sideways movement, or *leeway*. When plotting a course allowance has to be made for this in order to steer a course that will bring the boat to its destination. Leeway cannot be measured, only estimated by comparing the course through the water with the direction of the boat's wake.

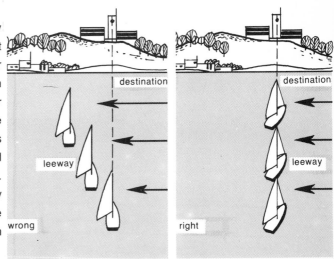

Typical leeway figures, based on experience, might be:

	Moderate Sea	Bad Weather
close/hauled	10°	20° or more
reaching	5°	10°
running	0°	0°

To incorporate leeway in your course corrections, it should be given a sign:

Leeway setting the boat to starboard: +
Leeway setting the boat to port: −

You therefore talk not about 5° leeway, only about a leeway of +5° or −5°.

Exercise 8

With a Force 2 blowing from North-East, we want to sail from Punta St Imperatore (40°42'.6N 13°51'.2E) to Punta dell'Arco (40°47'.0N 13°24'.6E) on the south foreland of Ventotene. What compass course must be steered allowing for variation, deviation and leeway?

Fixing the ship's position

This is invariably found from the point of intersection of two or more *position lines.*

Position lines

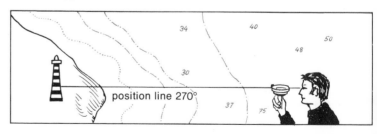

position line 270°

A position line (PL) is quite simply a line on which we are located. If, for example, we take a bearing on a lighthouse at 270° (true) then we are somewhere along the line running 270° towards the lighthouse on the chart, and this is a position line. If there is a second PL cutting the 270° bearing line, our position will be exactly where they cross, since we are then on two PLs at the same time.

The art of navigation lies in obtaining the best possible position lines; any kind of PL can be combined with any other, so long as they make an angle of more than 20°.

Position lines need not necessarily be straight lines. If we know we are 6 miles away from a certain point, our PL will be a circle of 6 miles radius centred on that point. If we are closing a coast and the echo-sounder shows exactly 20m, our PL may take a very irregular shape, that of the 20m line on the chart.

Conscientious navigators always try to pinpoint their position as accurately as possible, so they will hardly ever be satisfied with only two PLs but will try to obtain three or even four. In practice the 'intersection point' is then always a polygon, and the larger this is the more doubtful we should be of the fix. Not all PLs are equally effective; some are so fraught with uncertainty (estimated distance, for example) that it would be foolish to use them if it is possible to get something more reliable.

Normally, a navigator on a yacht will work with the following kinds of position line:

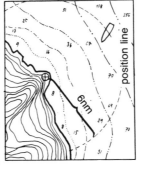
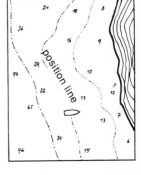

Left: if the distance-off is known, the PL is a circle.

Right: 20m line as a PL, only suitable with steeply rising bottom.

Course sailed (straight line)

In waters where there is no tidal stream, and under engine, this serves quite well; but as soon as imprecise factors such as leeway, tidal drift and uncertain steering in a rough sea are involved, better kinds of position line should be looked for. If you do use the course sailed, apply it with a proper amount of caution.

Distance made good (circle round the last known position)

This, too, I use only reluctantly because it always involves measurement inaccuracy and can be affected by tides or currents. A patent log (a spinning vane towed at the end of a line and driving a counter) gives about 5 per cent error. Electronic logs will – if properly adjusted – measure accurate to 1 per cent or better, but only give 'distance through the water'; no log measures 'distance over the ground' – so watch out if there is a current.

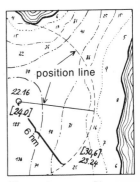

The most common PLs: course sailed and distance made good – the dead-reckoning position, usually quite inaccurate.

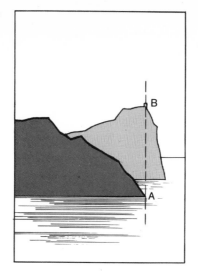

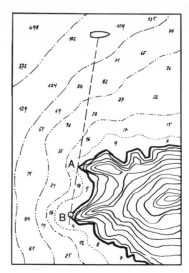

Colour plate: After making landfall: the skipper looks for an anchorage in calm water, where he will find old and new friends.

No instruments needed, you just wait until two landmarks line up.

Steering-compass bearing (straight line)

After taking account of deviation (not experienced with hand-bearing compasses on a GRP boat) and variation, this is very satisfactory in calm weather; if the boat is pitching about a lot there can easily be measurement error of 10° or more. In that case it is best to steer straight towards the object on which you want a bearing for a minute or two, and use the compass heading as the bearing.

Range (circle around the object on which a bearing is taken)

For this accurate PL you need a sextant and must know the height of the object above sea level (you can get this from the chart, *Pilot* or *List of Lights*).

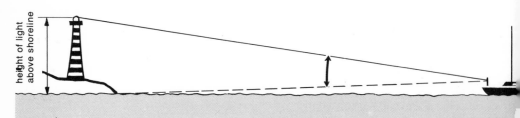

The distance in nautical miles is calculated from the following formula:

$$\frac{13 \times \text{height of light above sea level}}{7 \times \text{angle in minutes}} \quad \text{in metres}$$

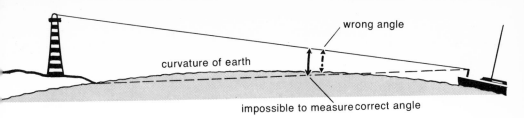

wrong angle

curvature of earth

impossible to measure correct angle

If you are more than 2½ miles from the object, this method cannot be used because the foot of the object will already be hidden by the dip of the horizon. If in doubt, take a measurement but use it only if the distance works out as under 2½ miles.

Horizontal angle (circle running through two objects)
Another very accurate position line. Using a sextant (the cheap plastic

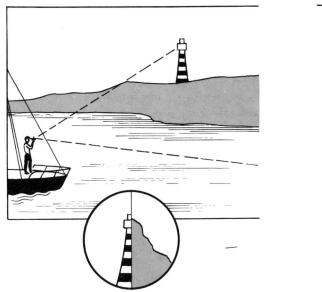

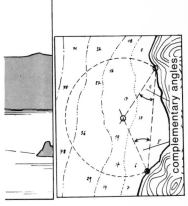

The two objects are superimposed in the sextant, and the complementary angle at the object drawn towards the yacht's position (a minus complementary angle must be drawn away from the yacht's position)

kind is quite adequate for this) measure the angle between two objects and then construct the centre point of the circle running through the two objects using the complementary angle (90° − measured angle).

Sounding (irregular line)
Caution! To be used only when the bottom has a marked 'shape'. Best used only with an echo-sounder (making allowance for state of tide and location of the transducer on the hull).

Radio DF bearing (straight line)
Caution! Usually subject to a lot of inaccuracy (see under radio direction-finding, page 212).

205

Consol bearing (straight line)

Comparatively high accuracy at sea, diminishing with distance from the Consol beacon.

Astronomical position line (straight line)

Not to be relied on, even under the most favourable conditions, as being accurate to more than 2nm. This is more than adequate out at sea, but closer inshore it is better to use a 'terrestrial' PL.

Running fix

If there is only one suitable object on which to take a bearing, and you are sailing past it, take two bearings on it. The PL resulting from the first

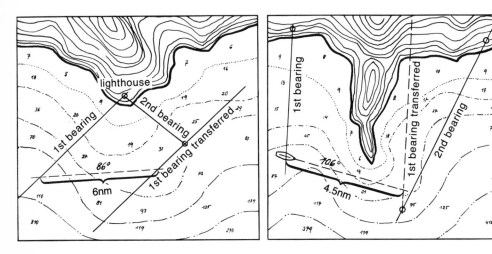

Left: a fix from two bearings on a single landmark.

Right: if the first landmark is later hidden from sight, the bearing PL can still be transferred and combined with a second bearing.

bearing is then simply shifted along the true course on the chart by the amount of the distance made good. A fix obtained in this way is subject to all the cumulative inaccuracy of log, steering error, leeway and tidal or current drift. Running fixes are frequently used in astronomical navigation.

Hints for chart work:

- use only a 2B pencil, and always rub out old course lines;
- have only one chart on the table at a time; otherwise there is a risk of reading off your distances from the one underneath;
- it should be possible to reconstruct every passage from the chart, so enter your course lines on the chart, and note the log reading in square brackets at each fix, with the time. Never enter a *compass* course on the chart – you are navigating 'true' throughout.

At about 0430hr, log reading 44.37, the skipper measures the height **Exercise 9**
above sea level of the light at Punta Imperatore and finds a sextant
angle of 2°25′. A bearing taken with the steering compass, which has
just been used for steering a course of 300°, shows 114°. What is the
ship's position? (Write in the log reading in square brackets, and the
time, on the chart.)

After obtaining his exact position, the skipper then beats into the wind **Exercise 10**
(ENE, F2), and can just lay 020° on the compass. What is the dead-
reckoning position at 0525hr with a log reading of 49.47?

To check the position, the horizontal angle between Punta Imperatore **Exercise 11**
(40°42′.6N 13°51′.2E) and a light on Capo Miseno (40°46′.6N
14°05′.4E just visible due east is measured and found to be 65°, while a
flashing light on the north-east foreland at Porto D'Ischia (40°44′.9N
13°56′.8E) bears 125°C. Does this fix match the position found in Exercise 10?

The course of 020°C (Exercise 10) continues to be held. At log reading **Exercise 12**
53.25 the light at Capo Miseno becomes hidden. At 0716hr, log reading
59.75, the flashing light at the mouth of the River Volturno (41°01′.1N
13°55′.6E) bears 067°C with a hand-bearing compass (nil deviation).
What is the yacht's position by running fix using the fix obtained at
0525hr (Exercise 11) as the starting fix.

At 0830hr, log reading 67.01, the church of San Vito is dead ahead, with **Exercise 13**
the steering compass showing 010°. The echo-sounder, the transducer
of which is 1m below the waterline, reads 19m. Position?

At 1900hr, log reading 67.01, we weigh anchor and steer a compass **Exercise 14**
course of 264° under engine towards the northern tip of Zannone.
a) what is the DR position at 2400hr, log reading 91.87?
b) what has been our speed?

With a compass heading of 270°, the pelorus gives bearings of 330° **Exercise 15**
for the light at Zannone, 58° for Capo Circeo, and 164° for Gaeta St
Erasmo. What is the actual position at 2400hr?

Navigation in tidal waters

Tidal flow causes particular difficulties, because streams can seldom be measured exactly; either you take what the tidal atlas gives as the direction and strength in normal conditions, or you work it out for yourself. To do this, you mark on the chart where you ought to be (on the basis of distance made good and your course) were there no tidal stream, and your actual position. To find the latter, you need PLs obtained without using the course and distance made good. From the tidal drift you can then plot or calculate its rate over one hour.

At 0402 hr the skipper has a DR position, from course sailed and distance made good; at the same time he gets a 'definite' position from two landmark bearings (a 'fix'). The difference between the DR position and the fix is the drift in 111 minutes. After conversion to 1 hour, the tide triangle can be drawn, and will show all values per hour.

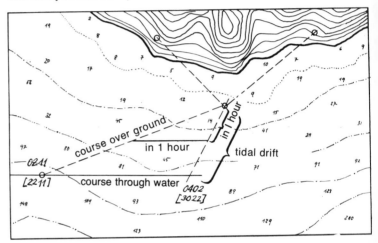

If you now want to steer towards a point so that, with a stream running, you get there by the shortest – and fastest – route, you have to select a 'course through the water' which will take·you to the destination on the course drawn on the chart between point of

A tide triangle should always be drawn only from 2 fixes (shown on chart as small circles) and a DR position. The desired course over the ground taking account of tidal drift is achieved only if tide direction and rate stay the same and the expected speed proves correct. But in narrows like this the stream will probably change.

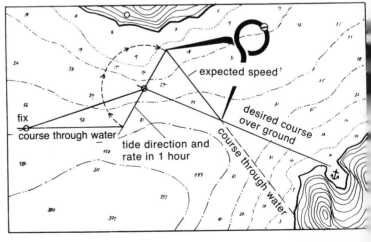

208

departure and point of arrival in spite of the drift. This is simple to do on the chart; all you have to do is to draw in the stream, with its direction and rate, from the point of departure, take your expected speed over one hour in the dividers, and strike an arc on the chart course line from the end of the tide arrow.

From this *tide triangle* you can now read off:
- the probable speed over the ground;
- the course through the water, to which you have only to apply deviation and variation in order to arrive at the compass course you need.

How much was the tidal drift over 5 hours?	**Exercise 16**
Strength and direction of the stream?	**Exercise 17**
The skipper now wants to steer for Punta Madonna on Ponza. What is the true course?	**Exercise 18**
What compass course should be steered, with an expected speed of 6 knots, if Punta Madonna is to be reached by the shorter path in spite of the tide (use the tide triangle!)?	**Exercise 19**
a) What will be the speed over the ground? b) What is the estimated time of arrival at Punta Madonna?	**Exercise 20**

Radio direction finding

DF Receivers

Everyone will have noticed when using a transistor radio that reception is better or worse depending on which way round you hold it. This is because the built-in antenna is *directional*. If reception is poor, you can often improve it by turning the set about a vertical axis. Assuming that the signal comes from a particular direction, the music is obviously loudest when the antenna is positioned so that it picks up a maximum of energy from the transmitter: if you then turn the set through 90°, you find the point of minimum signal or 'aural null'.

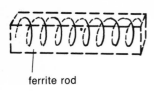

ferrite rod

If the antenna is positioned so that a maximum of radio waves pass through it, the transmitter lies in the plane of the loop. A ferrite rod antenna really comprises several 'loop antennae' one behind the other.

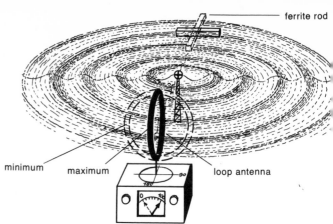

ferrite rod

minimum   maximum   loop antenna

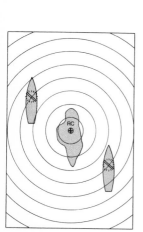

Same bearing twice – but it is unclear whether the island lies to port or to starboard.

This effect is used for radio direction-finding, or RDF, and the DF sets used on yachts are in fact perfectly normal radio receivers that are however able to receive the special LW frequencies used by DF beacons. Ordinary radio shops will of course also have sets covering this 'navigation band'. The really important item in the whole set-up is the DF antenna: with this you do rather more efficiently what you were doing before by rotating your little £10 transistor set. But now the set stays still, and you rotate just the directional antenna; this is the principle used with most yacht DF sets, though the way bearings are taken differs somewhat from the rather primitive method of turning a transistor radio to and fro. First of all, it is rather difficult to tell exactly at which antenna setting the sound is loudest (ie. the set is receiving a maximum of signal energy). It is much simpler to find the point of minimum energy. One also finds that when rotated through 360°, the antenna picks up not just one maximum and minimum, but two, and with a simple DF receiver you still need to know whether the DF beacon is in front or behind you. Better DF sets have an optical device with a needle to indicate the signal maximum, while top-class DF receivers even tell you which of the two minima is the one you want.

The simplest stations to take a radio bearing on are those which, like broadcast stations, are permanently switched on and transmit a sound. With these you do not have to wait until you hear a tone; even in the intervening pauses bearings can be taken on the beacon using the receiver's meter needle. If the DF antenna is set to receive an energy maximum, the needle will (depending on the nearness and strength of the beacon) give a full-scale deflection, falling back almost to zero at the minimum-signal antenna setting.

For those sets which do not have a built-in compass, the antenna needs to be graduated, with 0° straight ahead just as with a pelorus. Taking a bearing with a radio DF set is similar to taking an optical bearing. Obviously we cannot read off the compass bearing of the transmitter station direct from the DF antenna, and a compass course has to be used in our calculations. Remember: when working with a pelorus, you need merely to add the pelorus bearing to the compass heading to get the compass bearing. If this gives you more than 360°, you subtract it instead.

RDF position line

From the calculation viewpoint, therefore, a relative RDF bearing is treated in just the same way as a pelorus bearing. As with the pelorus, you must later allow for compass deviation on the course being steered at the time because, depending on magnetic deviation, the compass shows a slightly wrong reading on every heading. Moreover, variation must be allowed for as in all compass work. So a radio bearing will be converted into the true bearing of the radio beacon as shown here (remembering our rule on signs – from wrong to true, etc.). Your radio bearing is the one subject to errors, and hence wrong. Only true bearings are entered on the chart.

Radio beacons

The transmitters on which bearings are taken, which of course send no spoken signals, need to be identified so that their position can be found on the chart and the bearing plotted. To do this you will need certain reference material, such as the *Admiralty List of Radio Signals*, *Vol. 2*; this lists practically all the marine radio beacons in the world, giving their mode of transmission (A1, A2 or A3, which can usually be selected on the RDF set), their position and their identification signals.

The identification is a series of letters in Morse designed to ensure that you can recognise the beacon. For this it is not necessary to know Morse well, as identifications are sent so slowly that even someone totally unskilled will be able to decipher them after a minute or two, using a Morse code table (given in the *List of Radio Signals, Reed's Nautical Almanac* and elsewhere).

Depending on the cruising ground, you find that the coasts may be poorly or well-provided with radio beacons; in northern waters, for instance, you could navigate by radio beacons alone if you wanted to. But there is hardly any area where you would be unable to take a bearing on two or three beacons and use the PLs thus obtained in just the same way as landmark position lines. Things have been made easy for shipping by arranging for several beacons that are specially well sited for taking fixes to be all grouped on the same frequency. For example Beacon A transmits on a given frequency for 2 minutes, and then makes way for Beacon B which sends out its identification and a long note for 2 minutes, in turn handing over to Beacon C to complete the 6-minute cycle. The advantage is self-evident – you need to tune to only one frequency, and can then take three different bearings on this same frequency.

Though our home waters are extraordinarily well supplied with marine radio beacons, you find very few operating in the Mediterranean, for example. A lot of them are switched on only in fog or poor visibility, and some in fact will transmit only if you call them up by radio and ask for a transmission. Outside Europe there are vast areas with no marine radio beacons at all, because it would simply not be worth the expense of installing a beacon for the handful of ships that pass that way. It is however then possible to get help elsewhere – from *aircraft radio beacons*. The *List of Radio Signals* and *Reed's Nautical Almanac* contain a selected list of aircraft radio beacons that are of interest to shipping. Before using one of these beacons you should however make sure that it is not sited too far inland, otherwise there are likely to be substantial errors. In many yachtsmen's experience aircraft beacons on the coast are every bit as useful as a marine radio beacon; and they are to be found all over the world, since air traffic nowadays flies over the most remote regions.

The *List of Radio Signals, Vol. 2,* has another very useful feature – an alphabetical list of beacon identifications. I have very often heard an identification I did not recognise, and the beacon concerned would have been no help to me had I been unable to tell which station was involved.

Take care with RDF bearings

From what has been said up to now, radio DF sounds an ideal arrangement: you sit down below in the dry, and whatever the visibility you can take bearings at any time to fix your position. If you are tempted to think this way, let me offer the direst warnings! Radio bearings are hedged about with so many uncertainties that in my experience RDF is the least reliable of all navigational aids.

First of all, you cannot take bearings *at twilight*, even in an emergency. Because of the interaction of ground waves and sky waves, a radio bearing can, given the worst circumstances, be up to 90° out due to twilight effect! It is of course equally possible to get a correct bearing, but with the normal rotating ferrite antenna it is impossible to tell which is which. Many experienced yachtsmen also distrust *night effect,* though this ought not to occur as often. For safety's sake I would go so far as to say that at night, too, you should, if you have to take a radio bearing, use it with caution.

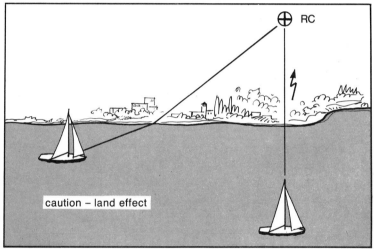

caution – land effect

Land effect is least when the coast is at right angles to the position line.

Even under normal circumstances a radio bearing is subject to a lot of inaccuracy. A literally incalculable factor is *land effect*, which produces a greater or lesser amount of refraction as a radio wave passes from above land to above water. This is felt particularly if we use an RDF position line that runs almost parallel to the coastline, while it is least when the PL is at right angles to the coast.

Quadrantal error

The biggest inaccuracies come from distortion of the radio wave by metal parts on the yacht (especially the rigging) and this again has to be set out in a quadrantal error card. This is done in just the same way as plotting the compass deviation on various headings. On a GRP-hulled yacht measuring the quadrantal error is indeed almost more important than preparing a compass deviation card, because it can amount to 10° or more. To find quadrantal error we take a bearing on the beacon (usually visually recognisable from far off by its tall masts) with a pelorus and with the DF set at the same time, while swinging the boat. The difference between the two bearings is then a direct value for quadrantal error. A typical quadrantal error curve will look like this:

Additional correction according to heading and angle of heel (Ramert's table) is about the same for all yachts.

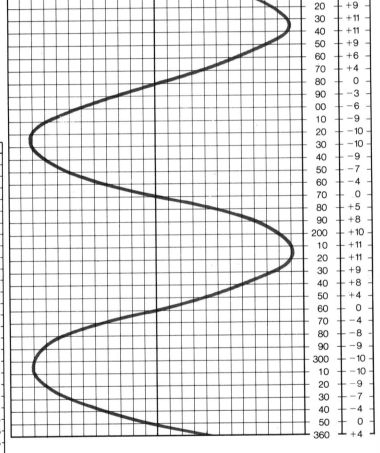

	heeling correction			
f	10°	20°	30°	40°
10	0	-0,5	-1,5	-2,5
20	-0,5	-1	-2,5	-4
30	-0,5	-1,5	-3,5	-6
40	-0,5	-2	-4	-7
50	-0,5	-2	-4	-7,5
60	-0,5	-1,5	-3,5	-6,5
70	0	-1	-2,5	-5,5
80	0	-0,5	-1	-3
90	0	0	0	0
100	0	+0,5	+1	+3
110	0	+1	+2,5	+5,5
120	+0,5	+1,5	+3,5	+6,5
130	+0,5	+2	+4	+7,5
140	+0,5	+2	+4	+7
150	+0,5	+1,5	+3,5	+6
160	+0,5	+1	+2,5	+4
170	0	+0,5	+1,5	+2,5
180	0	0	0	0
190	0	-0,5	-1,5	-2,5
200	-0,5	-1	-2,5	-4
210	-0,5	-1,5	-3,5	-6
220	-0,5	-2	-4	-7
230	-0,5	-2	-4	-7,5
240	-0,5	-1,5	-3,5	-6,5
250	0	-1	-2,5	-5,5
260	0	-0,5	-1	-3
270	0	0	0	0
280	0	+0,5	+1	+3
290	0	+1	+2,5	+5,5
300	+0,5	+1,5	+3,5	+6,5
310	+0,5	+2	+4	+7,5
320	+0,5	+2	+4	+7
330	+0,5	+1,5	+3,5	+6
340	+0,5	+1	+2,5	+4
350	0	+0,5	+1,5	+2,5
360	0	0	0	0

Unfortunately this is not the end of the problem. Any metal parts moved to somewhere on the boat other than exactly where they were when the quadrantal error was being measured (eg. aluminium spinnaker poles and booms) will invalidate the quadrantal error card. The quadrantal error also changes when the yacht heels – which is fairly often with a sail boat!

214

This particular source of error can however easily be allowed for using the table produced by Ramert and reproduced on page 214.

Quadrantal error on *Carina III* (masthead)

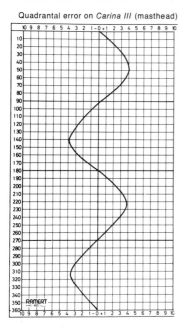

Quadrantal error on *Saudade II*

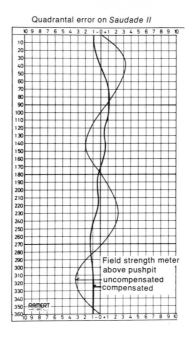

Field strength meter above pushpit
uncompensated
compensated

Quadrantal error curves for two well known yachts. *Left:* the masthead is not, as many believe, the ideal place for the DF antenna.

Right: better results are obtained above the pushpit, especially when quadrantal error is compensated (this must be done by an expert).

The conversion, mentioned a moment ago, of the bearing obtained with the DF set into a true bearing finally takes the following form:

	radio bearing
±	quadrantal error
(±	heeling error if any)
+	compass heading
±	deviation
±	variation
=	true bearing
	(=position line)

One more thing about DF sets that have to be operated handheld, usually in combination with a bearing compass: they are *not* suitable for accurate position fixing on a yacht. They suffer not only from the errors just discussed, but also from totally undeterminable inaccuracies stemming from the fact first that the compass will have a certain deviation that cannot be shown in a deviation card,

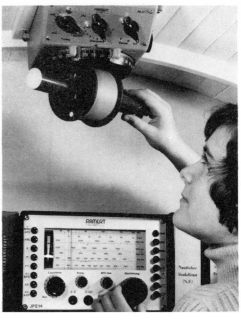

Top left: DF antenna on receiver;
right: well-proven Ramert set-up with DF antenna under the cabin roof;

bottom left: automatic DF set – the three knobs are used to set the frequency, and the needle swings to the bearing.

and secondly that quadrantal error is being ignored. Any portable DF set must therefore be assumed to have an unknown error of 20° or more.

With RDF surrounded with so many ifs and buts, one obviously starts to wonder whether it is worth buying such an expensive piece of gear. The answer is a very definite yes: if I am wandering about in thick fog, or have 10/10 cloud and no sight of land, I would much sooner have a poor position line than none at all. All I would stress is never to overestimate the quality of a radio bearing.

Exercise 21

At 0200hr a radio bearing shows the Ponza aircraft beacon bearing 039°, while the compass heading is 217°.

a) what is the true bearing of the beacon? (use the quadrantal error card on page 214)

b) why must this bearing be used with caution?

Consol beacons

One of the big advantages of Consol bearings is that you can use a simple radio set and do not need special antennae. The set needs to cover frequencies from 250 to 370kHz, and have an automatic volume control (AVC) that can be switched out, and a beat-frequency oscillator (BFO). The main feature of the Consol that matters to us is that a group of transmitters send out Morse dots and dashes, and depending on which sector around the Consol beacon we happen to be in we start by hearing either dots or dashes – dots in what is called an A-sector, dashes in a B-sector.

A transmission lasts for 30 seconds, and goes like this: first

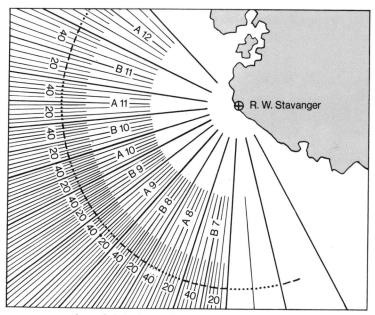

Simplified diagram of Consol chart; the dots or dashes are counted in each sector, working clockwise.

comes a series of dots (meaning an A-sector) which then become weaker and change to a constant note, or equisignal. This equisignal becomes louder and then changes to a series of dashes. In all, 60 symbols are sent out during each cycle, and what one then needs to know is how many dots and how many dashes were transmitted on the position line on which the boat is located. It is impossible to count the dots and dashes exactly, because the first set change into the constant note and one cannot tell by ear how many dots merged into the equisignal. If, in our example, there were 14 dots, the equisignal and finally 42 dashes, we will have made out 56 symbols; this means that 4 were lost in the equisignal, since 60 were transmitted. Halving this number, we have to add two symbols to each of the batches of dots and dashes counted. In the example, we were in an A-sector, and had 14 + 2 = 16 dots. For plotting we need a Consol chart, where we look in the A-sector and find the position line for 16 dots.

This takes only a few seconds. Unhappily Consol beacon navigation is of limited use, despite the two big European beacons at Stavanger and at Ploneis in Brittany, because these can really be picked up well only in the North Sea and North Atlantic. In the Baltic, land effect makes Consol navigation unreliable, and it is similarly unusable in the Mediterranean.

This is a great pity, because (unlike ordinary RDF) Consol is very precise. Admittedly there is still twilight and night effect to contend with so that bearings cannot be taken at these times, but the accuracy is such that at 400 miles range the maximum error likely is about 12 miles – and an ordinary radio bearing, even taken on a very strong transmitter, could never equal that.

Astronomical navigation

Anyone who can do the following sum will be capable of doing astronomical navigation calculations, using up-to-date tables:

$$
\begin{array}{r}
244°\quad 31'.7 \\
+\quad 118°\quad 44'.9 \\
\hline
=\qquad ?
\end{array}
$$

Remember in doing the sum that there are 60 minutes to one degree, and that 360° should be deducted from the answer (if possible). The answer is therefore:

003 degrees 16.6 minutes

Basically, astronomical navigation works in exactly the same way as the angular measurement with a sextant close to land described on page 202. There, we were dealing with the vertical angle between the top of a lighthouse (or the like) and its base. In astronavigation we measure the angle between a star and the horizon.

As in terrestrial navigation, we need to know the exact moment of measuring the position of the celestial body (sun, moon or star) which is of course changing all the time. The positions are listed in the *Nautical Almanac*. There is only one slight difference from

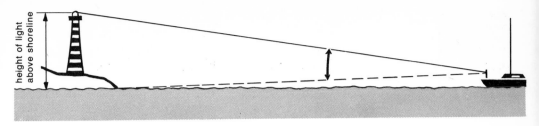

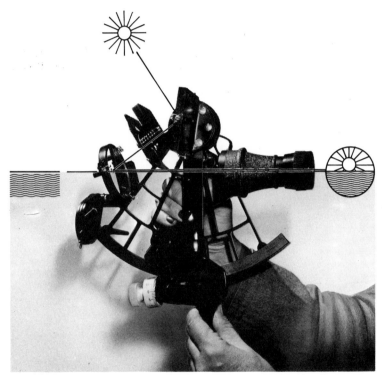

Terrestrial navigation measures the angle between the light, observer and shoreline.
Astro-navigation measures the angle between the sun, observer and shoreline.

navigating within sight of land: if we want an accurate astronomical position line (this is all one ever gets from any one sight, never a complete fix) the angle needs to be measured far more precisely than in terrestrial navigation. Being ½° out would not matter in a horizontal-angle measurement of two landmarks, but in a sun-sight it could mean an error of 30 miles.

Sextant or octant

It should be obvious that a cheap plastic sextant (selling at about £20), though quite adequate for measuring horizontal angles between landmarks, should at most be used for practice purposes in astro-navigation, never in earnest. You will need to dig rather deeper into your pocket and buy a micrometer-drum sextant; this could well cost up to £200. For yacht use a (somewhat cheaper) octant will do just as well, since the overhead observations that a sextant is capable of are normally never made on a yacht.

Cheap plastic sextant – all right for practising with.

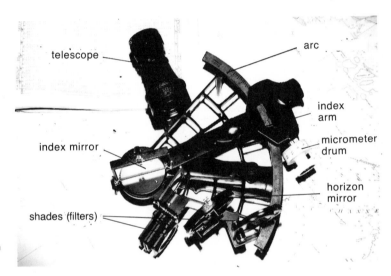

telescope

arc

index arm

micrometer drum

index mirror

horizon mirror

shades (filters)

Plath micrometer sextant with built-in illumination.

Sextants and octants are available in various versions, and it is often hard for a beginner to know what extras he really needs. In addition to the standard features (shades, micrometer and a telescope sighting tube of 4x magnification at most) a sextant really needs only scale illumination as an extra. A bubble horizon is useless on a yacht.

Metal sextants made by Hughes, Freiberger and some Japanese firms (eg. Undator) usually leave the works with a certificate showing test measurements in a table. These precision instruments must naturally be handled with the greatest care, for even a slight blow on the scale can render a sextant unusable. Every navigator must be able to check his sextant for the errors that may arise in the course of time.

Sextant errors

Index error is not really an error at all. It arises from the whole reading on the sextant being offset slightly. If we sight a single object (should be more than 2 miles distant) the micrometer should – with no index error – read exactly 0°0′, because no angle is being measured.

Usually it will not, and the sextant then has an index error. An error of under 2 minutes should not be corrected, and altering the precision screw settings of the mirrors will only do harm. It is often recommended that index error should be taken into account when working the sight, but since all calculations can so easily involve mistakes due to carelessness, etc. mark a new zero-point on the micrometer drum with a smudge-proof pencil. Index error varies little during a voyage, but it ought to be checked at the start of a cruise.

Zero point marked with a felt pen (arrowed)

To check for **side error** (tilting of the horizon mirror – the semicircular one) we start in the same way as when measuring index error.

no error

side error in horizon mirror

If there is no side error in the semicircular mirror, the line of the horizon in the sight-tube should be unbroken. Arrow shows screw for correcting side error.

The sextant is aimed at the horizon and the index arm set so that the horizon gives a straight unbroken line. If the sextant is now turned roughly 45° about the axis of the telescope, the horizon line should remain unbroken if there is no tilting error. If the horizon is broken, the tilting error present can easily be overcome by very slightly turning the screw pressing against the centre upper edge of the horizon mirror from behind (using the tool provided).

The index arm ought to continue in the mirror as an unbroken line (arrowed)

Perpendicularity (tilting of the index mirror – the square one) is checked by setting the index arm to the centre of the arc, and then holding the instrument so that you look exactly downwards at the index mirror with the zero point on the arc scale seen at the inner edge of the mirror. The parts of the arc viewed directly and indirectly should then run together without a break. You can correct this error yourself, by slightly turning the screw pressing on the centre upper edge of the square mirror from behind.

Whenever alterations have been made, especially to the mirror settings, the index error must be rechecked. If it is still within 2 minutes, re-mark the zero point; larger errors need compensation and for this there is usually a screw to one side of the (half-round) horizon mirror that swings the mirror a little about its vertical axis perpendicular to the instrument plane. But be careful – you can damage the sextant by fiddling about with the screws too much.

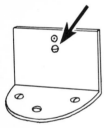

Correction of perpendicularity using tool supplied.

The technique of taking sights

To my mind this is the only difficulty there is in astro-navigation. Beginners in particular should not be satisfied with just working out a few position lines during the winter months – they should practise taking sights, because inaccurate PLs are mostly due to taking poor sights. In the commercial shipping world an inaccuracy of 2' of arc (ie. 2 nautical miles) is looked on as normal under good conditions; on a small yacht that is rocking about it will not be possible to reach quite this accuracy, and a beginner should assume an error of 5'. Only practice will improve this. The best opportunity for practice is a noon sun-sight at the sun's highest point, when it is – apparently – seen at the same angle for a couple of minutes. There is another well-tried way of checking your skill in taking sights: take five sun-sights at short intervals in the morning or afternoon, and plot the results with the intervals true-to-scale. If all five points are in a straight line, you know you can rely on your ability to use a sextant.

One of the main mistakes when taking sights is not holding the sextant completely vertical, and thus measuring far too big an angle between horizon and sun. This can only be avoided by swinging the sextant slowly during the observation. At its lowest point,

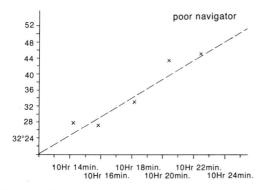

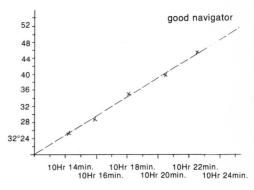

the sun should just kiss the horizon, and its lower limb should never overlap it.

The beginner will find that at first it is far from easy to catch sun and horizon in the sextant at the same time. I find the following

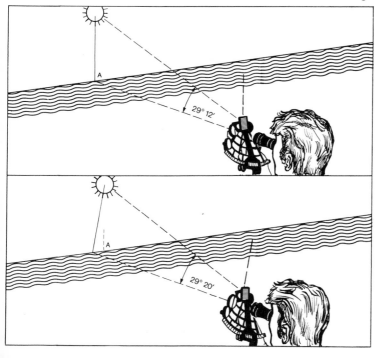

If the sextant is not held exactly upright, the angle observed will be too big.

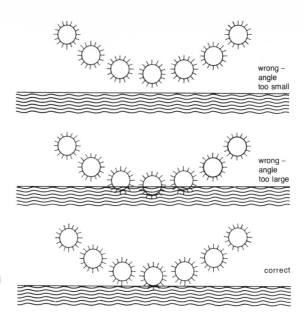

wrong –
angle
too small

wrong –
angle
too large

correct

Only a slow sweep will ensure a correct observation.

method best, though it is not really a method at all: I point the sextant towards the sun, and aim at the horizon. The index arm, with the second-strongest shade in place, is moved about while I sweep the telescope along the horizon back and forth under the sun until I 'catch' the yellow disc. I can then leave myself plenty of time for fine adjustment with the micrometer. You can also set the arm at 0°, aim at the sun, and then while moving the arm move the sextant downwards until the horizon appears. The danger here is either that if you are using a dark shade you will be unable to make out the horizon, or that by trying to avoid this you will be dazzled by the sun and incapable of taking a sight for the next few minutes. If you have practised taking sun and star-sights and built up your self-confidence, you will eventually be easily able to judge the quality of any particular sight you have taken.

Timing to the second

Important rule: in all astro-navigation, use only Greenwich Mean Time (GMT).

As in terrestrial navigation, you need to know the exact position of the object (celestial body) on which a bearing is being taken. Since it is moving very fast, you need to know the time of observation very precisely in order to look up its position in the *Nautical Almanac*. In years past you had to spend a lot of money on a yacht chronometer, the accuracy of which was still never all that satisfactory on a long voyage. Generally, because of the temperature fluctuations and vibration on a yacht, the '2 seconds a day' standard could not be achieved; but an inaccuracy of 4 seconds a day corresponds to an error of 1 minute of longitude. Today, quartz watches have brought about a revolution; these all work on the same principle, and a frequency of 32kHz or 4.19MHz, whether they cost £10 or £100, and are all accurate to within 1 second a day. Mechanical shocks do not affect their accuracy, but are more likely to ruin the works completely than with a spring watch. They should naturally be checked against the radio occasionally, and time signals on the full minute are transmitted constantly on 2.5, 5, 10, 15, 20 and 25MHz. It is best to keep the watch used for navigation set always on GMT, irrespective of local time; all the time signals on the frequencies just listed, and all data given in the *Nautical Almanac*, are based exclusively on GMT.

Though the quartz watch (for yacht use, a quartz diving watch is best) is compared to the radio time signal each day, it should not be reset each time it strays – either note down the discrepancy, or on a diving watch mark it with the adjustable ring. Since reading a watch is not all that simple, have a stopwatch set going at the instant of taking a sextant sight by calling 'now'; the navigator can first pack his expensive and sensitive piece of equipment away safely, and then compare the stopwatch to his navigation watch to find the exact time of the sight (which should be written down without delay).

The position of the celestial bodies

As I have just said, you need to know the exact position of the sun or other celestial body at the time of taking the sight, just as when taking bearings on landmarks. While the position of landmarks can be quoted in degrees of latitude and longitude, there is with heavenly bodies the apparent problem of their being suspended in space, so that three-dimensional coordinates ought really to be used. A couple of centuries ago some genius found a way of avoiding this difficulty by giving the position of stars, etc. using their geographical positions. The geographical position (GP) is the principal key to astro-navigation, and once you have grasped the idea

Geographical position

you should have no further problem in finding your position using the stars.

The reasoning is as follows: all celestial bodies are for practical purposes an infinite distance away from the earth, so it does not matter whether a body really is near the earth (like the sun), or is circling round many times further away in deep space (like the fixed stars). Because this factor is therefore taken as the same for all heavenly bodies in astro-navigation, the distance between the celestial body and earth's surface can be ignored (in the case of the really near moon, the distance is allowed for in the horizontal parallax). If we draw an imaginary line from the centre of the earth to the centre point of the celestial body, it will pass through the earth's surface at one quite specific point on the globe. In other words, if we know where this line pierces the earth's surface, we know the position of the star as well, because it must be directly overhead (an infinite distance away). Thus we need only know the coordinates on the earth's surface – the geographical position – to

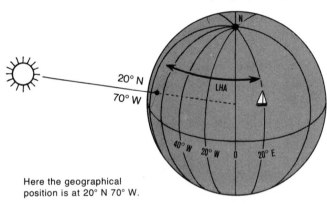

Here the geographical position is at 20° N 70° W.

fix the position of the celestial body.

To carry out astronomical calculations we invariably use only the coordinates of the GP, and everything is apparently worked out on the earth's surface. We could quite well locate this GP, like any other place on earth, by quoting it in latitude and longitude; but to avoid confusion we indicate the latitude as *declination* and the longitude as the *Greenwich hour angle,* or GHA.

Declination is quoted, like the latitude of any other point on the earth's surface, in degrees north or south, from 0–90°.

In the case of the GHA there is a slight – and only superficial – difference. While longitude is measured as 0–180° east or west, the GP's Greenwich hour angle is counted from 0–360°, always going west from Greenwich.

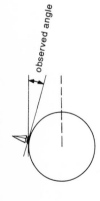

226

There is thus no such thing as a GP longitude of 167°W, only 167°. A longitude of 122°E would thus correspond to a Greenwich hour angle of 238°.

Using a *Nautical Almanac*, we can find the GP coordinates for **Nautical** every second of a given day; all you have to do is look under the **Almanac** date and the celestial body in question. The GHA is found by first taking the value for the full hour from the white pages of the *Nautical Almanac* (remember that all times are in GMT). Since the sun moves at a fairly constant rate, it is quite easy, using an interpolation table given in the coloured pages at the back of the *Nautical Almanac*, to find the Greenwich hour angle for times in between the hours.

Example: On 1 August 1975 we take a sun-sight at 10hr 28min 13sec GMT, and want to know the GP coordinates. Under the 'Sun' column we read, for 1000hr, a GHA of 328°25'.4, and then have to find how far the GP of the sun will move westwards in the remaining 28min and 13sec. Really we hardly need an interpolation table for working this out.

We know that the sun moves once round the earth, from east to west, in 24 hours, so that its GP travels through 360°. In 1 hour it will therefore move exactly 15°, in 4 minutes 1°, and so on. However, since one always wants to make navigation as simple as possible, we do not do rule-of-thumb sums but merely look up the interpolation table in the *Nautical Almanac*, under the 'Sun' column. On the page for '28min' we read from the line for '13sec' the longitude degrees and minutes – namely 7°03'.3 – that the sun (and its GP) will have moved since 1000hr. The GHA is thus 335° 28'.7.

GHA. 10hr	328°25'.4
Inc 28min 13sec	7°03'.3
GHA. 10hr 28 min 13sec	335°28'.7

Matters are even easier with declination, as the difference between the full hours is usually less than 1 minute. I can tell you, from experience, that it is best not to spend a long time on arithmetic, but merely to estimate the declination for parts of an hour. If the declination at 1000hr was 18°07'.7N, and was only 0°00'.6 more an hour later, we can judge that at 1028hr it was just on 18°07'.4. Such estimates are perfectly permissible, since for our purposes declination is always rounded up or down to the nearest minute.

We now have all we need for determining an astro-position line.

The noon latitude

This is the easiest astro-PL of all (it can almost be worked out in your head) and because it is so accurate it is still used in the commercial shipping world. We even do not need both coordinates of the sun's GP: the latitude (declination) is quite enough. As the name suggests, the sun sight has to be taken at noon. If we happen to be on the Greenwich meridian, noon will be fairly accurately at 1200hr. The sun moves 360° westwards right round the globe in 24 hours, covering 15° in 1 hour. At 15°W the sun, which has to travel 360° from east to west in one day, is exactly one hour later – ie. there noon will be at 1300hr GMT. If we know roughly the time of noon, we need only go up on deck and watch through the sextant.

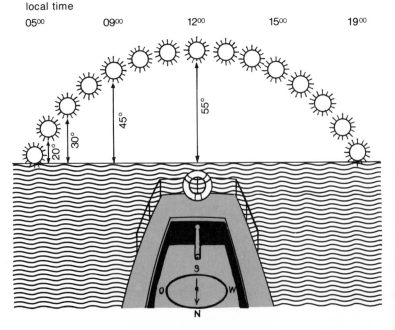

local time

05⁰⁰   09⁰⁰   12⁰⁰   15⁰⁰   19⁰⁰

If a yacht is sailing northwards in our latitudes in winter the sun rises astern in the SE, reaches its highest (noon) point due S, and sets in the SW. In summer it rises in the NE and sets in the NW.

The angle will have to be continually adjusted on the micrometer until the sun (apparently) remains at the same angle for several minutes, and then starts to drop again. This maximum angle is the 'noon observed altitude'.

There are various simple formulae for calculating the noon latitude, depending on where our boat, or the GP, happens to be. Don't bother to learn these by heart – it is quite enough to mark the ones that matter in the *Nautical Almanac* before starting a voyage.

If we are in the northern hemisphere, the following variants can apply:

- the sun has a north declination, and at noon we see the sun in the south (the normal case): latitude = 90° + declination − (observed altitude + total correction).
- the sun has a south declination (this never happens in summer): latitude = 90° (−) declination − (observed altitude + total correction).
- the sun has a north declination, and at noon we see the sun in the north (this does not occur in the North Sea or Mediterranean): latitude = declination + (observed altitude + total correction) − 90°.

As you can see, calculating the noon latitude is very simple. Only the *total correction* has not so far been mentioned. In broad terms, it comes from the fact that the sun's rays are slightly refracted as they pass through the various layers of air in the atmosphere so that we are not observing the real horizon, but only the apparent one we see – the visual horizon. Total correction can be looked up on the loose card supplied with the *Nautical Almanac*, or on pages A2 and A3. There is no need to work it out to tenths of a minute, because it cannot be measured so exactly anyway. Usually the height of eye needed for the tables in the *Almanac* will, on yachts, be 2m. So if we round off the total correction upwards or downwards we shall in the case of the lower limb of the sun (which we should always use if possible) manage quite well with the following three figures, avoiding a lot of tedious looking-up:

observed angle	total correction
above 20°	+ 11 minutes
above 25°	+ 12 minutes
above 40°	+ 13 minutes

Example: On 1 August 1975 we are at approx. 39°44′N, 14°00′E. At 1100hr we sight the sun at its highest point with a sextant angle of 68°17′. What is our latitude?

	90° 00′	
+	18° 07′	declination
−	68° 30′	corrected sextant angle
	39° 37′	latitude

Exercise 22

On 1 August 1975 we are south of Ischia. On a compass heading of 062°(C) the 164m high tower at Punta Imperatore is exactly on the bow. At 1111hr GMT we find the noon latitude to be 67°16′. What is our noon position? (Use deviation card on the practice chart, and height of eye as 2m as on page 229).

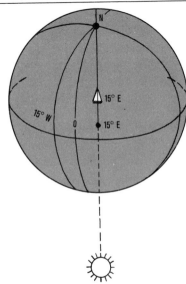

At noon the sun is due S (or N) and its GP is on the ship's longitude (see also illustration on page 228).

In practice this system does have one slight snag. Not knowing the exact moment of the sun's highest position, ie. noon, we need to go up on deck with the sextant in plenty of time so as not to miss our noon sight: this does neither us nor the sextant any good. So we really need to know the time of noon to within a few minutes. This can easily be calculated in advance; and *the reader should not skip this bit*, because this prior calculation can also be used later to find the longitude.

We see the sun at its highest point when it is exactly south of us (in our latitudes), and its geographical position exactly matches our yacht's longitude. Using the *Nautical Almanac*, we can quickly look up tables and work out the GMT for the sun's GHA in question.

Let us assume that on 1 August 1975 we estimate our longitude to be 13° 22′ E. This corresponds to a Greenwich hour angle of: 360° 00′ − 13° 22′ = 346° 38′ because of course the Greenwich hour angle is not expressed as an east or west longitude. The sun's GP reaches this longitude between 1100hr and 1200hr GMT. At 1100hr GMT it is on 343° 25′.4, so to reach our longitude it still has to move 3° 12′.6. We find this difference in the interpolation table, on the page for 12 minutes; so at 1112hr the sun's GP will be exactly on our longitude, and it will be noon at our position. The sun will be at its highest point.

The fact that we do not know our longitude exactly does not matter, because the sun will remain visible at its highest point for several minutes on end, and an error of 20 or 30 miles in our position will have little effect.

When is it noon aboard, on an estimated longitude of 9° 09′ E on 1 August 1975?   **Exercise 23**

At this time we observe the sun at altitude 68° 44′, with the sun   **Exercise 24**
seen in the south. What is our latitude?

The noon longitude

Just as we pre-calculated the time of noon using our estimated longitude, so we can also – working in the reverse direction – calculate our exact longitude if we know the time of the sun's highest position exact to the second. Unfortunately we come up against practical difficulties; the sun stays visible at the same sextant angle for several minutes, and this is much too vague for calculating the longitude. We want to know our longitude to within 3–4 miles. So we use a dodge that is popular especially with American yachtsmen: if we plot the sun's path around noon on a graph, we get something like the curve seen here. We can see from this that at 1122hr the sun stayed at the same angle of 67° 29′ during four minutes, and was only 1′ lower than this for 4 minutes before and 4 minutes afterwards.

Noon curve of sun: it stays stationary in the sextant from 1122hr to 1126hr. By 1146hr it is already dropping at 1 minute of arc every 20 seconds of time.

We can also see that the curve is virtually symmetrical; so to find the time of noon exact to the second, all we need do is to take a sight at a time before noon when the sun is still climbing steep and fast, and then wait after noon until the sun again appears at the same angle.

Noon is exactly halfway between the times of these two sights.

Just as previously we calculated the time of noon from the yacht's longitude, so conversely we can find the exact longitude from the exact time of noon pinpointed in the way just described.

Exercise 25

On 1.8.75 in the Mediterranean (estimated position 40° 20′ N, 9° 40′ E) we observe the sun at altitude 63° 50′ at 10hr 28min 38sec, at 67° 10′ at 1129hr, and again at 63° 50′ at 12hr 28min 24sec. What was our noon position?

Despite its simplicity, this 'finding the noon longitude from two equal altitudes' is very accurate, especially when sailing east or west. If however we cover more than 5 miles to north or south between taking the two sun-sights, slight errors can creep in. To compensate for these, a German yachtsman called Albrecht has worked out a further correction that does not complicate matters in the slightest: for every mile the ship moves *towards* the sun between the two observations, add one minute *to* the angle preset on the sextant before the second sight. If the ship is moving *away* from the sun, one minute should be taken *away* from the preset sextant angle for each mile before taking the second sight.

With both the noon longitude and the noon latitude you have to accept the fact that you can take sights only at one particular time. For the noon longitude you in fact need two sights, and a cloud coming over at just the wrong moment can upset the whole exercise. None of these snags apply to the AP 3270 method, which is accurate enough for yacht navigation purposes, and extremely simple. It is used all over the world not only by yachtsmen but by commercial shipping as well, where (especially among younger navigation officers) it has taken the place of the notorious haversine formula with its tedious trigonometrical calculations.

The AP 3270 Method

The AP 3270 *'Sight Reduction Tables for Air Navigation'* (which are for the most part identical to the US Navy Hydrographic Office Pub. No. 249) are in three volumes, of which for the moment only *Vols. 2* and *3* concern us. *Vol. 2* is used between the Equator and Lat. 39° (north or south), while *Vol. 3* more or less serves for the rest of the world.

The AP 3270 method is based on the following height-calculating principle: if we assume that we are a short distance from a lighthouse we can, knowing the height of the lighthouse and the angle 'foot of lighthouse/observer/top of lighthouse', easily work out our distance from the lighthouse using the formula on page 202, and then draw a position line (a circle around the lighthouse, with this distance as radius).

The higher up we see the light, the closer we shall be to the lighthouse – or, conversely, the shallower the angle the further away we shall be. Translating this simple reasoning to our sights of celestial bodies, imagine the sun as being the light of the lighthouse. The foot of the lighthouse will then be the sun's geographical position. Here, too, we can by using rather more complicated formulae (because a curved surface is involved) work out our distance from the sun's GP. In theory, all we need then do is scribe a circle round the sun's GP with this distance as radius and we shall likewise have a circular position line.

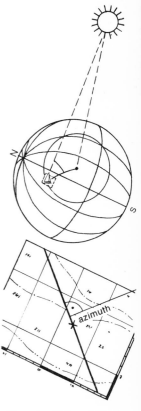

In practice this is of course impossible, since the distance to the GP may well be thousands of miles and a chart on which a circle that size could be drawn would be of little use for navigation. Yet if we take an ordinary chart, it will accommodate only a relatively tiny section of the circle around the sun's GP; so small that because of the vast radius of the circle the position line would no longer appear as a curve, but as a virtually straight line.

Having only a tiny part of the circle on our chart would be no bad thing, since this small part is really all that interests us. But again, we would not be able to draw it, since we could not put the point of the compasses on the centre of the circle.

To recap: we have said that the distance to the GP can be calculated from the observed altitude and the sun's position. At the same time, however, we have seen that our PL (a circle with the calcu-

The astro-PL is a circle with such a large diameter that the section involved appears to be a straight line. This is not so at angles above 75°, which must therefore be avoided.

lated distance as radius) cannot in practice be drawn on a chart. So we take a slightly different approach: instead of calculating the radius, we start from an estimated position (EP) for the yacht and then work out (don't worry – we use tables!) what the angle horizon/observer/sun would be at the same time of the sight if the yacht were actually at that estimated position. At the same time we can find out on which true bearing the sun ought to be. If we in fact observed exactly the pre-computed angle, the PL would be easy to draw – it would run through the EP and at the same time be at right angles to the true bearing of the sun (ie. of its GP), since it forms a tiny part of the enormous circle drawn around the GP.

Naturally the angle observed is never in practice exactly the same as the computed angle, showing that we are not exactly at our DR position. Remember the analogy with the lighthouse: if the observed angle is greater (ie. we have to look higher up to find the light) this means we are closer to the sun; and the difference between the computed and the observed angle will tell us how far we are from the estimated position. One minute of arc is exactly equivalent to one nautical mile on the earth's surface. If, for example, the observed angle is 5′ less than the computed angle, this means that we are just 5 miles further away from the sun's GP than the estimated position. We mark a point 5 miles along the true bearing (azimuth line) of the sun's GP going away from the latter, ie. away from the sun. All we have to do now is draw a straight line (which is really part of a gigantic circle) at right angles to the azimuth at this point, and thus obtain our position line.

This shows what is needed for drawing an astro-position line:
1. the bearing of the celestial body (azimuth);
2. the estimated position of the yacht, from which we calculate the angle we should observe were we exactly at the EP;
3. the difference between the observed and computed angles (the intercept), giving the distance to be shifted along the azimuth either *towards* or *away from* the EP.

The mathematical slog that was once dreaded in using the haversine method of calculating altitude and azimuth (a compass bearing on the celestial body would be far too inaccurate) is done for us by the tables in AP 3270, which provide altitude and azimuth already worked out for numerous points on the globe. The only art in using these tables lies in selecting, instead of the yacht's EP (which is probably not accurate anyway), the nearest assumed position for which AP 3270 gives a precalculated altitude and azimuth.

Opening *Vol. 3* of AP 3270, we first find the *latitudes* on lefthand and righthand pages; as these are given in full degrees, the latitude of the assumed position will have to be the same, and since we want this to be as close as possible to our EP we take the nearest full degree up or down (eg. 46° for an EP of 45° 31′N, and 45° for an EP of 45° 29′N).

The top and bottom lines of the tables show *declination* (the latitude of the GP). If we are in the northern hemisphere and the declination is 'north', we use only the pages headed 'declination same name as latitude'. If the declination were 'south', we would take the pages headed 'declination contrary name to latitude'.

This has dealt with two of the three tabulated values, and we now know the latitude of the assumed position. But how about its longitude? Going back to the tables, where we have already had declination and latitude, we find a third entry to the tables with the *local hour angle*, or LHA, in the right and left hand columns. This, it will be realised at once, combines the longitude of the assumed position and of the geographical position of the celestial body:

The LHA is the longitude difference between ship's position and the GP, while the GHA is that between the Greenwich meridian (0°) and the GP.

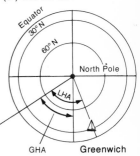

> *Very important:* the LHA is the number of degrees and minutes of longitude (westward from the assumed position) to the geographical position of the celestial body.

If, for instance, we are on 10° W and the GP's longitude (or GHA) is 20°, then the LHA is exactly 10°. If, on the other hand, the GHA were 0° and the sun is about to overtake us, the LHA will be 350°.

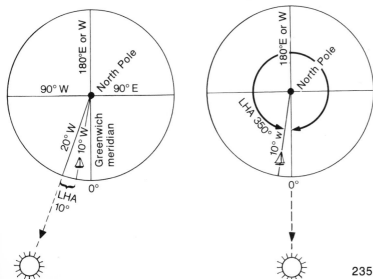

LHA is counted westwards from the ship's position towards the GP.

Left: LHA = 10°

Right: LHA = 350°

To work out the LHA we first need to know the Greenwich hour angle exactly (see page 227).

Example: Having taken a sun-sight on 1 August 1975 at 17hr 28min 11sec GMT (remember you always use GMT for navigation) we see from the *Nautical Almanac* that at 1700hr the sun's GP was on 73° 25'.6. The interpolation table then shows us how far the sun, moving 15° in 60 minutes, will have travelled in exactly 28 minutes and 11 seconds, and adding the answer (=7° 02'.8) to the GHA for 1700hr brings us to a GHA, for the sun's geographical position, of 80° 28'.4. If our DR position was 22° 02'.4, we now need only subtract our longitude from the GHA to arrive at the LHA. Remember that the LHA is always counted westward from the observer, so in the above case the LHA would be 58° 26'.

Had we been on an easterly longitude, we would have had to *add* to the GHA to arrive at the LHA.

> *Note:* LHA = GHA − observer's longitude if on a westerly longitude.
> LHA = GHA + observer's longitude, if on an easterly longitude.

If a westerly longitude cannot be subtracted from the GHA because it is larger than the latter, first add 360° to the GHA.

Example: GHA = 10° 24'.4; observer's longitude = 40° 12'.2W. We thus need first to increase 10° 24'.4 to 370° 24'.4 by adding on 360°, so that we can then subtract 40° 12'.2W from this. Answer: LHA = 330° 12'.2. It will in each case be better for the beginner to clarify the situation by drawing himself a sketch, looking down at the North Pole.

Thinking back, we see that AP 3270 provides computed figures only for positions meeting certain conditions, viz:

1. they have to have a latitude in whole degrees;
2. they have to have an LHA of the celestial body that is also in whole degrees.

How do we meet this second condition? Obviously we cannot alter the GHA, since the longitude of the geographical position at the time of taking measurement had one very definite value. But what we can alter is the assumed position. This corresponds to our actual position just as little as the estimated position which we previously took as a basis; all that it needs to be is as close as

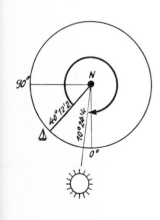

Colour plate: Ocean sailing – leaden calms give way to fair trade winds.

possible to our actual position. So we select a slightly different assumed position from that initially used for working out the LHA. The assumed longitude should, of course, be shifted as little as possible, so as to keep an LHA in full degrees. In the examples given above, therefore, instead of taking a longitude of 22° 02′.4W we shall use 22° 28′.4W to give an LHA of 58°, or 40° 24′.4 instead of 40° 12′.2 to give an LHA of 330°. To find the right assumed position we thus have to increase or decrease our assumed longitude, depending on which one our estimated longitude is nearer to (study the examples to the right carefully).

Now we have all the items needed for entering AP 3270 – first the latitude in whole degrees, secondly the LHA (which also has to be in whole degrees) and finally the declination. Declination, like the GHA, we find from the *Nautical Almanac*. A point to watch here is that, unlike the procedure for latitude and LHA, we do not take the nearest declination as the entry to AP 3270, but always *first* round down the declination. Thus if we have a declination of 15° 59′, we go to column '15°' in the table. We cannot of course simply ignore these 59 minutes, so after using the tables a further correction is made to allow for the fact that a whole-degrees figure was first taken in the table for declination. As a result we shall find three values in the table:

1. the computed altitude ('Hc');
2. the correction for having rounded-off the declination, which then has to be added to the declination ('d');
3. a number which finally gives us the azimuth or bearing of the celestial body ('Z').

Let us assume that our latitude is 41° N, our declination is 18° 07′ N and our LHA (which we have made into whole degrees by shifting the longitude) is 357°. On the page headed 'Lat. 41° – declination (15° − 29°) same name as latitude' we find in the column for 18°

Hc	d	Z
66 51	+ 60	173

The angle 'horizon/observer/sun' would thus be 66° 51′ if we were exactly at the assumed position and the declination were 18° 00′ N. The third figure shows us how to arrive at the azimuth. We have to correct this 'Z' according to whether we are in the northern or southern hemisphere. This is done because the tables, if they are

Examples of whole-degree LHA sums:

1.
Greenwich hour angle: 68° 39′.2
estimated long.: 97° 01′ W

```
        360°
  +  68° 39′.2
     428° 39′.2
  −   96° 39′.2
LHA =332° 00′.0
```

It would be wrong to subtract 97° 39′.2, because this longitude is about 38′ from the estimated long. and thus further away than 96° 39′.2.

2.
Greenwich hour angle: 68° 39′.2
estimated long.: 34° 58′E

```
     68° 39′.2
  + 35° 20′.8
    104° 00′.0
```

34° 20′.8 would be wrong, because it is more than 30′ away from 34° 58′.

not to be too bulky, have to serve for both hemispheres. With AP 3270 open in front of you, the simple rule for converting Z into Zn (azimuth) will be found at the top and bottom left. In our case, we use the rule at top left 'N LAT'. The first line 'LHA greater than 180°' applies to us, since our LHA is 357°, so the azimuth Zn is equal to Z, ie. 173°.

There remains the correction needed because we read the table only at 18 whole degrees instead of 18° 07'. Here again, a table at the back of AP 3270 simplifies the arithmetic. In this 'Table 5' we start at the top with 7 and find, beside 60, a final correction of 7. *Watch the sign!* In our case we have to add 7 minutes to the computed altitude ('d' was '+ 60') so that the altitude is no longer 66° 51' but 66° 58'. What we still need is the number of miles we have to shift the position line from the assumed position. To get this, all we need do is compare the calculated and observed altitudes. Naturally we shall, as before with our noon latitude, have to add the total correction to our observed altitude (see page 229); only then can we arrive at the final difference. Remember the analogy of the lighthouse – if the altitude observed is greater than that calculated, and we see the light at a steeper angle, then we are closer to the lighthouse. In this case, we take away the difference in minutes of arc as miles along the azimuth (running through the assumed position as 173°); and that is the point at which we finally construct our position line, at right angles to the azimuth.

Another example is to find a PL using AP 3270:

		Example
1.	Take a sun sight, noting exact GMT.	GMT 14hr 29min 22sec
2.	Apply total correction to observed angle (adding).	Sextant altitude = 42° 18' + 13'
		42° 31'
3.	Determine estimated position in latitude and longitude	40° 40'N 13° 33'E
4.	Round off estimated latitude up or down to bring it to whole degrees (= assumed latitude)	41° N
5.	Find declination from *Nautical Almanac*	18° 05'N

6. Using *Nautical Almanac*, find *exact* GHA (= longitude of sun's GP) at the time of the sun sight

28° 25'.5
7° 20'.5
———
35° 46'.0

+ 13° 14'E
49° 00'

7. Change the observer's longitude so that, by adding it to the GHA (observer to the east) or subtracting it from the GHA (observer to the west), an LHA *in whole degrees* results

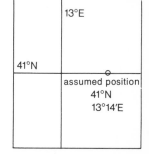

8. Plot the assumed position on the chart (latitude in whole degrees, assumed longitude as the longitude that gave the LHA in whole degrees)

9. Consult table, rounding declination off to whole degrees (note table headings 'Same' and 'Contrary')

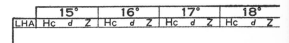

	15°			16°			17°			18°		
LHA	Hc	d	Z	Hc	d	Z	Hc	d	Z	Hc	d	Z
40	46 44	+42	115	47 26	+42	114	48 08	+41	113	48 49	+40	112
41	46 03	42	114	46 45	41	113	47 26	41	112	48 07	40	111
42	45 22	41	113	46 03	41	112	46 44	40	111	47 24	40	110
43	44 40	41	112	45 21	41	111	46 02	40	110	46 42	39	109
44	43 58	41	111	44 39	40	110	45 19	40	109	45 59	39	108
45	43 15	+41	110	43 56	+40	109	44 36	+39	108	45 15	+39	107
46	42 33	40	109	43 13	40	108	43 53	39	107	44 32	39	106
47	41 50	40	109	42 30	40	108	43 10	39	107	43 49	38	106
48	41 07	40	108	41 47	39	107	42 26	39	106	43 05	38	105
49	40 24	39	107	41 03	39	106	41 42	39	106	42 21	38	104
50	39 40	+40	106	40 20	+39	105	40 59	+38	104	41 37	+38	103
51	38 57	39	105	39 36	39	104	40 15	38	103	40 53	37	102

10. Look for the three answers along the appropriate line (computed altitude = Hc; correction for declination = d; and z)

Hc   d   Z
42°21'   +38   104

11. Using rules given at top and bottom left of table, work out the azimuth

360
—   104
———
256°

12. Using Table 5, find the correction for having rounded off declination and, depending on the sign, add this to or subtract this from the computed altitude.

42° 21'
+   3'
———
42° 24'

d / '	1	2	3	4	5	6	7	8	9	10	11	12	13	14	15	16	17	18	19	20	21	22	23	24	25	26	27	28	29	30	31	32	33	34	35	36	37	38	39
0	0	0	0	0	0	0	0	0	0	0	0	0	0	0	0	0	0	0	0	0	0	0	0	0	0	0	0	0	0	0	0	0	0	0	0	0	0	0	0
1	0	0	0	0	0	0	0	0	0	0	0	0	0	0	0	0	0	0	0	0	0	0	0	0	0	0	0	0	0	0	1	1	1	1	1	1	1	1	1
2	0	0	0	0	0	0	0	0	0	0	0	0	1	1	1	1	1	1	1	1	1	1	1	1	1	1	1	1	1	1	1	1	1	1	1	1	1	1	1
3	0	0	0	0	0	0	0	0	0	0	1	1	1	1	1	1	1	1	1	1	1	1	1	1	1	1	1	1	1	1	2	2	2	2	2	2	2	2	2
4	0	0	0	0	0	0	0	1	1	1	1	1	1	1	1	1	1	1	1	1	1	1	2	2	2	2	2	2	2	2	2	2	2	2	2	2	2	3	3
5	0	0	0	0	0	0	1	1	1	1	1	1	1	1	1	1	1	1	2	2	2	2	2	2	2	2	2	2	2	2	3	3	3	3	3	3	3	3	3
6	0	0	0	0	0	1	1	1	1	1	1	1	1	1	1	2	2	2	2	2	2	2	2	2	2	3	3	3	3	3	3	3	3	3	3	4	4	4	4
7	0	0	0	0	1	1	1	1	1	1	1	1	2	2	2	2	2	2	2	2	2	3	3	3	3	3	3	3	3	3	4	4	4	4	4	4	4	4	5

13. Find difference (= intercept) between computed and observed altitudes (applying total correction)

    42° 24'
    42° 31'
    ———
    7'

14. Draw azimuth on chart through assumed position.

15. Move along the azimuth *towards* or *away from* the sun by the number of nautical miles corresponding to the intercept

    7 nm towards

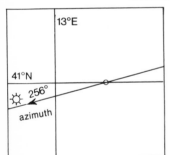

13°E — 41°N — ☼ 256° azimuth

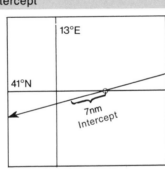

13°E — 41°N — 7nm Intercept

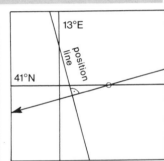

13°E — 41°N — position line

16. Construct a position line perpendicular to the azimuth through this new point.

Let me say again that complicated though all this may sound right now, such a position line can be calculated and constructed in about 5 minutes by anyone who can do simple addition and subtraction.

Using an astro-position line

Up to now we have been talking about only a single position line. Only exceptionally, however, will one PL be much help to us. What we want in navigation is our position, and we can get this only from the intersection of two or more PLs. As we saw when talking about navigating close to land, we can combine any kind of position line with any other kind, so long as they make a reasonably large angle; so we could combine our astro-PL with any terrestrial PL. But what do we do out on the ocean, where in daytime the sun is all there is to take a bearing on? The answer is quite simple: since the sun moves fairly fast we wait a while after taking the first sight, and then take a second. Our position line is perpendicular to the sun's azimuth, so the second sight will yield a PL that cuts the first one at more and more steep an angle as the sun's bearing changes. Naturally the sun will not shift position all that much over a few minutes, but if we wait a couple of hours (especially around noon) we shall find that the two PLs cut at a very satisfactory angle. Standard navigator's practice is (on large commercial ships as well) to take a sun sight during the morning, plot a PL from this using AP 3270, and then later use the noon latitude as a second PL. Provided we are not becalmed between taking the two observations we shall however have to allow for the fact that our position has changed a little in the meanwhile. However, just as when taking a running fix in sight of land (page 206) all we have to do is shift our first position line along our course by the distance covered.

I find from talking with cruising friends that astro-position lines using the sun, and taking noon sun sights, are part of every

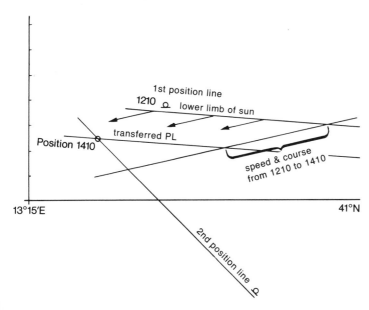

1st position line
1210 ☍ lower limb of sun
transferred PL
Position 1410
speed & course from 1210 to 1410

13°15'E

41°N

2nd position line ☍

navigator's daily fare; but they very seldom take star sights. If you are at sea for long periods, you do not need to know your exact position more than once in 24 hours; only when getting close to land is it advisable to work out a fresh fix as often as possible, and this is the only time one will fall back on star sights. It is not a bad idea to have a simple calculation work-scheme ready for the most common cases, which will serve for doing the work that crops up most frequently. A work-scheme like this can be used in two ways: either you can make the necessary number of photocopies, or you can set out the scheme on paper which is then stuck to card with cutouts at places where figures have to be entered. In the latter system, you then merely lay the stencil over a sheet of plain paper and write in the figures. Everyone could well design a scheme to suit his own ideas, basing himself on the following reasoning.

What do I need to construct a position line?

- the assumed position
- the azimuth
- the intercept

These three answers, which will determine the work-scheme, should be highlighted in colour. To make the work easier still, it is advisable to mark the entries in the tables of AP 3270 in colour as well.

Astronomical check on deviation

Compass with shadow pin at centre, to show the bearing of the sun.

Just as, with terrestrial navigation, bearings were taken on an object on land to find compass deviation, it is of course possible to use the sun for the same purpose. The procedure is very simple, and a good deal more reliable than using a land bearing. The only extra equipment needed is a shadow pin, which stands perpendicular above the centre-point of the compass card.

Since the azimuth (= true bearing) of the sun naturally changes we choose a time of day when this change is slow, ie. the early morning or late afternoon. Just as when taking land bearings, we have the boat turned slowly round a fixed point and note down the sun's bearing on compass headings at 10° intervals; the sun's bearing can easily be read from the compass card by means of the shadow pin. At the same time, however, we need to note the time (it is sufficient to note this in whole minutes). The only calculation we now have to do is to find the LHA, in whole degrees, for the first of our measurements, and this is done in just the same way as when obtaining a position line.

Remember that the LHA changes by exactly 1° in 4 minutes, since this is the time the sun takes (moving through 360° in 24 hours) to shift 1°. All we have to do then is add on to our 36 measurements the LHA applying in each instance, and read off the azimuth (the sun's true bearing) from the tables. This provides the deviation just as we obtained it from taking land bearings (page 197).

Even if he is not going to plot a completely new deviation card, the prudent navigator will occasionally check, by taking sun sights, that his existing deviation card at least still matches the actual deviation on his course at that time. This is especially important on a steel-hulled yacht, where deviation can alter substantially after a thunderstorm.

Exercise 26

On 1 August 1975 at 0630 GMT (log reading 02.44) compass bearings give us a reliable fix on 40° 31'.5N, 14° 20'.0E. The compass course is then changed to 283°. At 09hr 29min 55sec (log reading 18.54) the navigator observes the lower limb of the sun at 58° 41'.
a) What is the DR position?
b) What are the three table entries for LHA, latitude and declination?
c) What computed altitude and azimuth do we get from AP 3270?
d) What is the intercept (difference between computed and observed altitude)?
e) Do we plot towards or away from the sun?
f) What were the coordinates of the assumed position we now need for plotting?

Exercise 27

At 0946 GMT the shadow pin on the compass shows the sun bearing 146°. Is the deviation card correct at this heading (still 283°)?

Exercise 28

At 1112hr GMT (log reading 26.44) we observe the sun, at its highest point, at 67° 21'. What is the noon latitude?

Exercise 29

What is the noon position if the position line from 0930hr GMT is used as a running fix?

The moon

There is absolutely no reason for the reluctance that many navigators – some of them very experienced cruising men – have towards using moon sights. A lunar position line can be calculated and plotted following exactly the same principles as for a sun PL. *Vols.* 2 and 3 of AP 3270 are again used, and there are only three minor differences between reducing a moon sight and a sun sight.

Calculating the GHA

Whereas with the sun one can assume a uniform rate of westerly movement of 15°/hour, the moon does not move at as regular a speed. We find the GHA for the whole hours, and then calculate the distance covered in the remaining minutes and seconds; in the case of the sun, we have used the interpolation tables, which are based on a rate of 15°/hour, and allow us to look up the extra minutes and seconds direct. We cannot do this for the moon, as its rate of travel is not uniform, and the interpolation table is therefore based on the moon's slowest possible rate of 14° 19'/hour. So we start by finding this 'increment' in the table, and then have to make a further correction to allow for the fact that on the date concerned the moon was probably not moving at its slowest rate, but a shade faster. How much faster, we find under 'Diff.' shown at each GHA for the moon. We can find the correction for this difference from the interpolation tables.

> Example: On 1 August 1975 at 19hr 28min 12sec we find:
> Greenwich hour angle   181° 57'.6   ($\sqrt{}$ 10.2)
>
> $+$ 6°43'.7 (increment)
>
> $+$ 4'.8 (correction for '$\sqrt{}$ 10.2')
>
> $=$ 188° 46'.1

The moon's declination

We cannot find this by 'guesstimate', as we did for the sun. True, we need only a declination in whole minutes to look up AP 3270, and Table 5 of AP 3270 uses nothing more than this, but the moon's declination alters so rapidly that we must work it out exactly for the moment of taking the sight. Here again, we use the interpolation table. We start by finding the difference between the two declinations for the previous and following hour, shown expressly in the Nautical Tables as 'd' against 'Declination' for the day in question. We can then look up the 'Corr.' for our extra time – for example at the interpolation table page for '28 minutes', if we took the sight at 19hr 28min 12sec; this is then exactly 2.3 minutes for 'd 4.8'. There is one thing we must be careful about: whereas when finding the moon's GHA we always add on the corrections, with declination these can be either added on or subtracted, and one can only tell which from the declination shown for the previous and following hours. If the next hour's declination is smaller, we have to subtract the correction; if it is larger (as in the above example) it is added on.

Total correction

Total correction

With the sun calculations we took account of height of eye and observed altitude, and were thus able to reduce the total correction table for our needs to a couple of figures. The total correction for the moon, however, has to include horizontal parallax. We need not know exactly what this involves; it is listed in the *Nautical Almanac* as 'HP' for each hour. The sextant altitude is first corrected for height of eye and the resulting apparent altitude is used to enter the two-part moon correction table in the *Nautical Almanac.*

It is hard to see why the moon is used so seldom in navigation, since it means only these few extra corrections compared to working a sun sight. The moon is a very easy body to take a sight on, since in the daytime its lower limb never butts on to the horizon; and with a crescent moon you get an excellent intersection with the sun's PL, and thus a crystal-clear fix.

Warning: Never use the moon at night. It produces such a strong reflection on the water that this casts a light-haze over the horizon behind it, which is then invisible to the observer.

The planets

When they can be made out clearly in daylight (and this applies only to Venus and Mars), the planets are as satisfactory as the moon for taking a sight on. To find them more easily, it is a good idea well before the sight to calculate the angle for a predicted time of observation (from the tables), and then with this angle set on the sextant to search the horizon in the appropriate direction (azimuth) at the time on which the calculation was based. Working a planet sight is done in just the same way as finding a sun PL; one only has to be sure to use the 'Planets' column when looking up the total correction, the GP coordinates (declination and GHA) and the interpolation tables.

The stars

It is not necessary for the navigator to know the individual stars, since *Vol. 1* of AP 3270 helps here by listing the altitude and azimuth for 'Selected Stars'. The best way of finding the stars you want in the sextant is as follows: since all the fixed stars scarcely alter their relative position in the sky, a certain point in the sky has been arbitrarily chosen as the only reference point for the fixed stars (it is known as the 'spring equinox' or 'First Point of Aries'). For us this has the great advantage that to use *Vol. 1* of AP 3270 tables we need only calculate the GHA of Aries, using the *Nautical Almanac*. The LHA listed in *Vol. 1* is also the longitude difference between our assumed position and the Aries longitude (counted to our West). If, now, we want to take a sight on the selected Stars in *Vol. 1* at 1900hr GMT, we have only to find the LHA of Aries for this time, and then at once we have directly (ie. without all the other calculation involved in working a sun sight), on the page giving the latitude of our assumed position, the altitude and azimuth for all seven selected stars. If this altitude is set on the sextant and we search the horizon on the appropriate bearing (azimuth) we shall –

LAT 41°N

LHA ♈	Hc	Zn	Hc	Zn	Hc	Zn	Hc	Zn	Hc	Zn	Hc	Zn	Hc	Zn
	*CAPELLA		ALDEBARAN		*Diphda		FOMALHAUT		ALTAIR		*VEGA		Kochab	
0	35 07	056	26 46	091	30 03	168	17 41	195	26 16	258	30 10	297	28 46	348
1	35 45	057	27 32	092	30 12	170	17 29	195	25 32	259	29 30	297	28 36	348
2	36 23	057	28 17	092	30 19	171	17 17	196	24 48	260	28 50	298	28 27	348
3	37 01	057	29 02	093	30 26	172	17 04	197	24 03	260	28 10	298	28 18	349
4	37 39	058	29 47	094	30 32	173	16 50	198	23 18	261	27 30	299	28 09	349
5	38 17	058	30 33	094	30 38	174	16 36	199	22 33	262	26 51	299	28 01	349
6	38 56	059	31 18	095	30 42	175	16 21	200	21 49	263	26 11	300	27 52	349
7	39 35	059	32 03	096	30 46	176	16 05	201	21 04	263	25 32	300	27 44	350
8	40 13	059	32 48	097	30 48	177	15 49	202	20 19	264	24 53	301	27 36	350
9	40 52	059	33 33	097	30 50	178	15 32	202	19 34	265	24 14	301	27 29	350
10	41 31	060	34 18	098	30 51	179	15 14	203	18 48	265	23 35	302	27 21	351
11	42 11	060	35 02	099	30 51	181	14 56	204	18 03	266	22 57	302	27 14	351
12	42 50	060	35 47	099	30 50	182	14 37	205	17 18	267	22 19	303	27 06	351
13	43 29	061	36 32	100	30 48	183	14 18	206	16 33	267	21 41	303	27 00	351
14	44 09	061	37 16	101	30 46	184	13 58	207	15 48	268	21 03	304	26 53	352

On 41° N, with an LHA with Aries of 4°, Capella is observed at an altitude of 37° 39′, and an azimuth of 58°. The PLs of Capella, Diphda and Vega give the best intersection.

248

given good observation conditions – easily recognise in the sextant the stars that are still not visible to the naked eye. We would be most unlikely to pick up the wrong star, and if we did the fact would be obvious when we came to draw the position line.

Unfortunately there is still, in practice, a whole series of problems. These stem from the fact that star sights can be taken only at dawn and dusk, and even then only over a shortish period. At night the horizon is invisible, and during the day the stars are. I have found the following method useful:

I calculate in advance the LHA (observer/Aries) for a full hour during which the twilight observation is likely to take place (this sounds more difficult than it actually is – I need only calculate the LHA once, for the beginning of these 60 minutes; after that it increases by exactly 1° every four minutes). During the period of observation a helper sits at the chart table with a rule across the AP 3270 table at the LHA in question. Every 4 minutes this rule is moved down a line (with a glance at the clock). The altitude and azimuth can thus be called out to me whenever I want, and with the angle preset on the sextant I can look in the direction indicated by the azimuth to check whether the star is visible yet. As soon as I see a small, faint dot in the sextant, I take a sight on it and call out so that the exact time can be noted. Obviously one tries to sight as many stars as possible in the brief time available.

Hints to make things simpler are that stars higher up in the heavens are easier to make out, and that the first stars should be looked for in the east (where the sky is already somewhat darker) ending up searching the western sky. The 'Selected Stars' are not the brightest of the fixed stars, but have been chosen so that their PLs will provide the best intersections.

What about total correction when reading the altitude of stars direct from the AP 3270 tables? A glance at the table in the *Nautical Almanac* shows that the value is generally around the 4 minute mark. We can safely ignore this, to make the calculations simpler, since all one has to do is find the star for which these four minutes play no part. Obviously we must apply total correction when working out the star sight; with stars it is always minus, and thus has to be deducted.

The method just described is used only for locating the stars. To arrive at the position line we proceed as for the sun, except that when entering the tables we need only our latitude and the Aries

LHA. There is no declination entry into the tables, so our latitude lacks the same or contrary label. One important thing to keep in mind is that while *Vols.* 2 and 3 apply all the time, *Vol. 1* is calculated exactly only for one year; it is still possible to use *Vol. 1* in other years, provided the PL obtained is moved along a certain number of miles in a certain direction, and these two values can be found in Table 5 of AP 3270 *Vol 1.*

Electronic Calculators

Scientific calculators of the right type have a valuable place as part of the navigation equipment on any cruising yacht simply because they make complicated navigational calculation and life much easier. The range of calculators available on the market is large and it becomes increasingly difficult to choose the right one.

Basically, a suitable calculator for navigation should meet all of the following requirements:

1. It must be able to work in degrees, minutes and seconds of arc and handle all normal scientific and trigonometrical functions without error.

2. It must be able to handle *polar* to *rectangular* conversions and have summation keys (Σ) to give a running total when you are adding vectors so you can compute mean and standard deviation.

3. It must have adequate store and recall facilities to minimise the number of key operations. The more stores there are the better, especially for celestial navigation.

4. It must be capable of operation off a yacht's 12v DC power supply, or if using dry cells, have a very low power consumption. If it does not have this capability it is likely to be unsuitable for use at sea.

Several of the models made by Hewlett-Packard are very suitable for use on a yacht since they feature 'stack registers' and Reverse Polish Notation (RPN), a technique that is miles ahead of all other systems for navigation purposes. Some people find the algebraic logic such as used in the Texas Instruments calculators easier to understand; however, working out long complex problems with this type of calculator invariably uses more program steps than with RPN logic.

Calculator Types Suitable For Navigation

As very few calculators costing under approximately £90 are really suitable for serious navigation, the list below comprises those calculators that have been proven and tested at sea. In expert hands, other types of calculator can also be used if the user knows what he is doing. The prices are those current in the United Kingdom at the time of going to press.

Tamaya NC-2

One of the first 'dedicated' navigation calculators to appear on the market and primarily designed for sight reduction or great-circle

The Tamaya NC-2 is a
special navigational calculator.

and rhumb-line track and distance calculations, plus six other built-in programs. No 12v DC adapter charger is available but it runs off four 1.5v 'AA' size batteries which is sufficient for about 12 hours of continuous operation which is a lot of calculation time and probably sufficient for most ocean voyages. The operation is very simple, accurate and quick. It costs £140 which is rather expensive for the number of navigation applications for which it can be used.

Hewlett-Packard HP.19C and HP.29C

These are the latest calculators to appear on the market. They are both advanced scientific programmable calculators with continuous memory, which means that they retain data stored in 16 of their 30 addressable memories, as well as their 98-step program, when the calculators are switched 'off'. As you can merge up to four keystrokes in each of the 98 steps of continuous memory program, you can store programs of up to 175 keystrokes or more, all of which adds up to two very powerful and flexible calculators for navigation, so again there is no problem with power supplies at sea. The program capability means that you can cover more than one navigation application within one program. The HP.29C costs £149, or for those who require to see their calculations in print, the HP.19C with print-out costs £250 (a 12v DC adapter charger is available).

Hewlett-Packard HP.67 and HP.97

The king of pocket calculators. An advanced programmable calculator with an exceptional amount of programming power and flexibility employing magnetic cards for program storage. It has 26 addressable storage registers and 224 program steps with merged keystrokes. Just as with a tape recorder, a program recorded once on a small card, when wanted again, can be fed back into the calculator within seconds by inserting the card. There is a navigation Pac available containing 14 navigation applications, including some ingenious celestial navigation without having to use a Nautical Almanac, but perhaps less effective for not having used the most up to date astronomical data available.

Unfortunately, many of the programs will not give a yachtsman the type of answers he needs. With very little effort and proper consultation, the manufacturer could have rectified these omissions, which are well within the capability of otherwise excellent programs, but chose not to do so. Regrettably, the resulting Nav Pac is a disappointment for yachtsmen and is not to the usual high standard associated with Hewlett-Packard products. A golden opportunity has been lost to set the standard and type of software desperately needed.

Also available is a 12v DC adapter charger for the HP.67 costing £24.78 which enables the calculator to be used directly off the yacht's battery supply. The HP.67 costs £325 and for those who require print-out, the HP.97 costs £580. It is worth mentioning that both machines are identical in use and programs can be run on either machine. There is no doubt in my mind that this is the best calculator on the market for navigation today, so if you can afford it, buy it and I don't think you will be disappointed.

The great attraction for the HP.67/HP.97 owner, is the ability to design and record his own programs to meet individual navigation requirements. For those who do not have the necessary ability, desire or time to create their own, there is an excellent navigation software service provided by South Coast Marine Computors, South Coast House, Wimborne Road, Ferndown, Dorset

Texas Instruments TI.58

A programmable calculator with solid state software which has just appeared on the market and uses the Algebraic Operating System (AOS) logic developed by Texas. It has up to 480 program steps, or up to 60 memories. Effectively, this means that short problems with many numbers, such as statistical analysis could require nearly all memories, while long problems with many operations and few variables could require almost all program steps. It has two unfortunate features. Firstly, you cannot see what you are doing as you do it, because the results of intermediate calculations are not displayed. Secondly, you cannot see your key entry when programming without reference to a key code. Also you cannot record any program you have devised as both the program and data are lost when the calculator is switched 'off'.

No 12v DC adapter charger is currently available, but it is understood that one is likely to be developed in the near future. At the present time, the only way to use it at sea is to carry spare battery packs. The calculator costs £99.95. For those who require it, print-out can be achieved by the use of a PC-100A print/security cradle at an additional cost of £209.00.

Texas Instruments TI.59

This advanced programmable calculator with solid state software, includes the addition of magnetic cards to enable you to record your own programs. It has up to 960 program steps, or up to 100 memories similar to the TI.58.   No 12v DC adapter charger is currently available but it is understood that one is likely to be developed, but until it is, I consider this type of calculator with the higher power consumption required for reading magnetic cards is unlikely to be a viable proposition for use at sea. The calculator costs £249.95. For those who require it, print-out can be achieved by the use of a PC-100A print/security cradle at an additional cost of £209.00. In general terms, the algebraic logic uses more program steps than the equivalent RPN.

Both the TI.58 and TI.59 can be used with a Marine Navigation solid state software module which is available at a cost of £25 and is sold with a comprehensive manual containing 13 programs covering coastal navigation, 9 programs covering celestial navigation and 3 programs covering sailing and tactics.

It is the most comprehensive marine navigation manual so far produced but it is entirely conventional. For example, it includes no celestial navigation without the use of the Nautical Almanac.

Besides working out the more complex navigation problems, both the simple or advanced calculators can be used to do many simple (albeit trigonometrical) sums formerly done by using maths or maths tables. Some of these calculations can be done by using a simple scientific calculator such as the HP.21, just as well as all the calculators discussed in this chapter. These include:

1. Time, speed and distance calculations
2. Finding speed over a measured mile
3. Making speed curves
4. Strength of a current
5. Conversions and fuel consumptions
6. **Distance to horizon,** which is the distance, expressed in nauti-

254

cal miles, from a position above the surface of the Earth, measured along the line of sight to the horizon. It can be found by using the formula:

Distance to horizon (nm) = 1.144 $\sqrt{}$Height of eye (feet)

or = 2.072 $\sqrt{}$Height of eye (metres)

7. **Distance of visibility** is the distance, expressed in nautical miles, at which under normal atmospheric conditions an object should become visible for a given height of eye, commonly called dipping distance or extreme range. It can be found by using the formula:

Distance of visibility (nm)

= 1.144 $\sqrt{}$Height of eye (feet) + Height of object (feet)

or = 2.072 $\sqrt{}$ Height of eye (metres) + Height of object (metres)

8. **Distance of land object beyond the horizon** in areas (eg. the Mediterranean) with few seamarks where mountains are visible and specially suitable. It can be found by using the formula:

Distance in nm = $\sqrt{3.71 \text{ (H} - \text{HE)} + \text{(a} - 1.76\sqrt{HE})^2}$ −
$$(a - 1.76\sqrt{HE})$$

where   H   = height of mountain in metres
        HE = height of eye in metres
        a   = sextant angle in minutes

9. **Predicting distance off beam**   This enables you to predict how far you will pass abeam of an object before you arrive there. The Four Point Bearing Method suffers from the disadvantage that the required information is not known until the yacht is actually abeam, when it may be too late to avoid offlying dangers. Another way of doing this is by the use of special angles. Special angles are two relative bearings such that the distance run between the times of observations is equal to the beam distance. Examples of pairs of special angles are 25° and 35¾°, 35° and 67°, or 37° and 72°. The most useful pair of angles are 26½° and 45° because the distance run by the yacht between the times of observation of these angles is not only equal to the beam distance, but is also equal to the distance the yacht must run from the second observation to the abeam position. A calculator will do all this for you with ease and you don't need to stick to special angles. It cannot be too strongly

emphasised that this solution will only be accurate providing there is no large current or tidal stream acting on the yacht, or that you are not making significant leeway.

Example using HP.19C/29C

1. Enter 2nd bearing   055°   ENTER↑

2. Enter 1st bearing   030°   STO O − f SIN g $\frac{1}{x}$

3. Enter distance run   6.0   X RCL O f SIN X

4. Enter 2nd bearing   055°   f SIN X

Distance abeam   =   5.81 nm

10. **Distance off by vertical sextant angle** can be found by use of the formula:

$$\text{Distance off (nm)} = \frac{\text{Height of object in feet} \times .565}{\text{Vertical sextant angle in minutes}}$$

$$\text{or} = \frac{\text{Height of object in metres} \times 1.854}{\text{Vertical sextant angle in minutes}}$$

Omega navigation

Apart from ordinary DF with a simple directional rotating antenna there are quite a number of electronic navigation systems, but these have not caught on for yacht use: the reasons lie in limited availability (Decca), high power consumption (radar) or, quite simply, high price. Even today, satellite navigation gear can cost between £20,000 and £30,000. Only one system looks like becoming widespread in the yachting world; this is 'Omega', which the US

The Navicom Omega Receiver, specially developed for yacht operation.

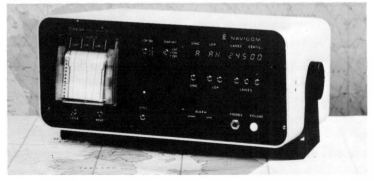

Navy has been developing over the past 20 years. It would take too long to explain the principle in detail, but the idea is that eight transmitters positioned round the world (six of which are already in operation) work on VLF (very low frequency) in the 10–14kHz band. The Omega receiver on a yacht always uses two of these stations to obtain a position line; the set automatically compares the two incoming signals, measures the phase difference between them, and from this automatically computes the number of a PL which is printed on a special chart. At the present time Omega transmitters cover all parts of the world of interest to cruising skippers except the 'Roaring Forties' in the South Pacific. The big advantage of the Omega system is that fixes can be obtained at any time accurate to within 3 miles (very rarely, 4 miles). The 'twilight effect' which so bedevils ordinary RDF does exist, but can be computed beforehand so that these limits of accuracy are maintained even at sunrise and sunset. Studies by the US Navy (for whose submarines Omega has been developed) on the corrections required under various propagation conditions are not yet complete, so the future will certainly see even more improvements to benefit the cruising world. For one's home cruising grounds, comparing Omega PLs with actual positions (eg. in harbour) before starting a cruise will bring the error down to even closer limits, because propagation conditions change gradually (not all of a sudden) for certain times of day on successive days. Only real blue-water cruising over very long distances makes this method at all unreliable. There is one proviso, however: a known position (accurate to within 4 miles at most) must be fed into the receiver before starting out, and further calculations are automatically based on this. The receiver must not be switched off, and has to work throughout the voyage. This is why Omega has so far not become popular in the yachting world – sets have had a consumption of 30W or more, and a yacht's battery can hardly cope with that day in, day out.

Now, with modern electronic components, it has been possible to develop sets more suitable for yachts. The Omega Yacht Receiver made by Navicom GmbH of Munich draws only 2W – which is really sensational, for a cabin reading light takes twice that! What is more, these 2W not only power the Navicom receiver but the motor for the write-out unit as well (this is essential to provide a check on whether the receiver really has been updating its calculations throughout the voyage, for only then will the fixes be accurate).

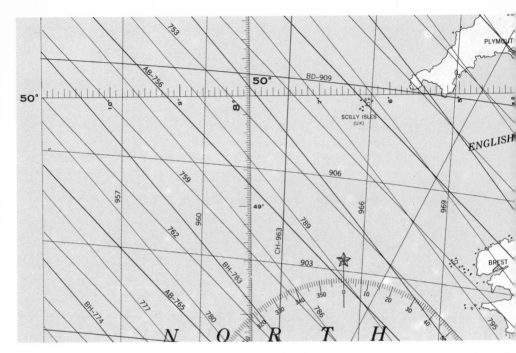

The letters (A to H) in front of the numbers of the PLs identify the transmitter pair; the set shows PLs to two places of decimals, to allow interpolation between two Omega lines on the chart. In a limited area these hyperbolic Omega lines will in practice take the form of straight lines, so can be very simply drawn on to coastal charts.

Unlike many other sets the Navicom has three channels, giving 3 PLs for one fix. If the boat's power supply should fail for a short time for any reason, the set switches automatically to an internal power pack which will keep it running for about an hour. Positions are printed out permanently on a paper chart, so the entire voyage can easily be reconstructed subsequently.

The installation costs about £2250, substantially less than one has had to pay for an Omega set up to now.

Bearing in mind its ease of operation, the accuracy achievable and the ability to obtain a PL at any time irrespective of weather and visibility, Omega is very attractive for yachtsmen even at this steepish price. I would warn you, however, against dodging the perhaps tedious process of learning astro-navigation, and relying on electronics alone. You will be dealing with transmitters and receivers, which can always go wrong; and when they do, the navigator has to manage on his own.

Preparing for a cruise

'The seaman's greatest enemy is haste' – so a cruise should never be planned to a strict timetable. A strict plan tempts one to carry on into bad weather just to keep up with the schedule – and this breaks the rules of good seamanship. So flexible planning, allowing one or other port to be dropped from the itinerary if necessary, is better and safer.

Charts will have to be carried for all the areas likely to be covered. It would of course be easy to recommend taking all the charts there are for this area – but happy the man who can afford to do so! So let us see what charts are essential.

The whole area taken in by the cruise must be covered on *passage charts*; these may not show every detail, but they will be adequate in an emergency (what I am envisaging when I say this is damage to the boat which makes it necessary to run for a harbour that is not included in your programme). Then, of course, you will need medium-scale coastal charts: it is difficult to decide how many, and which detailed harbour charts one ought to have. When entering a harbour in daylight, a harbour chart is not usually necessary – I know very few ports for which I would strongly recommend having one. All the textbooks tell you to use only the most up-to-date charts, and the sweeping changes in the buoying of harbours, wrecks, shoals and so on now under way, as everyone adopts the IALA system over a four-year period from 1977–81, probably adds strength to this argument, especially for European waters; but in normal and more settled times, and exceptional cases apart, I myself have had very little objection to using oldish charts if I can come by them cheaply, or even borrow them from a yachting friend. By the same token, of course, you should be prepared to pass on charts you no longer need; the borrower will seldom forget to post them back to you afterwards. Another useful tip is that merchant ships are required by law to carry the latest charts at all times, and old ones usually end up in the engine-room being used to make cylinder-head gaskets. A sympathetic navigating officer can often be persuaded to pass on out-of-date charts if you seek him out in harbour.

If you can afford new charts, the locally-produced versions are always to be preferred, since only these offer any certainty of really being up-to-date (I find, for instance, that Yugoslav charts of the Adriatic are far more accurate than German ones). Remember when using the older British Admiralty charts that they still give depths in fathoms (=6ft). Admiralty charts cover the whole world, and yachtsmen have long argued the respective merits of British and American charts. I prefer British ones because they show more detail; on the other hand, there are more large-scale, detailed charts available in the American series, and Admiralty charts often lack harbour plans and silhouettes of the coastline. Unfortunately not all charts use the same symbols, so you need to carry a 'List of symbols and abbreviations': this is known as 'Chart No. 1' for German and American publications, while the Admiralty publishes it as 'Chart No. 5011'. In France there are special coastal charts for yachtsmen; they have all useful items of information (such as light characteristics, etc.) printed on them, obviating the need to look up other publications.

Most **Pilots**, or 'Sailing Directions', are unfortunately published so seldom that the information (particularly the coastline drawings) given often no longer corresponds to reality. Most skippers will at some time have searched in vain for the 'small church with red roof' which of course disappeared behind skyscraper hotels 20 years ago. Nonetheless, Pilots do offer a lot of help, particularly if you enter-up any amendments before starting out. Sailing Directions are written with big merchant ships in mind, so when they say 'room for one or two small vessels' you may very well find an anchorage with 20 yachts in it – by 'small vessel' they mean anything under 1000 tons! Similarly, anchorages recommended in the Pilots are often not what we would think of as a calm spot to anchor; a tanker lying to anchor is hardly bothered by a 2m swell that we would stay in for any length of time only in the direst necessity.

In recent years, an increasing number of handbooks have been written specially for yachtsmen, and as they cater for our specific needs we can be very grateful for these. The good ones tell you where you can take on water, where you can shop, where you can buy fresh bread in the morning, where there is a good pub, and so on. One word of warning, however: while the Pilots for merchant shipping are as complete as possible and have been compiled by professional sailors, handbooks for yachtsmen almost always rely on observations made by holiday skippers. A harbour that has not yet been 'discovered' may be missing from the book, while breaking surf seen and misinterpreted by a shortsighted skipper could go straight into the handbook as 'reef in entrance'. In general, though, I have found the facts given to be very reliable; but being over-careful never does any harm.

The *List of Lights* (Admiralty NP 78) is the most important reference source next to the chart. This must be kept right up to date, and amendments must be painstakingly entered-up before starting a voyage. When closing a harbour entrance at night there are more important things to do than go hunting through loose sheets to find what changes have been made in the light characteristics.

Tide tables, for the area and year in question, are something I invariably carry even when (as in the Mediterranean) there is little difference between high and low water. Often individual currents close to land set different ways depending on high water and low water, as one can read in many cases from the Pilot.

List of Radio Signals (Admiralty NP 275). If you carry a DF set, it is worth going to the expense of having *Vol. 2* ('Radiobeacons') on the navigator's bookshelf; it lists all marine radiobeacons in the world, as well as aircraft beacons of importance to shipping. This, too, should be updated from time to time – in the western Mediterranean, for example, practically all the radio beacons have been changed over the last few years. RDF Charts which are published, particularly in France, for yachtsmen are very convenient – they not only show the beacons, but have the identification, range and frequency printed alongside them as well.

I would always carry *Vol. 3* of the *Admiralty List of Radio Signals,* giving details of all the world's weather services, including facsimile weather map broadcasts (the Meteorological Office publishes a similar *Handbook of Weather Messages*). An appendix gives an excellent explanation of how to plot weather maps, the FM 46 code and a glossary of meteorological terms in English, French, Spanish and Russian so that one can make something out of a foreign-language weather report.

If you carry MF or HF radio for communications purposes, then it is essential that you carry *Vol. 1* (*Coast Radio Stations*) giving details of the world's coastal radio stations, search and rescue procedures, medical advice by radio, and much other useful information.

Vol. 5 is also a particularly useful volume and contains details of standard times; radio time signals; radio navigational warnings and radio navigation fixing systems such as Loran C, Decca and Omega.

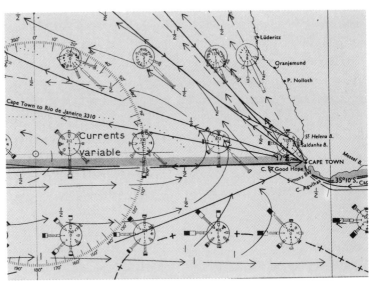

Part of a pilot chart for the South Atlantic, month of May.

The thicker the wind arrows the stronger the wind (the solid tail of the arrow means F8-F12); its length indicates the proportional frequency. The three numbers in the circle show, from top to bottom, the number of observations, and winds from changing directions and calms in percentages.

If you carry VHF radio for communications purposes then *Vol. 6* is also essential. This contains details of port operations, pilot services and traffic surveillance systems.

Note

It is also essential that all the above volumes of the *List of Radio Signals* and the *List of Lights* are regularly amended from the weekly Admiralty notices to Mariners otherwise they quickly become useless. The same notices also contain corrections for your charts.

Wind maps (Pilot Charts) are essential for every long-distance cruising skipper. They show the prevailing wind direction and strength for given months. If you plan to cross the Atlantic, for example, you get the pilot chart for the month in question and can then find the following data for specially-marked squares covering 5°:

Number of observations, percentage probability of storms and calms, probable wind direction and strength. The probability of tropical hurricanes is also shown for the West Indies and, if there has ever been one at that time of year (in which case one would avoid that month!), its path. There are pilot charts for every ocean of the world, usually one for each month.

Ocean Passages of the World has been published for many decades past by the Admiralty, and is required reading for the blue-water cruising skipper. This inexpensive book gives the recommended sailing routes all over the world, and the best times of year. The ocean-cruising skipper will also, of course, be interested in the steamer routes described, as he will need to exercise special care when near shipping lanes. The *Nautical Almanac* (the official publication, or *Reeds Almanac* which contains a wealth of other information as well) and AP 3270 should obviously be carried by every skipper who is going to use astro-navigation.

All the Admiralty publications mentioned can be bought from official chart agents in major ports; if in difficulty, or for further information, write to the Hydrographer of the Navy, Taunton, Somerset. A wide range of yachting reference publications, British and foreign, is stocked by Captain O. M. Watts Ltd., 49 Albemarle Street, London W1.

Studying the reference books and other material will give you an idea of what wind and weather conditions to expect, and what daily distances you are likely to cover. There are no general rules on this outside the tradewind regions (where you can expect a daily average of 100 miles, irrespective of the boat's size), and in the Mediterranean or Baltic you will have to put up with total calms or winds that turn the 'wrong' way. So if you want to use the engine sparingly, an average of 70 miles in 24 hours should be enough to keep you content.

The charts and so on can themselves be prepared to suit your needs. Warnings about dangers can be underlined in the Pilots, to make them stand out even more clearly. I have always found it specially useful to mark the characteristics alongside lights shown on the chart; those likely to be used for the passage can be found in the *List of Lights* in advance, and the same can be done for radio beacons. If you have not mastered the Morse code write in the characteristic or identification direct, as dots and dashes.

Important facts about this and that

Health on board

The demands on medical knowledge and medicine supplies will vary with the circumstances of each cruise; someone sailing lonely routes far from land will obviously need to make different preparations from a skipper cruising from harbour to harbour who can always get medical aid ashore. For the latter, a medicine cupboard like that at home will suffice, while for longer voyages greater knowledge and a wider range of drugs and dressings are needed. What are given here are no more than hints; they do not pretend to cover all eventualities, and the discussion of first aid to the injured has been deliberately kept very brief. A few books on first aid that can be highly recommended are listed at the end of this section, and before starting on any long cruise at least one member of the crew should have some basic medical knowledge (a first aid course will provide this). Even better would be advice from a doctor, especially one who is himself a yachtsman and knows the problems that are likely to arise.

Dr. Walter Dirr

Precautions

Every member of the crew should be in the best possible health when starting the cruise if medical problems are to be avoided as much as possible. If this peak physical condition is impossible through some chronic condition, a conscientious skipper may have to refuse to accept the person concerned as a member of his crew. The following are examples of what I would regard as conditions that absolutely rule out joining a sailing cruise:
- coronary disease;
- diabetes that is difficult to control;
- untreated hypertension (high blood pressure);
- bronchial asthma with frequent severe attacks of breathlessness.

265

It is advisable for crew members to have a thorough medical check-up, and they must tell the doctor what they are planning to do.

A dental check-up, too, is advisable, and the crew should have the inoculations that are recommended or compulsory for the countries to be visited (and certainly an anti-tetanus injection, which really everyone ought to have). If your own doctor cannot tell you what inoculations are needed, you can find out from your local health authorities. It may also be necessary, or at least wise, to consult the London School of Hygiene and Tropical Medicine (Keppel Street, London WC1), who can tell you, for example, what the latest position is on preventing malaria. Naturally everyone must take a supply of any special medicines he needs (cardiac drugs, insulin, etc.), as the yacht's medicine box cannot be expected to provide these. There is no need to have your appendix taken out as a precaution – the risk of serious appendicitis is statistically not all that great, even on a long trans-oceanic voyage.

Precautions can also be taken when actually on board. In a hot climate bacteria multiply very rapidly (mainly in food, but in drinks and ordinary water as well) and can cause attacks of diarrhoea which can be dangerous as well as merely unpleasant; so it is unwise to store food for longish periods once cooked. Fresh water carried aboard should be boiled before drinking; disinfectant agents can be added to it in an emergency, following the instructions, but will give it a strong taste. When taking over a boat it is a sound idea to disinfect all inside surfaces (an aerosol can disinfectant is simplest). A warning that should be self-evident, but is repeatedly ignored, is to *avoid strong sunshine* on the skin, especially in the early days. Avoid *chilling* after swimming or when drenched. Too much alcohol can promote the onset of some diseases, and it is certainly not a good way of warding off colds – rather the opposite.

Injuries

Simple wounds – minor cuts and scratches – usually need only disinfecting and a sterile bandage or plaster dressing, and special measures to staunch the blood are not normally needed. *Venous bleeding*, where the blood oozes continually from the wound, can be stopped by pressure or a tight bandage over the wound itself. *Arterial bleeding* comes in pulsing spurts, and should likewise be stopped if possible by pressure on the point of bleeding. Only in extreme emergency, and only with arterial haemorrhage, should a limb be tied off with a wide bandage; care must be taken not to leave a limb more than half-an-hour without circulation (the tourniquet should be slackened off for 3–5 minutes after this time, and can then if necessary be tightened again). The 'pressure points', where hand or finger pressure will compress an artery and stop bleeding, are given in the first-aid manual.

For **broken bones** the prime rule of treatment is to immobilise the limb. Don't try to set the fracture; this will only cause unnecessary and severe pain. In the vast majority of cases a splint can be applied so that the joints near the fracture point cannot move: with a broken forearm, for example, this would mean making it impossible to move either the elbow or the wrist joint. The bandages used must be wound suitably firmly, yet still be loose enough not to hinder the blood flow (this can be checked by watching the hand or foot, which should become neither blue nor white). The same principle is followed with *torn ligaments or muscles*. Generally no more serious risks will be involved.

Left: immobilising a broken leg, using a paddle as a splint.

Right: immobilisation where there is suspected spine injury, using a floorboard and torn-up shirt. The head must be tied.

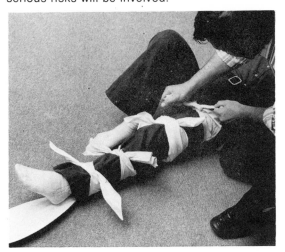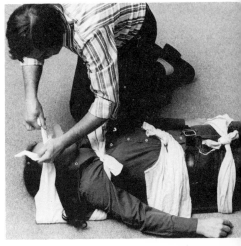

Spinal injuries, however, bring a risk of damage to the spinal cord, and paralysis, and if there is even a reasonable suspicion of such an injury the person should be laid on his back on a firm support and tied to this (with the head immobilised as well).

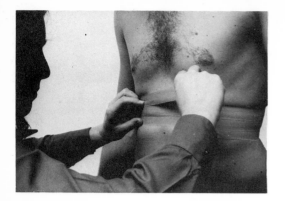

In the case of **fractured ribs**, a *plaster bandage* should be wound firmly (with the edge overlapping) round the body with the person breathing out. If this interferes with breathing the plaster bandage can be snipped with scissors on the side away from the broken ribs.

Broken ribs: wide plaster, with edges overlapped.

Open fractures, ie. with parts of the bone showing, need the wound disinfected as well as splinting. The wound is then merely covered with a sterile dressing, and antibiotics given to combat infection.

With all severe injuries, especially bone fractures, it is important to *combat pain*, in order to prevent traumatic shock, and with the complicated kind of fracture just mentioned medical help should be found as quickly as possible. Usually there is no immediate danger to life, but there is a risk of irreparable damage that could lead to amputation.

Injuries to the abdomen or chest cage can be dealt with only by applying a sterile dressing and giving antibiotics and painkillers. They are always an immediate danger to life, and a doctor must be found as soon as possible. Once *peritonitis* has set in, the chances of survival are slim after 24 hours have passed; cooling with an icebag or a cold compress will delay things somewhat.

In the case of serious or even slight *injury to the eyes* a sterile eye ointment or antibiotic eyedrops should be applied direct to the cornea, and the eye covered over with a bandage or eyepatch. Again, give plenty of antibiotics if the injury is a serious one, and sufficient painkillers.

Very deep wounds may need stitching, but this should be done only within four hours of the injury at most. If necessary any needle and thread can be used for the job, and both should be sterilised by being boiled briefly wherever time and circumstances allow. If they are stored in a sufficiently clean place this can be dispensed with at a pinch. The technique is to hold the edges of the wound together with one hand, while with the other the needle is pushed in through the skin towards the centre of the wound on one side, about 1cm away from the edge, and out through the skin on the other side. The two ends of the thread are then knotted so that the knot comes above skin, not above the wound. Repeat the procedure from one end of the wound to the other, placing stitches at intervals of about 1½cm. The edges of the skin can then be further brought together with plasters known as 'dumb-bell sutures', and a disinfectant powder applied to the wound. Such stitches should be removed after four days; under conditions like these there may of course be suppuration, and this should be treated with antibiotics and dressings. Pus-filled wounds can also be cleaned effectively by dusting ordinary caster sugar over them.

For **burns** the treatment adopted nowadays is to conduct the heat away from the skin rapidly by plunging the part into cold water at around 12–16°C. Cooling in water should last for about 10 minutes, the burned area is then taken out of the water for 2 or 3 minutes and then immersed again and so on until the pain fades. If large areas – say, of the chest or back – are burned, the dinghy can if necessary be made into a bath. The burned area is then covered with Melolin non-adherent dressings or, in the case of smaller areas, with a jelly or ointment such as Fucidin-Gel. Extensive burns can lead to serious complications such as kidney failure, so early medical attention is needed. In the meantime the body's fluid balance must be maintained; so long as normal urine production continues, the patient should be given plenty of fluids, in the form of water with salt added (2 or 3 grams/litre) and sweetened fruit-juices. If urine is scant (collect and measure it), about ½ to 1 litre more fluid than there is urine should be given to drink.

Excessive **heat and sun** can produce a general build-up of heat in the body which can produce either a genuine *heatstroke* or a *heat collapse*. In the latter, which is fairly harmless, the sufferer feels weaker and weaker, feels sick and vomits and breaks out in a cold sweat. He should be laid flat and given plenty of warm drink. A true heatstroke will lead suddenly from a completely normal condition to unconsciousness. Sweating ceases completely and the body temperatures rises to up to 42°C (107°F). The skin feels hot and dry, and as life is in danger a doctor or hospital should be sought as quickly as possible. In the meantime, the body should be cooled with icebags or wet cloths. *It is utterly wrong to try to pour liquid into an unconscious person's mouth.*

The **heart or breathing may stop** as a result of excessive chilling, but it can of course be caused by other factors. Resuscitation must be started at once. Absence of breathing can be checked by placing one hand on the abdomen and the other over the chest – if no movement is felt, the person has stopped breathing. Heart failure or insufficiency can be detected from an absence of the pulse in the carotid artery (down the side of the neck). To find this, grasp the throat about level with the larynx (Adam's apple) with the thumb on one side and fingers on the other, and keep a gentle pressure on the larynx.

External **heart massage** is started with a few sharp blows with the clenched fist to the chest over the heart, and often this is enough to start the heart beating, so that the carotid pulse is felt again. Otherwise, the following points should be remembered for heart massage:

- the patient must be laid flat on the back, on a hard surface;
- the helper kneels alongside;
- the heel of one hand is laid over the bottom end of the breastbone, with the other hand on top of the first;
- with the arms straight, the bottom end of the breastbone is pressed down about 4cm (1–1½in) towards the spine;

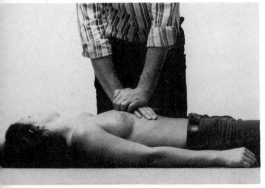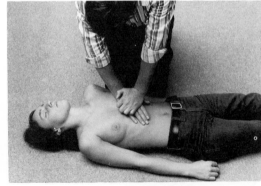

External heart massage – only on a hard surface.

- this short, sharp compression of the chest is repeated 70 to 90 times a minute.

If respiration has to be given at the same time:

- keep the airways clear, ie. clean away any blood, water, etc. covering the mouth or nose;
- the head is tilted well back, and the lower jaw pushed closed with one hand;
- the helper now blows his own breath into the person's nose (or into the mouth, in which case the nose should be pinched closed). Rising and falling of the chest will indicate that artificial respiration is being successful;
- keep breathing into the patient's lungs about 15 times a minute.

If the helper is on his own, he should give 15 strokes of heart massage, followed by three breaths into the lungs, another 15 strokes of massage, and so on. If there are two helpers, give one breath every five massage strokes (stopping massage briefly while this is done).

Particularly with elderly patients, correctly-administered heart massage usually causes broken ribs, but this risk must be accepted. How long resuscitation measures should be continued will depend on circumstances. If the pupils of the eyes are fully dilated and do not narrow down after starting resuscitation, one must assume the person is dead after 15–20 minutes. If the pupils do narrow, resuscitation must be continued until medical assistance arrives.

To sum up, three important points again; don't give resuscitation unless it is obvious it is needed. With artificial respiration, make sure the airways are clear. *Never* pour anything into an unconscious person's mouth.

Frostbite and hypothermia (severe chilling) call for rapid warming up in the heated cabin, or a warm bath. Localised frostbite should be warmed up in a bath of water at about 25°C, raised over ½-hour to 40°C. The affected limbs should then be moved about, and later raised. Here again medical help is needed quickly, to prevent irreparable damage to the limb.

Internal illnesses

This covers so many and difficult conditions that I cannot hope to cover them all. Obviously circumstances can arise that are not mentioned here, and a layman should not try to make a diagnosis come-what-may – this might well be impossible even for an expert, especially under the conditions on board. I will try, therefore, to discuss illnesses (and indicate possible treatments) solely on the basis of given symptoms.

Almost every acute internal disease shows three main symptoms to a greater or lesser degree:
- fever,
- pain,
- disturbance of function.

These generally also indicate the treatment.

Since **fever** is in 90 per cent of cases caused by bacterial infection, it calls for an antibacterial medicine, ie. an antibiotic: in the yacht's medical store suggested a few pages further on, these are ampicillin and propicillin. These are penicillin-based preparations with a broad spectrum of action, and only if there is known penicillin allergy may they not be used. A side-effect is usually diarrhoea of varying severity. **Pain** calls for a painkiller, depending on its nature and severity.

Functional disorder will be treated according to its nature. We can divide the body into the following regions: head, neck, chest, abdomen (including the pelvis with the urinary and sex organs), and the limbs. In discussing the various regions I shall work from the most common complaints to the rarer (and generally more serious) ones.

Head

Inflammation of the nasal sinuses leads to 'the snuffles' and a thick, yellow secretion. There is pain in the upper jaw and perhaps also the forehead. Moving the eyes upwards or sideways produces a feeling of pressure behind the eyes. The organisms causing this will nearly always yield to penicillin (eg. ampicillin).

Nosebleeds are a common occurrence, and usually stop of their own accord. Cold compresses on the nape of the neck help. If there is no sign of the bleeding stopping after half-an-hour, take Dicynene tablets and block the nose with cottonwool to staunch the flow. Nosebleeds do not generally reach worrying proportions.

Inflammations of the **outer ear** or the eardrum are very painful; use ampicillin and eardrops.

Toothaches may be harmless; but an abscess will initially indicate its presence only with pain, followed later by swelling and finally by a fever. At first only ordinary painkillers are needed. When swelling appears, indomethacin will usually reduce it very quickly. Use ampicillin only if there is fever.

The nosebleeding just mentioned can, if coupled with haematoma (blood under the skin) round the eyes, indicate a *skull fracture*; apart from keeping the patient still, there is no treatment that can be given. If unconsciousness sets in, the chances are not all that good. Get a doctor as quickly as possible.

Meningitis is equally dangerous, and shows itself first in headaches and, especially, a stiff neck. There is a very high fever, and again antibiotics and rapid medical attention are needed. Since light in the eyes is unpleasant and painful for the patient, put him in a darkened room, and give painkillers.

Both **tonsillitis** and **laryngitis** make swallowing painful. Unlike laryngitis, tonsillitis leads to swelling of the glands under the jawbone. Treatment in both cases is ampicillin and Dequadin lozenges; a patient with laryngitis must not talk or smoke. 'Swallowing the wrong way' presents a danger of blocking the airways at the entrance to the windpipe (the larynx) and a reflex response will be violent coughing that will clear the obstruction. It is virtually only in children that small objects can pass through the larynx, block the windpipe and bring breathing to a complete stop. The child goes blue, and there is no breathing movement; the only chance of clearing the airway is in holding the child up by the feet and thumping it hard on the back. **Neck**

Here it is mostly the **lungs and airways** that are in trouble. This usually involves *bronchitis*, which is inflammation of the smaller airways or the windpipe itself. Main symptoms are coughing and throwing up of phlegm, and if the windpipe is inflamed the coughing **Chest** is accompanied by pain behind the breastbone. So long as there is little or no accompanying fever, medicine to break up the phlegm and stop the coughing (Alupent, in our list) will be sufficient. If there is a highish fever (over 38.5°C, 101°F) *pneumonia* must be suspected, in which case an antibiotic must be given at once. To get as broad an effect as possible, ampicillin is the best one to use. Accompanying pneumonia, but sometimes on its own, there may be *pleurisy*, recognisable from pain in breathing (usually in the lower part of the rib-cage). This seldom needs separate treatment; if it occurs alone – ie. as breathing pain without any fever, coughing or phlegm – an anti-inflammatory drug like indomethacin should be taken.

One is usually as unaware of one's **heart** as of any other organ; but when heart pains do occur the sufferer is understandably deeply worried. Here one needs to distinguish between true cardiac pain due to inadequate circulation, and the harmless functional complaint. Heart pain can sometimes be sparked off 'in the mind'! There are two ways of telling the difference:

1. Serious heart pains occur more markedly during physical effort and under the effect of cold, generally disappearing rapidly with rest.
2. True heart pain will usually fade within a few minutes of letting a glyceryl nitrate tablet dissolve under the tongue, while functional pain (which is not serious) will be unchanged by the drug.

While serious heart pain calls for complete rest and the use of quite strong painkillers, the other kind responds to 'occupational therapy' – work!

A **cardiac infarct**, or heart attack, is really only heart pain due to insufficient circulation, taken a stage further. Tightness in the chest accompanies very severe pain round the heart, coupled with a 'feeling you are going to die'; it is often combined with circulatory collapse, recognisable from cold sweating, darkness before the eyes and a rapid pulse. This calls for complete rest and painkillers and tranquillizers. Obviously a doctor is needed as quickly as possible. An infarct can also lead to a severe state of shock or death from heart failure within seconds; the resuscitation measures already described must be used. A heart attack on board a yacht is quite on the cards, remembering that there may be people getting on in years and perhaps rather out of condition, doing work calling for effort they never make in their everyday lives.

Apart from the main symptoms of pain and fever already mentioned, functional disorders affecting the abdomen mostly involve vomiting and diarrhoea.

Abdomen

Vomiting, in the form of seasickness, will be the most common illness on a boat. Strictly speaking, seasickness vomiting has its immediate cause not in the abdomen but in the organs of balance in the ears. From the treatment viewpoint, however, it is like any other vomiting. All the drugs used (eg. Dramamine, Kwells and Stelazine) work on the central nervous system, which means they can cause drowsiness. The earlier they are taken, the more effective they are, so they should be taken at the first signs of a rough sea getting up (by seasick-prone people even sooner, if rough weather is expected). Once severe seasickness and vomiting has started, it is difficult to take anything to deal with it, because tablets will be quickly thrown up again. In this case suppositories, or if necessary an intramuscular injection, will have to be given. As a precaution in bad weather, do not overload the stomach with rich food; it is general experience that instant coffee, too, will start off seasickness. Once severe vomiting starts, avoid taking food in any form; on the other hand a fluid intake is needed, even if only in small amounts at a time. Unsweetened tea without milk is best. Contraceptive pills must, to be effective, be taken again if vomiting starts less than two hours after first taking them.

Diarrhoea is, particularly in the hotter countries, almost always due to bacterial infection; I said earlier that bacterial contamination of food or drink was generally responsible for this condition. Treatment must be started at the first sign of diarrhoea, to prevent it getting worse and becoming a cause for concern; the best way is very largely to keep off food altogether. One *must* however have enough fluids, at least 1½ litres and preferably 2 litres a day, again best taken in the form of unsweetened tea without milk. At the same time take Kaolin mixture and Penbritin. I strongly advise against taking antibiotics, since these will only make the diarrhoea worse, and even with a genuine salmonella infection they are not the treatment of choice, only turning people into infection carriers.

Heartburn, which those prone to it often get after drinking a lot of alcohol, is harmless and will respond well to Gelusil tablets. Foods and drinks that cause acidity (coffee, alcohol, strong spices) should be avoided.

Gastro-intestinal bleeding may be a complication of vomiting or diarrhoea, or start of its own accord. The vomit has a 'coffee-grounds' appearance. The appearance of the stools differs with the site of the bleeding; only bleeding fairly close to the anus will give really red traces of blood. Otherwise there will be 'tarry' stools (pitch-black in colour and foul-smelling – the latter distinguishing them from the harmless black stools seen after drinking red wine) to indicate bleeding further up the digestive tract. The source of the bleeding is usually an ulcer just after the outlet from the stomach, in the duodenum. Take Dicynene tablets and plenty of iced drinks, and Gelusil. This is always serious, so try to find a doctor as soon as possible.

The **'hollow organs' of the abdomen and pelvis** are a case apart. They include the gallbladder and bile ducts, the whole of the intestine, the kidneys and urinary system and (in women) the fallopian tubes and womb. These organs call for special attention because they are subject to a particular form of pain known as *colic.* Colics are pains that vary in intensity in almost a wave-pattern, coming as it were in gusts. If pains like this occur, take Buscopan (the suppository form available in some countries is particularly suitable). If the gallbladder or bile-ducts are affected the temperature generally soars as well, perhaps combined wtih shivering fits; the pains are in every case on the right side, radiating usually from the shoulder-blade at the back. If there is fever, an antibiotic should be taken. With the kidneys and urinary tract the pain is localised more in the loins and involves the groin. Plenty of fluid should be given as well as Buscopan.

An enormous number of people suffer from **supposed constipation**. I use the word 'supposed' deliberately, because most of these people are basing themselves on the belief that a good, daily movement of the bowels is essential for health. This is absolute nonsense. Even if he goes to the loo only once in three days, a person is *not* ill! I really wanted to delete a laxative from the list of

278

medicines altogether, because generally they are only misused: but one cannot really do without them in a case of inflamed haemorrhoids, or with illnesses involving fever. Otherwise, use natural remedies such as food with plenty of roughage (fruit, vegetables, salads and wholemeal bread), cold fruit juice taken on an empty stomach, etc.

Intestinal blockage   will sooner or later lead to a total retention of faeces and wind, and within two to three days there will be symptoms of peritonitis (discussed below). Treatment by the layman is virtually impossible, and one must in particular avoid giving laxatives in such cases.

Salpingitis   (inflammation of the fallopian tubes) and **inflammation of the womb**, which also cause colicky pain in the lower abdomen, are usually accompanied by fever, and there is great sensitivity to pressure. It is hard to tell them apart from appendicitis, and there is no certain test for the layman to apply. Give antibiotics such as ampicillin, painkillers (in our case Buscopan) and an anti-inflammatory such as indomethacin.

All the abdominal complaints listed here, apart from kidney-stone colic, can lead to *peritonitis*. Besides very severe and violent pains felt over the whole of the abdomen, the latter feels 'as hard as a board'. If peritonitis is local, eg. in acute appendicitis, the hardening of the muscles, too, will be more or less localised to start with. In every case the situation is very serious, and one can only try to gain time by applying icebags or cold compresses, at the same time giving an antibiotic like ampicillin. A strong analgesic, such as Fortral by intramuscular injection, will be needed to cope with the pain, though bear in mind that so far as possible no painkillers should be given for about four hours prior to reaching a doctor or hospital (otherwise the symptoms will be masked and the doctor will be prevented from making a rapid diagnosis).

Inflammation of the urinary system, bladder or kidneys   is accompanied by varying degrees of fever. In the case of the kidneys the temperature rises very quickly, usually with shivering fits. Another general symptom of inflammation of the urinary apparatus is a burning sensation when passing water, and an urge to urinate frequently though usually producing only a few drops. Here again, use antibiotics and painkillers.

Bleeding from the bladder is not very common, but is always serious. Apart from giving Dicynene tablets, there is nothing that can be done, and a doctor must be found.

A total **inability to pass urine** may occur, exclusively among men over the age of 50 and especially with severe chilling or over-indulgence in alcohol, through swelling of the prostate gland. I would not really advise an attempt at passing a catheter by a layman who has never done it before, and it is a good deal simpler to *puncture the full bladder*. The following instructions must be strictly followed:

■ No water must have been passed for at least 12 hours before. This ensures that the bladder really is full, and raises it in the abdomen.
■ The pubic hair should be shaved off, and the skin over the pubic bone disinfected with acriflavine.
■ A sterile hypodermic needle, Size 1, is now taken and inserted vertically through the skin about 2 fingerwidths above the top edge of the pubic bone; the needle is then allowed to penetrate further under gentle pressure, until drops of urine start to emerge through it.

With very fat persons it may be necessary while doing this to compress the abdominal wall by pressing inwards. If a few drops of blood are seen at first while doing so, there is no need to interrupt the operation. Collect the urine obtained in a measuring vessel, because the operation must be discontinued after removing about 1½ litres. This is most important, otherwise bleeding from the bladder may be caused. After the bladder has been relieved in this way, withdraw the needle with a quick jerk, and cover the puncture point on the skin with an ordinary Band-aid. Punctures like this can be repeated as often as necessary.

Inflammation of the veins

Haemorrhoids (piles) are a special form of this, and can make life an absolute misery. Apart from keeping things absolutely clean (especially after using the toilet) and local application of ointment such as Lasonil, an anti-inflammatory (indomethacin) will help a great deal.

With **phlebitis**, or inflammation of the leg veins (divided into the superficial and deep types), indomethacin is again the drug to use. With superficial phlebitis reddening is seen all along the affected vein, with pain and swelling and hardening of the network of veins. This is generally harmless. Cool the affected area and apply ointments such as Lasonil. Deep phlebitis, which is not visible much externally apart from swelling of the affected leg, is a serious condition. There is pain when standing and walking and, typically, pressure on the sole of the foot produces pain. The danger here is that blood-clots will get carried to the lungs, and absolute rest at once is essential. Give the patient indomethacin, and ampicillin if there is fever. Make sure to keep up an ample fluid intake. If the swelling of the foot has not subsided a good deal within six hours of this treatment, find a doctor.

Skin inflammation sometimes comes from insect bites or minor wounds, and results in a painful reddening of the skin beneath the wound. Propicillin and cooling dressings will bring relief.

Boils or abscesses are easy to recognise. Delay treatment until the abscess is 'ripe'; within a couple of days the skin over the tip of it will become red and taut, with the very tip finally turning whitish. Then take a sterile knife-blade or scalpel and make a tiny nick in the skin at the tip of the abscess, whereupon the pus will almost spurt out. Lay a strip of sterile gauze over the opening, and cover the whole with a dressing; generally healing will proceed without complications, though ampicillin should be given just to be on the safe side.

A typical acute attack of **gout** can be easily recognised by the layman. The ends of the big toes swell, turn bluish-red and are extremely painful. Once again, take indomethacin and plenty of fluids, but no alcohol.

Allergies – hypersensitive reactions – are very common, and are triggered off by drugs, insect bites, foods, washing powders and a host of other things. In the milder forms the skin is itchy, reddish and forms a rash. The face often puffs up as well. Calcium, and in severe cases Medrone tablets, can give rapid relief. In very severe allergic reactions there may be large weals, and symptoms of shock and suffocation. Provided the patient stays conscious, he can be given calcium and Medrone tablets in generous doses; if he becomes unconscious, or seems to be suffocating, an injection (preferably intravenous) of Depo-Medrone will be the only answer.

Injections

Filling a syringe: it must contain no air, so hold it pointing upwards and press the plunger gently until a drop of fluid emerges.

Neither *intramuscular* nor *intravenous* injections are particularly difficult to give. Practical instruction, rather than a lot of theoretical description, is however almost indispensable. The need for giving injections will be obvious from what has been said in the last few pages: for example an unconscious person must never have any-

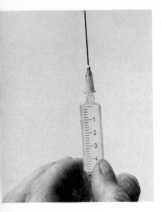

thing poured into the mouth, as this will only cause vomiting which will block the airway and almost cause suffocation. When vomiting and diarrhoea come together, injection, or even an infusion, would be needed for treating shock properly. I would always advise carrying a blood substitute, ideally Macrodex; even if you have not yourself mastered the technique of intravenous injection, somebody else may be able to help give a life-saving infusion.

When giving an intravenous injection, imagine a thin plastic tube (use one for practice!). Withdraw the plunger slightly before injecting – if blood appears, the needle is in the vein (put rubber-tube tourniquet round the upper arm first).

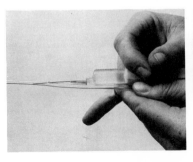 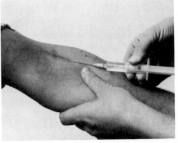

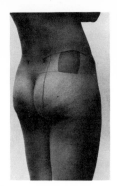

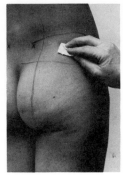

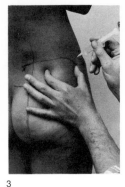

1

2

3

4

Collapse, shock, panic

A **collapse** can occur with, for example, a fluid deficiency, or circulatory weakness after a feverish illness, or in some people after as little as stooping and getting up quickly or changing quickly from a lying to a standing position. It makes everything go black, causes slight nausea and sweating and a feeling of weakness. The symptoms may be so severe as to produce temporary unconsciousness so that the victim falls over. The patient should remain in a lying position; it is wrong to sit him up. In fact, the upper part of the body should be placed lower, and the legs raised. Usually the pallor will go, and consciousness returns within a few minutes.

People tend to try to breath deep and fast after a collapse; if this is continued for several minutes it can produce severe cramps in all the muscles, especially seen as peculiar paw-like curling of the fingers and a fishlike gaping of the mouth. This is hyperventilation tetany (not to be confused with tetanus, which is muscle spasm caused by wound infection). A very simple way of overcoming such attacks is to throw a handkerchief or jacket loosely over the head; administering calcium will also quickly stop an attack.

Patients drift into a **shock state**, the shock being caused by a previous severe event of some kind; this may be injury, an allergic reaction, haemorrhage, a heart attack or many other things. The victim is nearly always fully conscious; there is cold sweating, a very fast heartbeat, a pallid skin and a drastic drop in blood pressure (with the carotid pulse scarcely detectable). The person's life is in danger, and he should be laid flat with the legs raised; an intravenous infusion of a blood substitute can save life. Once the person has become unconscious, there is not a great deal of hope left.

Intramuscular injection
1 the injection site
2 clean skin with pad soaked in surgical spirit
3 hold syringe like a pencil and stab it in with some force, working from the wrist
4 press plunger home slowly

283

If someone on board looks like going to pieces in a crisis, it may become necessary to calm him down; this can usually be done well enough with Valium tablets, or if needs be a Valium injection, which may even have to be given by force. In such a case the dose can safely be increased to 40 or 60mg without any risk of poisoning. Valium is also a well-established remedy for acute lumbago: at least 40mg need to be taken, and this will of course induce a marked feeling of tiredness, but the important thing is to relax the tense back muscles. No alcohol should be taken during this treatment.

I have quite deliberately left any kind of 'wakey-wakey' pills out of our list of medicines, because there is no situation that justifies using them. They can, on the contrary, be highly dangerous. If you artificially overcome the body's defence mechanism of fatigue, the short spurt of extra activity will be followed by a collapse that is certain to be all the more total. I would only remind readers of the death of a Danish racing cyclist at the Rome Olympics in 1960, shown to be due to taking an energy-enhancing drug. There are also almost bound to be mental side-effects, unpredictable in nature and severity but undoubtedly unwelcome; they include overconfidence, lack of critical judgment, and often a dangerous depression.

Coping with a distress at sea

Liferafts and lifeboats, too, must carry a certain amount of medical stores; as space is restricted, these will be limited to dressings, painkillers and seasickness preventatives. Apart from this, there is not a lot that medicine can do to help increase chances of survival. One absolute warning: *never ever drink seawater!* Innumerable experiments have shown that even small amounts of salt water can severely damage the health, cutting down the chances of coming through. Only rainwater or the fresh water collected by condensation on metallic foil should be drunk. Guard against extreme chilling. Over-exertion (through rowing and the like) must also be avoided.

Literature

Now for a few books on medical care that ought to be on the boat's bookshelf, especially on a long cruise. These may be a bit beyond the layman here and there, and occasionally even incomprehensible, but it is still reassuring to have something to consult in an emergency.

The Ship Captain's Medical Guide, published by H. M. Stationery Office, London.
This government publication is standard equipment on many merchant ships, and covers internal complaints as well as accident injuries. Abundantly illustrated, it is amazingly good value at only £2.65.

Baillieres Handbook of First Aid, published by Baillière, Tindall & Cassell, London.
Designed for use by medical students, nurses and ambulancemen.

First Aid for Yachtsmen – emergencies and aftercare Dr R. Haworth, published by Adlard Coles 1975, London.
Written in plain, straightforward language with clear illustrations by a doctor with sailing experience.

The yacht's medical store

Carla Schenk
pharmacist

Just as a seagoing yacht needs a toolkit and enough spare parts, so it must have a stock of medicines. It is not really feasible to recommend a generally-applicable list, because this will depend on a host of differing circumstances:
■ the cruising ground
■ the length of the cruise
■ the size of the crew
■ whether there are any children
One can begin by assuming that all members of the crew will be in peak physical condition when starting the voyage. If anyone suffers from a particular condition (such as diabetes, asthma, migraine, etc.) he or she should naturally bring along a supply of any special, personal drugs.

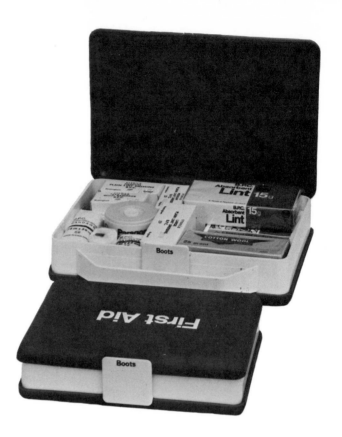

The small medicine store should be ready to hand in the bridge deck, even on a short voyage.

The yacht's medical store should be kept in watertight plastic containers in as cool and accessible a place as possible, ie. against the hull wall below the waterline. The medicine box needs checking at regular intervals, certainly at the start of the season and before any major voyage, to ensure it is complete and that the drugs are in good condition. Some (eg. penicillin) carry a printed expiry date, which makes things simple; but how can one tell whether other products are still as they should be? And when do they need to be replaced with fresh stock?

The principal warning signs are:
- tablets crumbling, or the surface of coated tablets becoming slimy or scaling off.
- tablets or solutions changing their colour.
- deposits or flocculent precipitation in clear solutions, syrups or eye and eardrops.
- a change in smell.
- breaking up of ointments or emulsions that are normally smooth and homogeneous.

If these warning signs appear, throw the offending drug away as soon as possible. If you want to buy replacement drugs when abroad, show the pharmacist the old packing and the leaflet inside it; he will then be able to match up the chemical composition and sell you a corresponding preparation.

The following suggested list is for a yacht carrying three to four crew on holiday cruises in, say, the North Sea or Channel, the Mediterranean or the Caribbean, where you can get to a doctor within two to three days in an emergency.

Drugs

Drug	Quantity	Uses
acriflavine solution		disinfecting wounds
Alupent tablets	20	bronchitis, persistent coughing
ampicillin		infections of respiratory,
125mg tablets	25	urinary and bile tracts,
250mg vials	5	blood poisoning
Betnovate-N cream	30g	burns, sunburn, grazes, stings
Bisolvon tablets	20	influenza, fever
Buscopan tablets	20	colics, cramps
Buscopan ampoules	5	(gallbladder and kidneys)
calcium tablets	20	allergies, rashes
chloramphenicol 0.5 per cent eyedrops	10g	bacterial infection of eyelids & tear-ducts, conjunctivitis
chloromycetin 10 per cent eardrops	10g	inflammation of outer and middle ear
Dequadin lozenges	20	infections of mouth and throat

Dexa-Rhinaspray, 125-dose unit	1	colds
Dramamine tablets or	100	seasickness
Kwells tablets	2 x 25	
Dulcolax tablets	30	constipation
Dicynene tablets	20	bleeding (internal, eg. stomach, intestine or bladder) & nosebleeds
Fortral capsules	20	very severe pain
Fortral suppositories	5	
Fucidin gel or ointment	10g	boils and abscesses
Gelusil tablets	50	acid stomach, gastritis, ulcers
glyceryl trinitrate tablets	15	angina pectoris
indomethacin	20	inflammations and swellings
kaolin mixture	200ml	diarrhoea
Lasonil ointment	40g	sprains, bruises, haemorrhoids
Medrone tablets	10	severe allergies, insect bites on neck
noradrenaline ampoules	5	circulatory collapse
oxazepam tablets	25	nervous excitement,
or Valium tablets	20	sleeplessness
opium tincture	10g	severe diarrhoea
paracetamol tablets	25	pain (headaches)
Penbritin KS powder to make	120ml	diarrhoea
Phenergan ampoules	3	severe vomiting
propicillin tablets	10	infections of ear, nose and throat, airways, mouth, and teeth, and skin
Stemetil suppositories	5	severe vomiting
Valium ampoules	5	severe nervous excitement

1 medical thermometer

10 disposable gloves, sterile, large size

1 pair tweezers

1 disposable scalpel

10 surgical clamps

1 pair bandage scissors

1 airway tube

10 disposable syringes, 5ml size

5 disposable syringes, 20ml size

20 disposable hypodermic needles, Size 1

1 disposable catheter

100ml surgical spirit, in plastic bottle

1 triangular bandage

cotton wool, 50g

first-aid kits, 3 large size, 3 medium size

bandaging mull, 1m

1 Smith & Nephew Melolin bandage 60 x 80cm

3 Melolin first-aid kits

10 Seton's dumb-bell sutures

Band-Aid plasters, large box, assorted

elasticated plaster bandage, 5m x 2½cm, 5m x 5cm (for compression bandaging)

muslin bandage, 2m x 6cm, 2m x 8cm, 2m x 10cm

crepe bandage, 1m x 8cm, 1m x 10cm

1 eye patch

leather finger-stalls, 1 large, 1 medium

safety pins

1 set inflatable splints

I always keep some drugs and dressings in frequent use ready to hand in the bridge deck:

first-aid kits, elastic bandages, Band-Aids, muslin bandages, noradrenalin drops and oxazepam tablets, acriflavin solution, sunburn ointment, painkiller tablets and, most of all, tablets against seasickness. This mini-medicine store will be sufficient for day cruises.

For longish voyages I would also take along a few drugs *for use only by a qualified doctor.* You may well find a doctor on your holiday island, or get advice from one by radio on how to give these preparations yourself in an absolute emergency. They should be kept separate in a special Tupperware box marked clearly 'For doctor only': to prevent all possibility of their being used inadvertently, seal the box firmly with Sellotape.

Drug	Quantity	Use
Epontol ampoules	5	short-duration anaesthetic
strophanthin ampoules	5	acute heart failure and insufficiency
Macrodex + electrolyte	2	shock
mepivacaine hydrochloride ampoules	5	local anaesthetic
adrenaline ampoules	10	collapse, shock
Depo-Medrone 40mg ampoules	3	severe allergies, insect bites in neck

Thought has been given, in compiling the list, to the fact that drops are not the easiest of things to measure out accurately on a rolling, pitching yacht; and with colics, severe pain and vomiting, suppositories are often the simplest way of administering drugs. Most preparations listed here are available only on a doctor's prescription, and one or two of them are on the Dangerous Drugs list. The best way to go about building up your yacht's medicine chest is to see your own doctor and explain carefully why you want the various items; he can then probably provide you with a private prescription, and will doubtless give you valuable advice on how they should be used if the need arises while at sea. In several cases drugs have been listed here (those with a small initial letter) by their 'generic' name, under which they will be more readily available (and usually cheaper) than when prescribed by a particular tradename. Branded drugs are shown with a capital initial.

If your cruise takes you to the tropics, the medicine chest will have to include chloroquinone (eg. Resochin) against malaria and salt tablets for maintaining the body's electrolyte balance. Sugar-coated tablets and capsules tend quickly to become unusable in hot climates, and suppositories can be cooled down (in their individual packing) in cold water.

If there are small children on board, you will additionally need:
propicillin syrup (powder to make 100ml)
ampicillin syrup
Penbritin Paediatric Tablets
My medicine chest has taped to the lid, for emergency use, a pocket torch the battery of which is renewed yearly.

Tools and spares

'Take as many tools with you as you can; even if you don't know how to use them, you may well come across someone somewhere who does.' This was probably the best piece of advice I had given to me before starting my round-the-world cruise. I paid less than a single sheet-winch would have cost me for – I think – a full kit of tools. Thank heavens there are not yet any 'maker's special tools' for yachts, so you can still buy them in the shops paying the same price as other, ordinary mortals. For this very reason I am amazed how badly equipped with tools many cruising skippers are; having what you need can often mean the safety or otherwise of the boat. People will spend hundreds on a wind monitor which is not absolutely necessary on a cruising yacht, and then will be too mean to pay £8 for a set of ring spanners.

Obviously tools will be chosen to suit the needs of the boat. There is no point carrying a 32mm spanner if there is not a single 32mm bolt on the whole vessel. On the other hand, you may have to have twice the normal number of spanners if you are unfortunate enough to have some items of mechanical equipment on board that have metric threads and others with inch threads (don't be tempted to 'make do' with the wrong size). The following list makes no claim to be exhaustive, and is meant only to give a broad idea of what to carry. It is designed for a long cruise, though personally there is not much I would leave out even on shorter trips.

Tools

One set should be *ring spanners,* which have the advantage (especially in the usually cramped confines of a yacht) of needing very little room to turn the nut a bit at a time. If an *open-ended spanner* has less than 60° to work in, it has to be turned over each time for the next turn. Ring spanners make it easier to undo a tight nut, because if you use a lot of force on an open-ended spanner the jaws tend to spread, and then slip on the nut, ruining it. For this reason adjustable spanners are to be avoided, practical though they may seem – they are a sure way of chewing off the corners of a nut or bolthead.

2 sets of spanners

1 set of Allen keys

rubber-faced hammer

pincers

1 large pipe wrench

flatnose pliers

1 hacksaw

291

2 Mole wrenches	The most versatile tool you can have. You need a lot of force to close them, but they then remain closed by themselves. They can be used in umpteen different ways – to replace a winch handle lost overboard, to turn a bolt-head when you have ruined the screwdriver slot, to stop the prop shaft from sliding out when it has broken loose from its flange, and so on.
2 hammers	One should have a slightly rounded hitting surface.

The propeller shaft is held temporarily with a Mole wrench, to stop it from slipping out.

drill **rivetting tool**	If you carry only a hand-operated drill, remember that there will often not be enough space to turn it in the tight corners that yachts have; so an electric one is better. There are quite cheap ones (£10 or so) working on 12V; originally meant for cars, they can of course be used on a boat just as well. They are more powerful than hand drills, and usually have an 8mm chuck (try to get a 10mm chuck if you can).

The ideal, of course, would be a powerful drill like the do-it-yourself ones you use at home, though these need shore mains or a generator. If you use a little Honda generator set, remember that the E 300 puts out barely 300W, so buy a 250W drill. You will obviously need heavy-duty twist drills in all sizes; the smaller ones easily snap when used by the unskilled (like us).

wood saws	Crosscut and fretsaw (with blades).
vice **tin-snips,** **sharp knife** **or razor blade,**	One of the most important items, though very seldom used (but when you *do* need it, you really need it!) It will allow you, in a remote anchorage or far out at sea, to cut and file metal parts to shape in an emergency. One problem will, however, be where to

Drill powered from the battery

clamp it; on small yachts you can generally use one of the com- **screw clamp**
panionway steps. To avoid damaging the woodwork, slip small **threadcutter**
pieces of wood between the step and the vice clamp before tighten- **chisel**
ing it up.

Take one or two screwdrivers for the cross-slot kind of screw, as a **screwdrivers**
precaution. (various sizes)

You should have various shapes and sizes of these; remember you **files**
need them for both metal and wood.

Should be in stainless steel, and with toothed blades (the only way **shears**
of preventing smooth materials from slipping out of shears).

For severing shrouds, guardrails, etc. Should be capable of cutting **boltcutters**
through stainless steel up to the diameter of your heaviest shrouds
– make a point, when buying, of asking how many millimetres of
stainless steel they can cope with.

Extremely useful device, running on a small can of gas like those **Soldering**
used for refuelling gas cigarette-lighters. **torch**

Important for freeing rusted bolts or getting jammed threads mov- **penetrating**
ing again. The label on the can may say 'for electrical equipment', **oil**
but I would not use penetrating oil or anti-rust agents for water- **oilcan**
proofing – there are special silicone products for sensitive yacht's **greasegun**
electronics, though whether these are generally effective is a mat- **sewing-**
ter of opinion: once I sprayed my transmitter with one, and could **machine oil**
not get another sound out of it – the stuff had formed a thin protec-

tive coating on the capacitors, but had also affected the dielectric space between the plates, making a tedious re-trimming job necessary. I have used this spray again since, but take care never to get it on the capacitors. It tends to evaporate and lose its effect within a month or two.

epoxy adhesive Can also be used for locking screw threads, and as a sealant that will not burn off when used on an exhaust.

epoxy resin Will not keep for much over a year.

plastic metal This is also described as cold welding material, and is in fact a plastic adhesive to which a filler has been added to give extra strength. It comes nowhere near the hardness of metal, however, as you can prove with a file; so the astronomic prices charged for it in some countries until recently were certainly not justified.

cyanide adhesive

adhesive Uhu or Evostik This is the wonder adhesive, recently come on the market, that people warn will stick the skin together for ever after if you put a drop between finger and thumb and press them together for 15 seconds, and will need tearing apart! You can also use it for *extra* security when attaching wire rope terminals. Its drawback is the still-high price, and the fact that it does not keep long in a hot climate.

silicone rubber Unlike natural rubber, this – used for seals – does not perish and remains springy for ever. Snag: in general it cannot be stuck to plastic, nor to wood unless this has been specially treated beforehand.

Vaseline For smearing over the battery terminals, and for coating eggs which will then remain fresh for up to three months.

tallow This can be used for lubricating ropes which are constantly under load where they run through a block.

talcum powder For rubbing into the rubber sealing strip round hatches and portholes

Can be used to wrap round bare wire ends at the shroud bottle-screws, to prevent scratch injuries.

Sellotape & insulating tape

Not only for the helmsman during the night watch – it can be used to stick a screw to the screwdriver where there is no room for the fingers (and as a temporary plug for small leaks).

chewing gum

These write on any surface. They can be used to note the operating-hours reading on the engine when changing oil; to number parts when dismantling a starter motor so as to reassemble it in the right order; to show the direction of rotation of winches; and so on.

smudge and waterproof pencils

From a car accessory shop, and best used by clipping direct on to the battery terminals. You can of course also heat a soldering iron in an open flame (a spirit or kerosene stove). This kind of iron must not be poked round inside electronic gear, as transistors and diodes are ultra-vulnerable to heat; this also applies to the soldering torches already mentioned, working from a small gas bottle. Both these types are really only for rough work, where stray heat will do no harm. You will of course also need solder; buy the kind incorporating its own flux.

soldering iron tweezers (flat-nosed & pointed) hand mirror magnifying glass

Available from electrical stores, from about £5 upwards. Unless you know all about electronics, a cheap universal meter will do perfectly well for your needs.

voltmeter or universal meter

For stopping up any small leaks that occur. Particularly useful for this are the sets of rubber plugs in various sizes packed in every inflatable lifeboat. They are quite cheap, and available from most yacht chandlers.

corks and rubber plugs

To be any use for sewing sails, this must give a zig-zag stitch; but a hand-driven model able to do this will be hard to find on the secondhand market, and modern machines present current consumption problems. It also needs to be very tough, to cope with heavy sail materials. All this means that machines can hardly be used for the job, and you have to fall back on doing things by hand. Still, if you've the room, it is worth carrying a hand sewing-machine.

sewing-machine

Rubber sealing plugs from a liferaft

adhesive
carpet tape

For emergency repairs to sails. The modern product often has enormous adhesive power, though remember that even for this wonder tape the base has to be dry and as grease-free as possible.

diving mask
& snorkel

Very important: if you want to be really in control of things when cruising, you have to be able to go over the side occasionally to check whether anything is amiss. On long voyages you are bound to want to clean off the underwater hull. A 10m yacht can be cleaned in about two hours with a stiff brush, by one man. But don't get any wrong ideas; no-one can work over the side in a seaway, however superfit he may be.

diving
wet-suit

rubber
gloves

This is expensive to buy, but advisable even if cruises are to be mainly in warm water. Only wearing a wet-suit will you be really able to work underwater for any length of time, and you may have to spend hours in the cooler water of a harbour dealing with rudder, propeller, speedo or echo-sounder problems.

diving torch

Useful not only if you are unlucky enough to have a problem underwater at night (*warning:* never go into the water at night with a torch if there is the slightest likelihood of sharks about). The range of these bulky torches tends to be overestimated, too; even in very clear water you cannot see further than 2m. But a diving torch is valuable on board at night as well – in foul weather with pouring rain, ordinary hand-torches soon pack up. A floating diving torch is best, as it can be thrown into the water after anyone who falls overboard at night and the skywards-pointing beam will then make it easier to find the spot.

water hose
(30m)

It is often more convenient, and safer, to take on water through a

296

hose rather than haul the yacht up to the watering-point.

This I would take only if there were lots of spare room. All harbours are at sea level, so 'down-town' is usually uphill!	**folding bicycle**
A bundle of problems: petrol on board, road tax and insurance complications. It is often simpler, and in the end cheaper, to hire one locally if you think you really need it.	**mini-motorbike**

Spare parts

In various thicknesses, for electrical work.	**insulated copper wire**
In all possible sizes, and rather carry too many than too few.	**stainless steel screws**
Size and material will usually be governed by the yacht's internal fittings. If brass screws are used, you must have the right size available. After a long time exposed to salt water they corrode, even if sited in what you might think is a dry place; then the screwdriver cannot get a grip, and it is better to fit a new screw.	**woodscrews brass wire s/s wire wire rope stainless steel sheet (small pieces 1, 2 & 3mm thick)**
Available from tool shops in an assortment of sizes. Generally made in materials that rust, but they can be used for a short while in places where you have lost the washer overboard during dismantling. If necessary you can make a washer by winding ordinary steel wire in a spiral, heating it till red in an open flame and then plunging it into cold water to temper it.	**split pins (all sizes) spring washers**
For all electrical gear on board, but use only leak-proof batteries for electronic equipment. They can be stored for only a limited time, and batteries in electrical equipment must be checked occasionally. Even leak-proof batteries will leak eventually, and this can ruin electronic gear.	**spare batteries**
For all lamps on board.	**spare bulbs**
Especially for navigation lights, whose sockets are bound to wear out in time from getting salt water on them.	**spare sockets**

fuses	Many items of electronic gear have their own built-in fuses.
2 Norseman terminals	Using these, a new shroud can be made up in an emergency with the wire rope listed above; this means carrying a wire rope at least as long as the boat's longest shroud or stay.
bottlescrews	Carry a spare for each kind used on board.
bulldog clamps	These can be used to make an eye on a wire rope.
wooden plank 40cm x 2m	This doesn't look very smart stored on a yacht, and a lot of people grin to see a plank like this lying about on deck; but in fact an ordinary plank with a couple of holes bored in the corners is a universal aid – you can use it as a gangplank, put it outside the fenders to take the rub of the wall, and laid athwart the cockpit it makes a comfortable table to eat from (it looks better covered with a tablecloth!). In very foul weather it can be fixed in front of the cabin windows to protect them against heavy seas, and it could be fashioned into an emergency rudder.
blocks & shackles	In all possible sizes needed.
lamp-glass	For the cosy, kerosene-fuelled hurricane lamp.
spare burners	For the stove; don't make do with a repair kit, because it is quicker and easier to replace the burner complete than to spend ages fiddling about dismantling the jets.
sail needles	Various sizes, stored free from rust in a small screw-capped bottle filled with oil.
spare alternator	Only an alternator, which you will certainly not be able to repair with the means to hand, calls for carrying a spare; the older DC dynamo will only need its carbon brushes renewing every three years.
engine spares belts	The engine manufacturer can advise you what spares to carry. Apart from the oil filter, an impeller for the water pump or, better still, a replacement water pump, you should have at least a full set

of gaskets and seals. For a diesel, carry as many spare injectors as there are cylinders. For petrol engines essential spares include spark-plugs, contact-breaker points and a coil.

fuel filter
stainless
hose clips

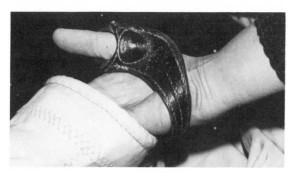

Sailmaker's palm

sailmaker's palm
rubber shockcord with hooks, rope, whipping twine, sailcloth (2m² is enough)
piston hanks
mast-track slides
pump spares

For all pumps on board (including the toilet).

Neoprene diaphragms, in particular, last only one to two years when used in salt water.

If you follow this suggested list, you will end up with a mass of small bits and pieces; the trouble will be not so much finding room for them as the risk of items disappearing into odd corners of the boat. So it is advisable to write out a full inventory showing where they are all stowed; include every item, down to the smallest. Tools are obviously best kept in a special tool-box, stowed so that they are quickly and easily accessible. You will need tools far more often than you think.

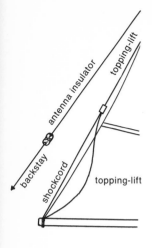

topping-lift

Hints and tips

Topping-lift

Time and again, especially with the wind free, you find that the boom lifts and leaves too much slack in the topping lift, which then catches in the porcelain 'egg' insulators often fitted to the top and bottom of the backstay; infuriating when you then need to reef at short notice. To prevent this, you need only fix a 2m length of shockcord parallel to the lift to keep it under tension.

Drinking water   is scarce, yet no-one has to do without a shower on deck with fresh water; a watering-can rose and a cheap plastic bucket are all you need. It's amazing how far 5 litres of water will go.

Echo-sounder

If you buy a new echo-sounder, this can be temporarily built-in if there is no opportunity for hauling the yacht out at once. It will work if the transducer is set against the inside of a wood or GRP hull, and immersed in water. This is simple to test out by letting it right down into the bilge. I wouldn't leave it like this permanently, how-ever, because the sensitivity is reduced.

Binoculars

These tend to wear out rapidly on board, as they are exposed to all weathers; it is all too easy to shove them back in the case without wiping off the salt spray. It may work out cheaper to buy a low-price Japanese pair every three years. If you try them before buying, insist on having the actual ones you've tested and don't accept another pair 'in the maker's packing'. It takes a lot of practice to keep binoculars of × 10 magnification still enough on a yacht, and a slightly lower power is easier to handle.

Cine-filming and photography

On board a yacht this has its special problems. Without a wide-angle lens you might as well not even try. Hardly any amateur succeeds in really capturing the feel of bad weather or a big sea-way. When, later on, you see the horizon in the picture as a straight line, you would think it was not much over Force 3, so take the picture while down in a trough. Unhappily, all optical equipment is hypersensitive to dampness and salt water, so really dramatic pic-tures in foul weather are rare. The best answer would be an under-water casing, but these are usually expensive and bulky. A cheap and satisfactory solution is the 'ewa-marine' underwater camera

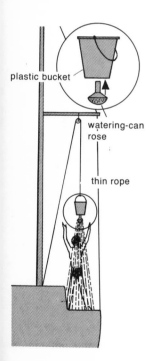

plastic bucket

watering-can rose

thin rope

Temporary freshwater showerbath

bag, made by the German firm of Goedecke (Munich), who guarantee it as being watertight down to a depth of 10m. It is available for all sizes of camera. A great deal more expensive is the Calypso miniature camera, which is itself watertight and can be used down to 50m without any protective casing.

Even in the darkness of the cabin, however, there is another enemy lurking to harm a costly piece of camera equipment; this is a fungus which has the glass of lenses as its favourite target. It thrives where conditions are dark and damp, and spreads a fine spider's-web of strands all over the lens which will completely ruin it since the fungus cannot be removed once it has a hold. Dry storage and lots of ultra-violet light are an effective defence, so cameras should be brought out into the open air occasionally and even exposed to direct sunlight. They are best stored in an aluminium case with a tight seal, or in a Tupperware box, also containing a cloth bag filled with silica gel. This is a cheap chemical which turns pinkish-red when saturated with moisture which it absorbs from the air; it can then be heated over the stove until it goes back to its original dark blue colour.

A **Polaroid camera with flash** can be an enormous help if you have to carry out repairs to complicated equipment you don't really know anything about. If you photograph, say, an open fuel injection pump before you take it apart, you've a better chance of getting it back together again.

A waterproof camera container is essential for taking photographs in bad weather conditions.

Don't be over-optimistic about fishing under way. The Mediterranean was fished out 3000 years ago, and is not worth the trouble of trying. I have used expensive reels 'suitable for sea fishing' all over the world and been very dissatisfied with them – they are usually too small. The Polynesians taught me how to do it: 100m of perlon line at least 1mm thick is made fast to the boat at one end, with a steel hook and a tuna spinner lure at the other. The best chance of a bite is at dusk, and you use one of the winches for hauling the line in – the catch will usually be one of the biggish fellows (pompano or tuna).

Fishing

You need a hand lead on board as well as the echo-sounder – not only because the latter can go wrong, but because hand-sounding is the only way in a narrow channel or (from the tender) around a yacht that has gone aground.

Hand lead

301

Up the mast

These rungs prevent the foot from slipping off sideways.

No-one in the crew really likes going aloft, yet the rigging must be checked regularly. The cheapest, and by no means worst bosun's chair is a hardwood board (20 × 50cm) suspended at the four corners. Unlike the posh ones from America, which resemble trapeze harness, the board is more comfortable to work from as you can move more freely. Obviously you wear a safety harness, and above the crosstrees you clip on to the mast, not just to the chair. Metal rungs fixed to the mast are also very good for climbing up quickly to free a halyard or look beyond the horizon.

Patent log

In spite of all the electronic gear, the good old patent log undoubtedly will remain with us. One of its snags is that the vane is sometimes bitten off by fish. If you immerse the last couple of metres before the vane in epoxy resin, this will make the line rock-hard and hardly any fish will be able to bite through it.

Hauling out

When there is so much growth on the underwater parts of the hull that it is seriously affecting speed and handling, hauling out cannot be avoided. If you have never worked with the boatyard before, make them a true-to-scale drawing of the hull; and in any case mark the position of both ends of the keel on the deck with adhesive tape. Unfortunately we, as laymen, cannot check what the manufacturers tell us about their expensive hull paints; once, when I had run out of paint, I did the rest of the hull with a dirt-cheap antifouling a friendly fisherman gave me as a present; a glance at the underwater parts nine months later showed that it was much more effective. In future I shall put far more trust in what local fishermen tell me than in the makers of yacht paints costing three times as much! Unless you are a fanatic for high-speed sailing, you can greatly simplify matters by dispensing with needless rubbing-down. Brushing off and rinsing clean with fresh water is enough, and tiny traces of marine growth left behind give a good 'tooth' for the new paint.

Salt water in the linen

Towels go hard as a board, and pillows get scratchy. But banging and shaking will get rid of most of the salt crystals, so you can if necessary do your washing in seawater.

Sheath-knife

It may sometimes be necessary to cut through a rope within seconds. The sheath-knife is generally under your oilskins at a moment like this; a (salt-water proof) diver's knife in its scabbard fixed to the foot of the mast offers extra safety.

Stove

If you are out of kerosene, it is possible as a make-do to use clean diesel oil in the Primus. It doesn't burn very cleanly, but it works. You can even use diesel as a substitute for methylated spirits for preheating, by winding a wide wick soaked in diesel oil round the burner. This tends to be a smokey business, but is still better than having cold food. To heat the cabin with the Primus, bricks heated over the flame are effective.

Certificates and clubs for cruising yachtsmen

Certificates of competence

With more and more people taking to the water for sport and relaxation, it seems inevitable that the wide open spaces of the sea are going to become a little more cramped, and that the authorities will increasingly take a hand in regulating the yachting world. When the author sailed round the world, from 1971 to 1974, there was no harbour in the world where one was asked to produce a 'driving licence'; but these happy days look like becoming a thing of the past only a few years from now. Already some countries in the Mediterranean have begun to require the skipper of a cruising yacht to show an official licence to prove his competence; in the Federal Republic of Germany an official yachtsman's licence was introduced at the end of 1973, and is now obligatory for sailing a cruiser in national waters. France, too, has a similar licensing scheme, and other European countries are following suit. Though these licences cover only sailing in national waters, it seems certain that other countries will take to asking to inspect the licences of visiting yachtsmen. In Britain, where the yachting world is largely united in resisting the idea of compulsory licensing, there is nonetheless a well-developed voluntary scheme of training and certification that can serve to meet these growing demands for presenting a piece of paper to prove the skipper's competence to sail in another country's waters: it can provide objective and reassuring confirmation of the yachtsman's own confidence in himself!

The scheme, run by the Royal Yachting Association in conjunction with the government's Department of Trade, provides a graded series of certificates. The RYA's Coastal Certificates come in two grades, Grade 1 being intended for newcomers to sailing and covering basic seamanship and pilotage (navigating close to shore), while Grade 2 covers coastal passage-making, night sailing and elementary navigation.

The 'Yachtmaster' certificates are approved by the DoT (the government body also responsible for certificating professional masters of vessels), and set standards for skippers of offshore and ocean cruising yachts. The Offshore Certificate courses teach navigation, meteorology and yacht handling, and assume previous Grade 2 qualifications; the Ocean Certificate examination is concerned only with astro-navigation and long-distance passage making.

The knowledge that this book has tried to put over is not sufficient for passing these examinations (it has not, for example, dealt with the buoyage system which – as mentioned earlier – is at present undergoing fundamental changes with the introduction of the IALA system), but there are RYA-recognised training establishments for the practical aspects and the theory can be learned through correspondence courses or evening classes. Further information is available from the Royal Yachting Association, Victoria Way, Woking, Surrey (Tel: Woking (04862) 5022).

SSCA

Probably the most valuable of all sources of information for the cruising yachtsmen are the monthly bulletins of the Seven Seas Cruising Association. To become a member of this exclusive body you have to have lived on a yacht continuously for at least a year. Members are duty-bound to send the SSCA reports of experience on their voyages; these are then collated and printed and distributed to all members. Non-members can also subscribe to them for a modest fee, and it is even possible to obtain back numbers from previous years. The bulletins cover virtually every spot on the globe where a yacht has ever passed, with descriptions tailored for yachtsmen's needs. Eric Hiscock, and Irving Johnson who has sailed round the world seven times, acknowledge their gratitude to the SSCA's bulletins for some of the most enchanting anchorages they know. The SSCA's address is PO Box 6354, San Diego, California, USA.

Answers to Navigation Exercises

1 a) 41° 13'.3 N; 13° 04'.2 E
b) 40° 54'.5 N; 12° 57'.3 E
c) 40° 49'.8 N; 14° 25'.7 E
d) 41° 00'.7 N; 13° 55'.6 E
e) 40° 38'.2 N; 14° 36'.7 E

All data relate to the year 1975.
For Exercise 7 use the deviation card on the practice chart.

2 43.4nm

3 (5 × 0.5) = 2.5W, 11°W = 9°W

4 Course	328° T
Var	9° W
Course	337° M

5 Course	074° M	
Var	9° W	
Course	065° T	Estimated Position 40° 55'.8 N 13° 04'.2 E

6 True Bearing	344° T	Deviation curve and card on Practice Chart
Var	9° W	
Mag Bearing	353° M	
Comp Bearing	351° C	
Deviation	2° E	

7 Course	269° T
Var	9° W
Course	278° M
Dev	1° W
Course	279° C

8 Track Required	282° T
Leeway	+ 5°
Wake Course	287° T
Var	9° W
Course	296° M
Dev	3° W
Course	299° C

9 $\dfrac{13 \times 164}{7 \times 145}$ = 2.1nm

Bearing	114° C
Dev	3° W
	111° M
Var	9° W
	102° T

10

Co	020° C	Log	49.47
Dev	3° E		−44.37
Co	023° M	Dist Run	5.10nm
Var	9° W		
Co	014° T		
Leeway	− 10°	DR Posn 40° 48′.2N 13° 49′.1 E	
Wake Co	004° T		

11

Co	020° C	Bearing	125° C
Dev	3° E	Comp Error	6° W
	023° M		119° T
Var	9° W		
Co	014° T	Horizontal Angle 90° − 65° = 25°	

Fix 40° 48′.2 N 13° 49′.1 E

12

Co	020° C	0716	Log reading 59.75
Comp. err.	6° W	0525	Log reading 49.47
	014° T		Dist Run 10.28nm
		Bearing	067° C
		Dev	0°
			067° M
		Var	9° W
			058° T

Running Fix 40° 58′.8 N 13° 50′.7 E

13

Co	010° C	Approx. fix 41° 06′.2 N 13° 49′.7 E	
Dev	2° E		
	012° M		
Var	9° W		
	003° T		

14

Co	264° C	Dr Posn. 41° 01′.0 N 13° 17′.5 E	
Dev	3° E	Log dist 24.86 in 5hr = 4.97kt	
	267° M		
Var	9° W		
	258° T		

15

Co	270° C
Dev	0°
	270° M
Var	9° W
	261° T

	Zannone	Cape Ciceo	Caeta St Erasmo
Pelorus	330°	058°	164°
Co T	261°	261°	261°
	591°	319° T	425°
	−360°		−360°
Bearing	231° T		065° T

Fix 41° 04′.7 N 13° 13′.8 E

16 5nm

17 321°/1.0kt

18 Track 227.5° (T)

19 Course to Steer   217.9° T
         Var   9°   W
                    226.9° M
         Dev   5°   E
                    221.9° C

---

20 a) 5.86kt

b) $\dfrac{16.2 \times 60}{5.86}$ = 165.87min

Probable ETA 0246

---

21 a) D/F Bearing   039°   (Relative)
     Quadrantal Error   +   11°
                      050°
     Co   217° C
                      267° C
     Dev   5° E
                      272° M
     Var   9° W
     Great-circle Bearing   263° T

b) Night effect!

---

22 Bearing   062° C   90°00′
      Dev   4° E   Declination   +   18°07′
              066° M   108°07′
      Var   9° W   Observed   67°16′
              057° T   40°51′
                              Total corr   −   13′
                              Noon Latitude   40°38′ N

Position: 40° 38′ N 13° 41′.7 E

---

23 LHA   360° 00′
     Long E   −   9° 09′
     GHA   350° 51′
     GHA 11h   343° 25′.4
                  7° 25′.6   (= 29min 42sec)
       =   11hr 29min 42sec

---

24   90° 00′
     Declination   +   18° 07′
                  108° 07′
     Observed Alt   68° 44′
                  39° 23′
     Total Corr   −   13′
     Latitude   39° 10′ N

25 1st sight   10hr 28min 38sec
      2nd sight   12hr 28min 24sec
                   22hr 57min 02sec ÷ 2 = 11hr 28min 31sec

GHA 11hr   343° 25'.4
inc 28min 31sec   7° 07'.8
GHA 11hr 28min 31sec   350° 33'.2
                           − 360°
                             9° 26'.8E

                                       90° 00'
                   Declination + 18° 07'
                                      108° 07'
                   Obs. Alt.   67° 10'
                                      40° 57'
                   Total corr −   13'
                   Latitude   40° 44' N

---

26 a) 40° 32' N 13° 58'.8E
     b) Lat 41° N Dec 18° N (18° 08')
         GHA   313° 25'.4
         inc   7° 28'.8
         GHA   320° 54'.2
         Long E   + 14° 05'.8 (nearest longitude to make whole degrees)
         LHA   335° 00'.0
     c) Hc   58° 34'   Azimuth = 130° T
         d   +   6'
         Hc   58° 40'

     d) Hs   58° 41'
         Total corr +   13'
         Ho   58° 54'
         Hc   58° 40'
         Intercept   14' towards
     e) Towards
     f) 41° 00'N 14° 05'.8 E

---

27 Bearing   146° C LHA @ 0930 GMT 335°
     Dev (on 280C)   1° W At 0946 339° (1' LHA more every 4min)
                      145° M
     Var   9° W
                      136° T
     Azimuth from AP.3270 = 136° T
     Deviation Card correct on this heading.

---

28   90° 00'
     Declination + 18° 07'
                      108° 07'
     Obs. Alt.   67° 21'
                      40° 46'
     Total corr −   13'
     LATITUDE   40° 33' N

---

29 Log distance 1112   26.44
     Log distance 0929   −18.54
     Log distance run   7.90nm
     A 7.90nm shift along the 273° true noon position
     Fix 40° 33' N 13° 49'.2 E

308

A Position line using AP 3270

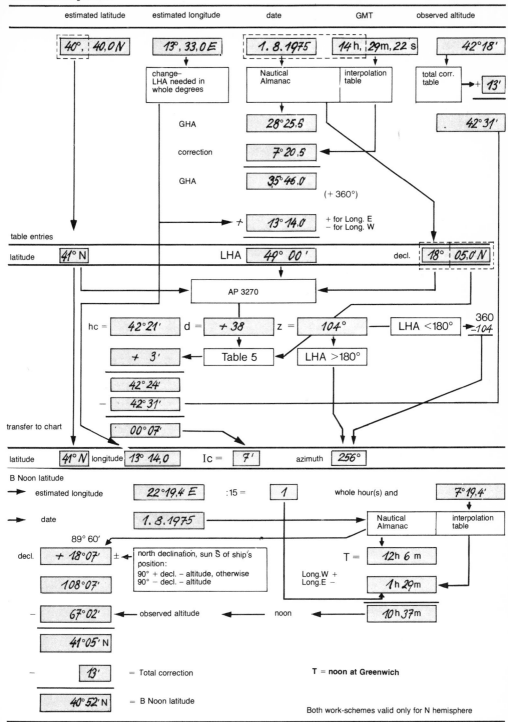

	estimated latitude	estimated longitude	date	GMT	observed altitude

40°, 40,0 N   13°, 33,0 E   1. 8. 1975   14 h, 29 m, 22 s   42° 18'

change—
LHA needed in
whole degrees

Nautical
Almanac

interpolation
table

total corr.
table   + 13'

GHA   28° 25,5

42° 31'

correction   7° 20,5

GHA   35° 46,0

(+ 360°)

+   13° 14,0   + for Long. E
                                  – for Long. W

table entries

latitude   41° N   LHA   49° 00 '   decl.   18° 05,0 N

AP 3270

hc =   42° 21'   d =   + 38   z =   104°   LHA < 180°   360
                                                                                                              –104

+ 3'   Table 5   LHA > 180°

42° 24'

–   42° 31'

transfer to chart   00° 07'

latitude   41° N   longitude   13° 14,0   Ic =   7'   azimuth   256°

B Noon latitude

estimated longitude   22° 19,4 E   : 15 =   1   whole hour(s) and   7° 19,4'

date   1. 8. 1975   Nautical   interpolation
                                                        Almanac   table

89° 60'

decl.   + 18° 07'   ±   north declination, sun S of ship's   T =   12 h 6 m
                                              position:
                                              90° + decl. – altitude, otherwise
                                              90° – decl. – altitude   Long.W +
108° 07'   Long.E –   1 h 29 m

–   67° 02'   ← observed altitude ← noon ←   10 h 37 m

41° 05' N

–   13'   = Total correction   T = noon at Greenwich

40° 52' N   = B Noon latitude   Both work-schemes valid only for N hemisphere

Suggested titles for reading list.

Hiscock, Eric: *Voyaging under sail,* OUP 1970
Hiscock, Eric: *Sou'west in Wanderer IV,* OUP 1973
Moitessier, Bernard: *Cape Horn – the logical route,* Adlard Coles 1969
Moitessier, Bernard: *Sailing to the reefs,* Adlard Coles 1971
Knox-Johnston, Robin: *A world of my own,* Cassell 1969
Adlard Coles *Glénans Sailing Manual,*
Coles, Adlard: Heavy weather sailing

Units for the yachtsman

1 nautical mile = 1 minute of arc at the equator = 1852m = 6080ft
(or sea mile)

1 knot   = 1 nautical mile/hour, the unit of speed used for ships, wind and current (NB: a north wind blows *from* the north, but a northerly current runs *towards* the north)

1 cable   = one-tenth of a nautical mile = 185.2m = 200yd approx.; unit of distance used on older Admiralty charts.

1 centimetre = 0.39in. Past British custom has been to quote rope sizes in *circumference* in inches, while metric rope sizes are the *diameter* in millimetres (circ. in inches = diam. in mm ÷ 8)

1 metre   = 3.28ft = 39in (despite metrication the foot is likely to persist in the sailing world for some time yet; with many yachts the length in feet forms part of the type designation – eg. the Nicholson 39)

1 fathom   = 6ft = 1.82m. Older Admiralty charts show depth in fathoms, and close inshore in fathoms + feet (eg. 2_4); Admiralty metric charts are recognisable from a greater use of colour and the words 'Depths in metres' printed in magenta.

1 horsepower = 0.735kW; from 1978 engine power will officially be quoted in kilowatts instead of horsepower (though, like feet, HP will probably continue in popular usage for a good few years to come).

1 kilowatt   = 1.359hp

Index